DESIGN
OF
CITIES

DESIGN OF CITIES
REVISED EDITION

Línea del centro

EDMUND N. BACON

A Studio Book
THE VIKING PRESS
New York

Revised edition issued in 1974 by The Viking Press, Inc.
625 Madison Avenue, New York, N.Y. 10022

Distributed in Canada by
The Macmillan Company of Canada Limited

SBN 670-26862-3

Library of Congress catalog card number: 73-185988

Printed in U.S.A.

ACKNOWLEDGMENT

M.I.T. Press: From *Two Chicago Architects and Their Clients* by
Leonard K. Eaton. © 1969 by M.I.T.

ACKNOWLEDGMENTS

I wish to express my gratitude to the Rockefeller Foundation for the grant to write this book. I also wish to thank the Ford Foundation for the Travel and Study Award of 1959.

I would like to express my appreciation to three great mayors of Philadelphia for their encouragement and support: The Honorable Joseph S. Clark, The Honorable Richardson Dilworth, and The Honorable James H. J. Tate.

I feel the deepest gratitude to my great teacher, Eliel Saarinen, who provided me with many of the basic ideas in this book. I much appreciate the kind cooperation of Mr. Felix Klee and the Klee Foundation in Berne for making the Paul Klee documents available to me. Also I wish to thank Professor Dr. C. S. Kruijt, ir. D. J. de Widt, W. Smeulers, H. J. van Veldhuizen, L. C. Johanns, L. H. Simons, of the Instituut voor Stedebouwkundig Onderzoek of Delft, for the survey and beautiful drawings they made especially for this book of the Square in Wijk-bij-Duurstede. To my co-worker and associate, Alois Strobl, I am grateful for working with me on the design of the book and its illustrations, and I am grateful to Agnes Kelly for writing it down.

I am deeply indebted to the scholars who have helped me with parts of the book: Frank E. Brown, John Travlos, Wolfgang Lotz, Steen Eiler Rasmussen, James S. Ackerman, and Sir John Summerson — although absolving them of blame for any errors I may have made.

To single out any other of the multitude of the scholars, authors, architects, historians, and friends who have influenced me and contributed to my understanding would be unjust, but I would like to make this a collective acknowledgment of their valued contributions.

E. N. B.

FOREWORD—REVISED EDITION

My principal purpose in this revised edition is to transmit, not the forms of my work which will be deemed obsolete, but rather the forces behind them, the thought models and the muscular and sensory images on which they were based, and the forces which propelled them into action. My purpose is to help young people propel their own ideas, developed in their own terms, into the realities of their own day. In doing this I have been immeasurably aided by the collaboration of a young person, Peter Mahony, both because of his inherent qualities, and because of those of the generation of which he is a part. Many of the ideas new to this edition are the product of our joint effort.

One thing that emerges with greatest clarity from the experience in Philadelphia is that the reason the plans got built was that the ingredient of acceptance was built into the plans from the beginning, and that the planning process and the process of carrying out the plans were always seen as one.

May 1973

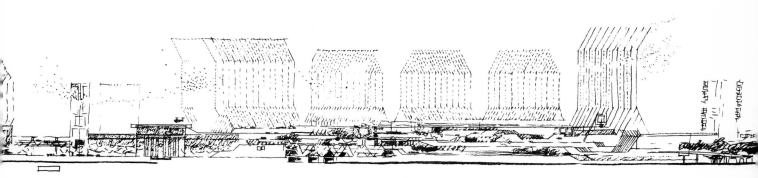

FOREWORD

My qualifications for writing this book are those not of the scholar or historian but of a participator in the recent history of the rebirth of Philadelphia. By some historical accident there has been set into motion here the convergence of an extraordinary series of creative forces which are in process of changing the face of the city. I believe that this experience, the product not of one person but of the interaction of many, is rich with ideas that are applicable to other cities in all parts of the world where there is a desire for a finer physical expression of man's inner aspirations.

In my work in Philadelphia I have been conscious of parallels in the currents of history, and have constantly drawn upon them. In this book I attempt to share those moments of historical development which have been particularly helpful to me, and through a fresh look at them hope to make clear some of the deeper forces that have been decisive in what has been happening in Philadelphia since its renaissance began.

7

Drawings, diagrams, and color overprints were specially drawn for this book by:

Alois K. Strobl — 49, 50–51, 78, 84, 99, 102–103, 108, 110, 254, 257, 259, 260, 261, 270–271

William L. Bale, Jr. — 66, 70–71, 74, 140–141, 176, 177, 196–197, 205, 213, 217, 220, 221, 224–225, 268 (upper), 272

John Andrew Gallery — 95, 98 (upper), 110, 218, 286–287

James Nelson Kise — 83 (lower), 188–189

Elliot Arthur Pavlos — 83 (middle), 86, 87, 106, 142, 143, 145, 147, 149, 151, 153, 154

Robert A. Presser — 90–91, 184, 185

Lawrence Sherman — 83 (upper), 98 (lower)

Irving Wasserman — 192–193, 200, 266–267, 300–301

J. H. Aronson — 94, 114, 119

CONTENTS

Acknowledgments 5
Foreword — Revised Edition 6
Foreword 7
THE CITY AS AN ACT OF WILL 13
AWARENESS OF SPACE AS EXPERIENCE 15
THE NATURE OF DESIGN 33
WAYS OF PERCEIVING ONE'S SELF 39
THE GROWTH OF GREEK CITIES 67
DESIGN ORDER OF ANCIENT ROME 85
MEDIEVAL DESIGN 93
UPSURGE OF THE RENAISSANCE 107
DESIGN STRUCTURE OF BAROQUE ROME 131
DUTCH INTERLUDE 163
18TH AND 19TH CENTURY EUROPEAN DESIGN 171
DEVELOPMENT OF PARIS 187
EVOLUTION OF SAINT PETERSBURG 196
JOHN NASH AND LONDON 201
VITRUVIUS COMES TO THE NEW WORLD 217
LE CORBUSIER AND THE NEW VISION 228
THE GREAT EFFORT — BRASILIA 235
PEKING 244
SIMULTANEOUS MOVEMENT SYSTEMS 252
DECISION MAKING 254
PUTTING THE IDEAS TO WORK — PHILADELPHIA 264
GRIFFIN AND CANBERRA 309
CITY FOR HUMANITY — STOCKHOLM 312
LOOKING INTO THE FUTURE 319
Appendix 324
Notes on Illustrations 325
Bibliography 331
Index 333

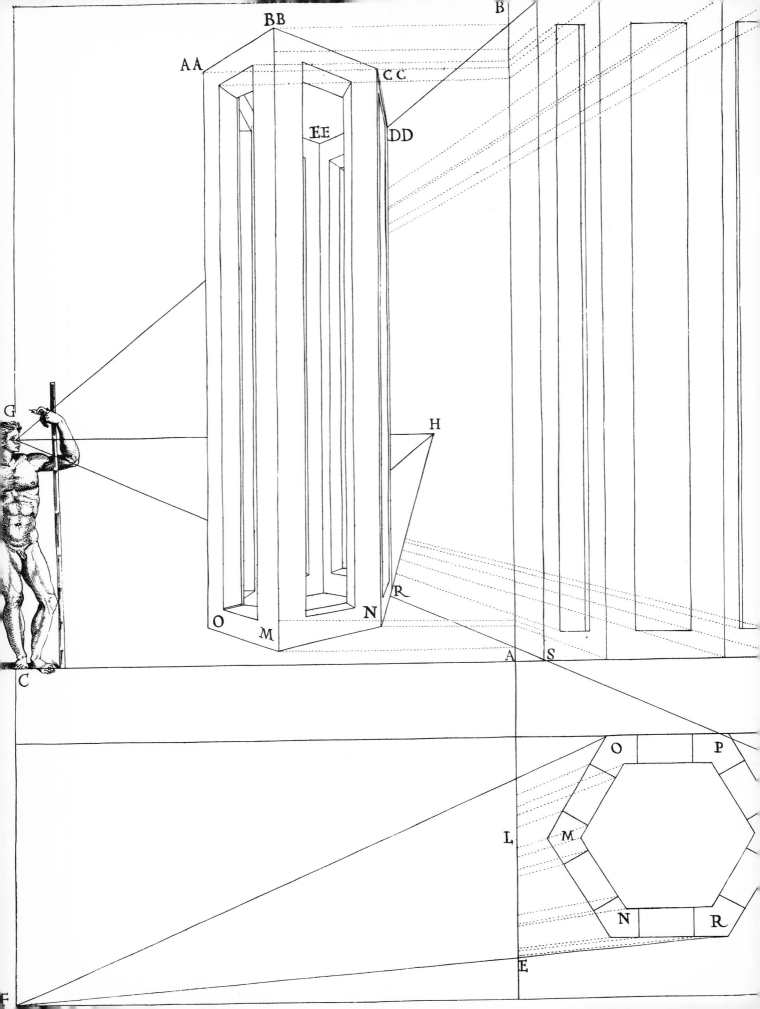

Many are the things that man
Seeing must understand.
Not seeing, how shall he know
What lies in the hand
Of time to come?

— Sophocles, *Ajax*,
translated by E. F. Watling

. . . beholding [seeing with understanding] is just
not a mirror which always remains the same, but a
living power of apprehension which has its own
inward history and has passed through many
stages.

— Heinrich Wölfflin,
Principles of Art History, 1915,
translated by M. D. Hottlinger

A man of antiquity sailing a boat, quite content
and enjoying the ingenious comfort of the contriv-
ance. The ancients represent the scene accordingly. And now: What a modern man experiences as
he walks across the deck of a steamer: 1. his own
movement, 2. the movement of the ship which may
be in the opposite direction, 3. the direction and
velocity of the current, 4. the rotation of the earth,
5. its orbit, 6. the orbits of the moons and planets
around it. Result: an interplay of movements in
the universe, at their center the "I" on the ship.

— Paul Klee,
"Creative Credo," 1920,
from *The Thinking Eye*

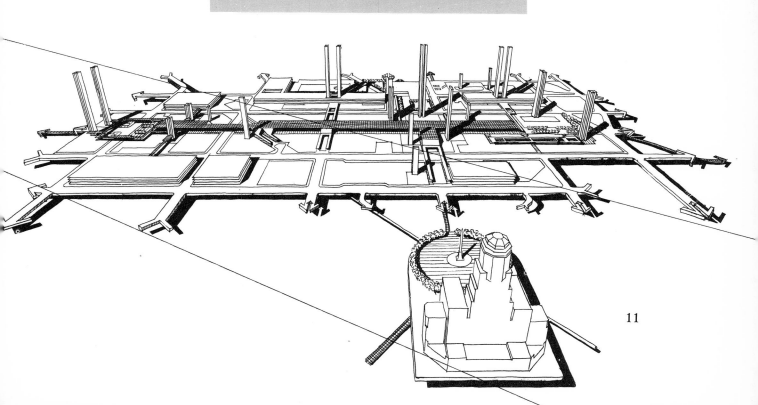

11

THE CITY AS AN ACT OF WILL

The building of cities is one of man's greatest achievements. The form of his city always has been and always will be a pitiless indicator of the state of his civilization. This form is determined by the multiplicity of decisions made by the people who live in it. In certain circumstances these decisions have interacted to produce a force of such clarity and form that a noble city has been born. It is my premise that a deeper understanding of the interactions of these decisions can give us the insight necessary to create noble cities in our own day.

The purpose of this book is to explore the nature of these decisions as they have occurred in the past, the influence of the circumstances in which they were made, the way in which they have related to one another and to the ideas that emerged from their union, and to examine the gradually evolving forms they have produced. My hope is to dispel the idea, so widely and uncritically held, that cities are a kind of grand accident, beyond the control of the human will, and that they respond only to some immutable law. I contend that human will can be exercised effectively on our cities now, so that the form that they take will be a true expression of the highest aspirations of our civilization.

With the enormous improvement in the techniques of mathematical manipulations of electronic computers applied to the problem of projecting past trends, we are in danger of surrendering to a mathematically extrapolated future which at best can be nothing more than an extension of what existed before. Thus we are in danger of losing one of the most important concepts of mankind, that the future is what we make it.

Recent events in Philadelphia have proved incontrovertibly that, given a clear vision of a "design idea," the multiplicity of wills that constitutes our contemporary democratic process can coalesce into positive, unified action on a scale large enough to change substantially the character of a city. A principal aim of this book is to consider what is meant by "design idea."

13

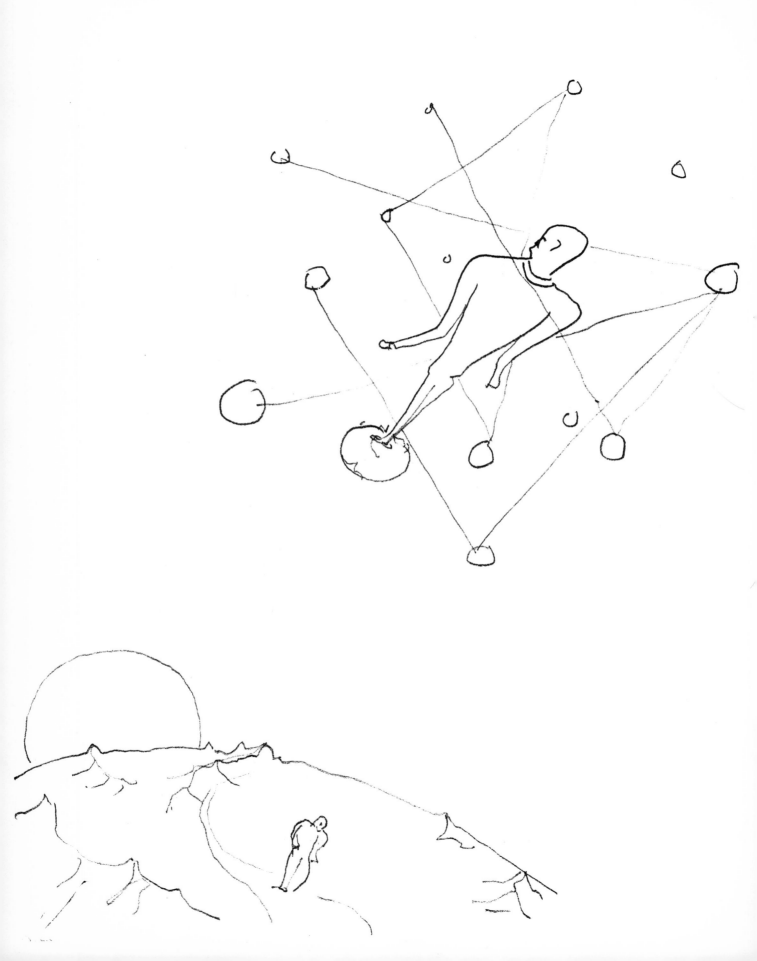

AWARENESS OF SPACE AS EXPERIENCE

The basic ingredient of architectural design consists of two elements, mass and space. The essence of design is the interrelation between these two. In our culture the preponderant preoccupation is with mass, and to such an extent that many designers are "space blind."

Awareness of space goes far beyond cerebral activity. It engages the full range of senses and feelings, requiring involvement of the whole self to make a full response to it possible.

The human organism progresses in its capacity to perceive space from the spaceless embryonic state, through the limited space exploration of the infant, to the primarily two-dimensional exploration of the crawling child, and finally to the bodily leap into space essential to the athlete's skill and the dancer's art. There is an intellectual parallel of deepening perception which is based on becoming connected with larger and larger systems. In architectural terms it means progressing from the earth and earth materials into the less tangible elements of the universe. Through this sense of connection with a system greater than himself man achieves aesthetic satisfaction, and the more nearly universal the system, the deeper the satisfaction. This is why a conscious expression of space is essential to the highest expression of architecture.

O to realize space!
The plenteousness of all,
    that there are no bounds,
To emerge and be of the sky,
    of the sun and moon and flying clouds,
    as one with them.

In these words Walt Whitman has given a great assignment to architecture. But it can never be fulfilled unless the designers themselves develop an awareness of space through the involvement of their whole being.

15

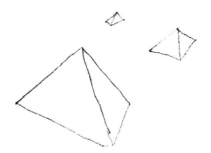

Mass

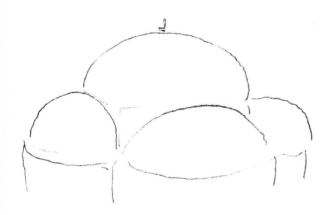

A blowing out —
space inside

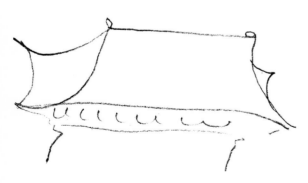

A curving in —
space outside

FORM AND SPACE

Architectural form is the point of contact between mass and space. Where the philosophical interrelationship between these two elements is unclear, so will form of the architecture be unclear. By defining the point of juncture between mass and space, the architect is making a statement about the interrelationship of man and his universe.

The Egyptian pyramid stands as the consummate expression of a form which emerges from the earth as dominant mass. It is a statement of unchangeable absolutes.

Chinese architecture, on the contrary, is a powerful expression of a state of harmony with nature, not dominance over it. The concavity of a roof is an expression of the modesty of man, of the receptivity of his structures to universal space which these roofs gracefully receive and which becomes the core of his architectural compositions in the courtyards.

In Islamic architecture the use of form and space is different again. The magnificent domes which are central to so much Islamic work seem a reflection of inner space, which, seeking expression, pushes the membrane outward, taut, to set the form. This is in marked contrast to the domes of Christian churches and cathedrals of Western Europe, which were conceived in terms of structure, of mass.

So in all the cultures of the world, architectural form is an expression of the philosophical interaction of the forces of mass and space, which, in turn, reflects the relationship between a man and nature and man and the universe. The clarity and vigor with which mass and space are resolved set the level of excellence of architectural work at any period of a culture's development.

DEFINING SPACE

Space itself can assume strongly marked attributes. The Greeks recognized this, and it was an important element in their art and religion. Thus there were groves and vales set aside for certain spirits, particular places which became sacred precincts and mountains dedicated to gods personifying human qualities. Much of Greek architecture was designed to infuse spaces with a spirit, and to serve as a link between man and the universe by establishing a firm relationship with natural space.

In Islamic architecture devices were developed for delimiting space as a positive (and often religious) element. The four minarets about a mosque establish a transparent cube of space infused with the spirit of the mosque. The dome animates the space so defined.

The square plane of the great elevated platform of the Mosque of Omar in Jerusalem sets vertical forces into motion which define a shaft of space rising from it, enveloping the dome. The free-standing archways have no function other than to frame the act of specific entering into this space.

So in cities today we must think beyond the design of buildings and circulation systems. We must establish volumes of space that are in scale with the needs of the present time and defined by means which are in harmony with modern technology. These volumes of space must be infused with a spirit which is generated by architectural forms. In this way richness and variety can be established in the city, and through the cumulative effect of various kinds of association with the different parts of the city, its citizens may build up loyalty to it.

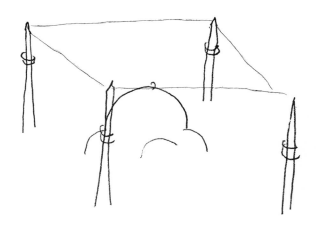

Creating space around —
defining, delimiting

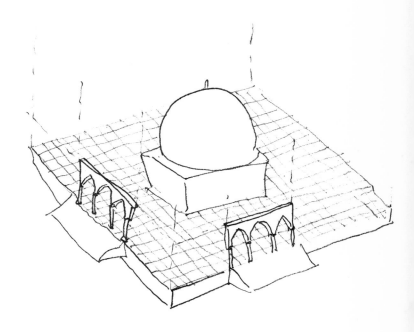

ARTICULATING SPACE

It is one thing to delimit space by structural devices such as walls. It is quite another to infuse the space with a spirit which relates to the activities that take place in it and which stirs the senses and emotions of the people who use it. Architecture encompasses both.

By the building of a blank wall, as indicated in the sketch shown at left, a space is defined, but it remains a characterless space. The second sketch suggests how rhythm, texture, and spirit are injected into such a space by architectural means — in this case through the recall of Chinese forms.

In Sigfried Giedion's book *Architecture, You and Me* (Harvard University Press), Fernand Léger develops this principle in modern terms through the concept of "colored space." He says, "It was about 1910, with Delaunay, that I personally began to liberate pure color in space," adding that the "habitable rectangle is going to change into a boundless colored space."

Architectural forms, textures, materials, modulation of light and shade, color, all combine to inject a quality or spirit that articulates space. The quality of the architecture will be determined by the skill of the designer in using and relating these elements, both in the interior spaces and in the spaces around his buildings.

In most cities there are buildings of character which lose their effectiveness because they are situated in out-of-the-way locations; there are also prominent sites occupied by uninteresting buildings which make no contribution to the surrounding area. In urban design there should be skillful deployment of architectural energy so that the influence of fine buildings radiates outward, articulating the whole fabric of the city.

Space comprehensible

Space articulate

18

SPACE AND TIME

One of the prime purposes of architecture is to heighten the drama of living. Therefore, architecture must provide differentiated spaces for different activities, and it must articulate them in such a way that the emotional content of the particular act of living which takes place in them is reinforced.

Life is a continuous flow of experience; each act or moment of time is preceded by a previous experience and becomes the threshold for the experience to come. If we acknowledge that an objective of life is the achievement of a continuous flow of harmonious experiences, then the relationship of spaces to one another, as experienced over time, becomes a major design problem. When viewed in this way, architecture takes its place with the arts of poetry and music, in which no single part can be considered except in relation to what immediately precedes or follows it.

The Botticelli painting above depicts a space beautifully scaled and simply and powerfully articulated for the great event which is taking place within it. It is also a representation of time: the flow from the past is symbolized by the archway to the left, and the anticipation of the future is represented by the glimpse (through the archway at the right) of open space extending to the horizon and beyond.

Since designers should provide a setting for a totally harmonious life experience, the dimensions of their designs should encompass the whole of a day, the whole of a city.

19

Creating space through
the tombs of the Ming Emperors

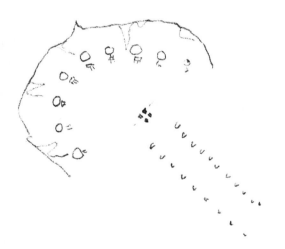

SPACE AND MOVEMENT

Up to this point architecture has been discussed as a series of linked spaces, each possessing a particular quality and each related to the other. The purpose of a design is to affect the people who use it, and in an architectural composition this effect is a continuous, unbroken flow of impressions that assault their senses as they move through it. For a design to be a work of art, the impressions it produces in the participator must be not only continuous, but harmonious at every instant and from every viewpoint. It is the failure of the architect to project himself into the mind and spirit of the people who are to experience his designs that causes much of the staccato feeling to be noted in work today.

In order to emphasize this point I use the word "participator" to designate the person who so senses the flow of messages that are transmitted by a design. The changing visual picture is only the beginning of the sensory experience; the changes from light to shade, from hot to cold, from noise to silence, the flow of smells associated with spaces, and the tactile quality of the surface underfoot, all are important in the cumulative effect.

Underlying it all is the modular rhythm of footsteps, the unchanging measure of space since earliest civilization. There is the muscular effort to cross a court, for instance, or the exhilaration induced by the prospect of ascending or descending a stairway. Only through endless walking can the designer absorb into his being the true scale of urban spaces.

A magnificent example of architecture related to movement is in China, north of Peking — the Tombs of the Ming Emperors. The long approach, cut through a forest, is distinguished by rhythmically spaced archways and stone figures, animal and human, which face the procession route. The climax is the groin-vaulted pavilion in the center of the semicircular mountain range. At the foot of the mountains are thirteen pavilions, behind which rise thirteen mounds containing tombs of emperors, so superbly placed that they bring into play, in memory of the dead monarchs, the entire volume contained within the mountain arc.

DEFINITION OF ARCHITECTURE

Each generation must rework the definitions of the old symbols which it inherits from the generation before; it must reformulate the old concepts in terms of its own age.

Using the range of ideas discussed so far, weaving them together into an organized relationship, we can formulate a definition of architecture that will serve as a working basis for the discussion which follows.

Architecture is the articulation of space so as to produce in the participator a definite space experience in relation to previous and anticipated space experiences.

INVOLVEMENT

To put an awareness of space to use creatively requires participation in a process involving the whole range of one's capabilities.

At various times in history this process of involvement has reached a high pitch. One such period, certainly, was the Periclean Age in Athens, and another was the eighteenth century in Europe, the age in which Francesco Guardi made the drawing opposite. When an artist of the caliber of Guardi sees the world with such clarity, we are indebted to him for the gift of insight he brings to us, regardless of the environment in which we live.

This is architecture, not to look at, but to be in. It draws us into its depths and involves us in an experience shared by all the people who are moving about in it. The same kind of experience can be encountered at the Villa d'Este, at Tivoli, where the fountains are not merely something to see but something to be experienced. As the water sparkles, gurgles, and flows on all sides of us, we are completely involved by it. So it is, or should be, with the city. The designer's problem is not to create façades or architectural mass but to create an all-encompassing experience, to engender involvement.

The city is a people's art, a shared experience, the place where the artist meets the greatest number of potential appreciators. In many kinds of human relationships it is the function of the active person to establish the creative force and also to develop receptivity to it. So it is the function of the designer to conceive an idea, implant it, and nurture its growth in the collective minds of the community in such a way that the final product has a reasonable chance of coming close to his original concept.

The designer thus functions in time and space: he conceives forms as pulsating expressions of organic vitality flowing through the structure of the city, and he brings to the mind of the community the significance and meaning of the evolving forms in the flow of the total development. Simultaneously, he brings into full focus the physical realization of an idea which had been implanted before and establishes a glimmer of the vision of the development to come. This can be compared to the interweaving themes in music where one theme interlocks with another in the flow of time. In this manner a vast number of separate acts of city-building can be brought into relationship with one another over a considerable span of time and over a large area.

Should anyone conclude that this process places the designer in an autocratic position that will enable him to force his ideas on the community, I hasten to say that under the democratic system there are so many safeguards and processes of rejection that the possibility of overriding the sentiment of the community is extremely unlikely. Almost invariably, the final product of the designer at the city scale will be quite different from the original form proposed. To fail to provide any coherent vision of a finer, healthier, and more inspiring city is to fail to provide people with something to which they can react. The development of an adequate hypothesis or "design idea" of what the city ought to be imposes a severe discipline on the designer and on the nature of the design itself, but until it is done there is nothing to accept, reject, or modify. The technical nature of his hypothesis, or vision of a "design idea," is of the greatest importance and consequently the subject of a major portion of this study.

True involvement comes when the community and the designer turn the process of planning and building a city into a work of art.

MEETING THE SKY

Throughout history, architects have lavished much of their tenderest care on the part of the building which meets the sky. From the *akroterion* of the Greek temples, which delicately fused the harsh pedimental triangle with the upper atmosphere, through the spires and turrets of the Gothic churches, from the tortuous writhing figures, volutes, and urns on Baroque parapets to the cupolas and iron filigree of the Victorian period, this area has been a characteristic expression of the spirit of the times. Now, all too often, we establish a typical floor and repeat it mindlessly upward—all thought ceasing before the sky is reached. We sweep our rubbish into the upper air and use it as the crowning feature of our designs, with pipes, air-conditioners, and TV aerials as symbols of our relationship with the infinity of space.

The skyline of the city has long been a dominant element in urban design and should be reconstituted as a major determinant in city-building.

MEETING THE GROUND

The way in which the building rises out of the earth determines much of the quality of the entire structure. The constant and inspired expression in Greek architecture of the raising of the temple onto a podium elevated above the surrounding land was followed by the Roman expression of beautifully patterned marble-paved spaces which bound buildings together and set the scale of the foreground. Medieval architecture rose sheer from the level of the earth, but this earth was enriched by paving, by the buildings around it, and by the wellheads and fountains upon it. The raised podium and flights of steps were used to give stability to Renaissance buildings and beauty to the squares in which they were placed.

Today it seems as though we had lost such vision and care little that our important buildings stand almost as miscellaneous features among areas confused and dehumanized by automobile spaces and by ill-placed and ugly street lights and signs.

POINTS IN SPACE

Here is the excitement of points in space positioned freely, yet firmly established in the complex spatial geometry of the composition. Point reaches to point across the void. Tensions are set up between them, and as the observer moves about in the composition the points glide and move in relation to one another in a continually changing harmonic relationship. This is one of the finest aspects of many of the very great compositions. The plane of the point at the top of the obelisk in the Piazza Navona relates to the two towers and the dome of Sant' Agnese and then dips down to the heads of the sculptured figures in the fountains at each end. The points at the top of the two domes of the Piazza del Popolo interplay with that of the Sixtus V obelisk in the center. With much of our modern building, we have tended to lose the articulation of explicit points in space, thus robbing ourselves of many of the dynamic possibilities for harmonic spatial effects.

RECESSION PLANES

Here the basic composition is set back behind firm pylons which rise on each side of us and serve as a link between ourselves and the architectural forms, heightening their dramatic power. This is the proscenium effect, the establishment of a frame of reference to give scale and measure to the forms behind. It was frequently used by the Greeks, who skillfully placed their propylaea to emphasize depth and to define the approach to their temples — even in the most isolated sites. In China and Japan much the same purpose was served by free-standing gateways. While we are unlikely to use triumphal arches today, the creation of a setting for a building, the establishment of linkages in scale with objects in the foreground, such as flagpoles, sculpture, or stairways, as a measure of depth, remains as important as it ever was, and much can be accomplished by the careful placing of large buildings and small buildings in relation to one another.

DESIGN IN DEPTH

In the interrelation of these two arches, one deep behind the other, we again have a symbolic representation of a pleasurable human experience, that of penetration in depth. This form has been used repeatedly in the history of architecture. We see it in the archway of the clock tower in Padua, which interacts with the bull's-eye window of the little church across the square; and we see it in the recession of the arches in medieval battlements and in the series of doors in a Renaissance palace. A sense of movement in depth is established, and, where the architectural forms are related to one another, the size of the space is made comprehensible by a comparison of similar forms reduced by diminishing perspective. Exemplified here is a device for unifying form in space and giving coherence to design on an urban scale.

ASCENT AND DESCENT

The use of varying levels as a positive element in the design composition is brilliantly portrayed here, with emphasis on the process of ascending and descending from one level to the other. We can sense the joy of anticipation of running up a flight of steps, of the muscular effort to reach the higher level and the feeling of satisfaction when this is achieved. There can be an equal sense of pleasure in descending a stairway and anticipating the unfolding forms of the level below. Even in Ostia, the ancient port of Rome, built on a flat plain, prominent buildings were set upon very high bases that had great flights of steps, providing the citizen with the pleasure of a change in level.

With the revival of interest today in the use of many levels, stairways have taken on new importance as design elements. The use of mechanically driven escalators imposes a new architectural discipline because of the perceptual sequences they produce.

CONVEXITY AND CONCAVITY

Here we see the continuous interplay of two forms, the positive and the negative, the massive and the spacious, convexity and concavity. The forms envelop us and involve us completely in their spatial animation. In design of this sort, interrelationships are established between parts at all levels. Design is not confined to forms that depend on the land as the basic connector; it functions effectively in new kinds of relationships at each level in space. It is not limited to the manipulation of flat planes but involves buildings freely positioned in spatial volume. In our own day there has been a resurgence of interest in the use of curved forms, but all too often these have been conceived as isolated forms in space. Architects have not taken advantage of the full excitement of interplay that is possible.

RELATIONSHIP TO MAN

In this last view of the drawing, we are concerned with the relationship of the architect to the man he is seeking to house. The forms are carefully scaled to involve the people within the building, to flow from that part of the structure the people can see at close range, that they can touch and feel. Unlike some Renaissance architecture, where the base of a column towers above the heads of the people, the column here is set on a pedestal within reach of the people passing by it.

The point of contact of the Greek Doric column with the marble block of the temple floor is in perfect relationship with the viewer. Even the most monumental of the classical Roman work was designed so that the bases of the columns were within reach of the hand. Today, with the towering dimensions of so many structures, the designer must devise new means for establishing a connection between the building he creates and the people on the ground.

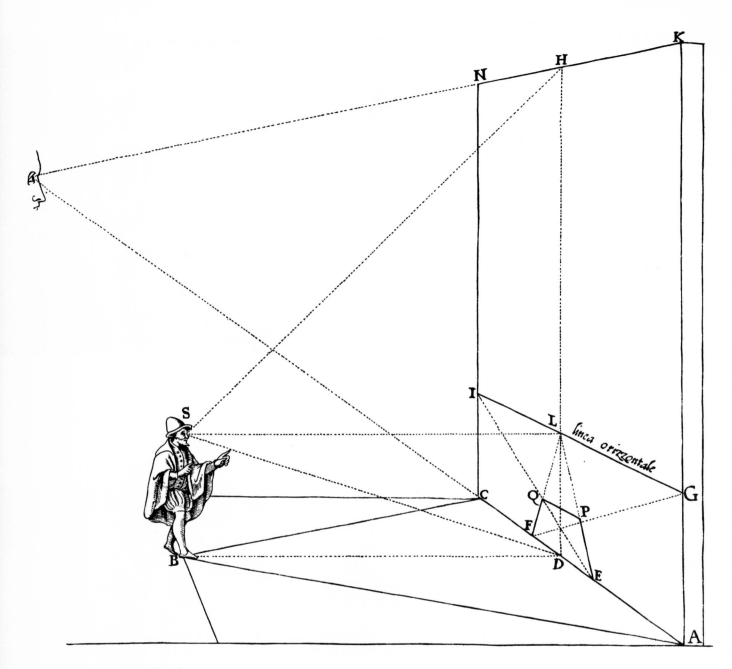

Apprehension

28

DESIGNER AS PARTICIPATOR

The seventeenth-century engraving on the facing page poses a question that persists today: Is the designer thinking of his work from the lofty bird's-eye viewpoint of a disembodied intellect, or is he able to project himself into the person of the participator, and so conceive his design in terms of the effect it will actually have on the senses of the people who use his buildings?

The answer to this is greatly influenced by the designer's philosophic and scientific apprehension of the culture of which he is a part, by the way he represents his ideas, and by the relationship of his method of representation to the actual realization of the building on the ground.

A contemporary illustration of this relationship is provided by the two photographs to the right. The upper one is a study model of the new town of Vällingby outside Stockholm, and the lower one shows the actual town as it was built.

Here much of the designing was done through the use of blocks (representing buildings), which were placed and moved about on a cardboard base. The view from an airplane of the completed project (below, right) is extremely impressive. It places the observer in the same angular relationship to the finished town as the designer was while he was making the study model. However, when one actually enters Vällingby on foot and moves about in the town, one looks in vain for a central organizing space. In fact, Vällingby is not as satisfying an experience on the ground as it is when viewed from the air, and this, I believe, is because the design was conceived primarily in terms of the model and not from the viewpoint of the pedestrian who was to walk about in the town itself when it was built. This stresses the importance of developing new ways of representing present-day design concepts, and the necessity of achieving a deeper understanding of the actual effect of a design on the people who use it.

In his 1781 book, *A Series of Plans for Cottages, Habitations of the Laborer,* . . . John Wood the Younger, the great architect of Bath, (see page 185) says, "In order to make myself master of the subject, it was necessary for me to feel as the cottager himself . . . no architect can form a convenient plan unless he ideally places himself in the situation of the person for whom he designs."

Representation

Realization

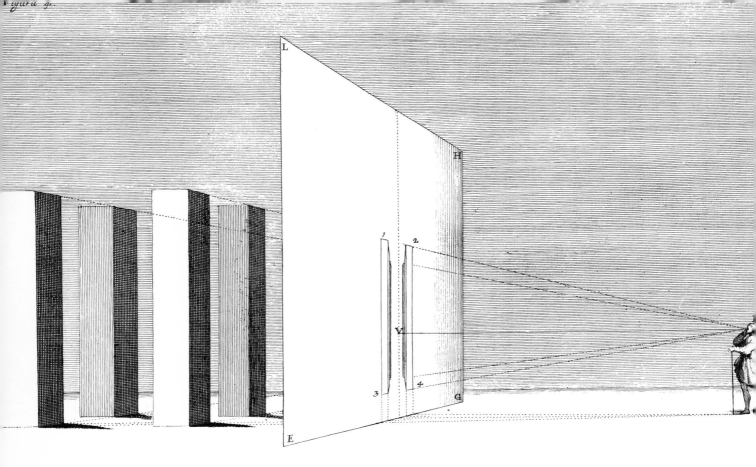

REALIZATION   REPRESENTATION   APPREHENSION

The engraving above, from Andrea Pozzo's *Prospettiva de' Pittori ed Architetti,* published in Rome in 1723, sets forth the problem of the interrelation of apprehension, representation, and realization.

Apprehension, as Heinrich Wölfflin points out (page 11), is a living and constantly changing power, influenced by the philosophical, religious, and scientific attitudes of various periods. It is the basic power which the architect exercises while he is designing in space.

Representation is the means by which spatial concepts are reduced to tangible images, and realization is the establishment of definite three-dimensional forms—the phase of which Walt Whitman speaks on page 15. It is only when these three elements are in harmony that great design is produced.

The Renaissance man in the Pozzo engraving apprehends space within the framework of the new humanity of his period, with its fresh emphasis on the individual and on individual experience.

The images in his mind are deeply influenced by the new method of representation — scientific perspective. Thus this picture can portray both the representation on the picture plane of an already existing reality, or, conversely, the projection of an imaginary three-dimensional concept which exists in the mind of the designer.

These two phases interact on each other, the concept influencing the structure and the structure influencing the concept in a never-ending interplay.

The designer conceives a three-dimensional form which is later built on the ground. From observation of this he gains new understanding of his own mental symbols as expressed in his two-dimensional drawing. However, there is a conflict between the drawing and the three-dimensional reality. Thus the four pylons in the drawing above, through which one can move in ever-changing directions, seem startlingly different from their perspective representation on the picture plane. This poses a dual dilemma.

In order that his three-dimensional concept

be realized through actual construction on the ground, the designer must reduce it to a two-dimensional, representational image which serves as the medium of communication to the builder, who must put it back into three dimensions again. This two-dimensional image also serves as the medium of communication to the client and to the general public, whose support may be necessary for its construction. When a design is truly rich in its three-dimensional aspect, to reduce it to a two-dimensional image may destroy its most vital qualities and thus result in a most imperfect process of communication. This occurred in the case of the winning design by Pedersen and Tilney for the Franklin Delano Roosevelt Memorial in Washington, D.C. The essential nature of the design was totally misunderstood by many of its critics because it was not reducible to a picture plane.

The second problem occurs in the mind of the designer himself. This is so because his work is limited by the stock of images, by the range of the vocabulary of conceptual models, at his command, just as a mathematician is limited by the mathematical symbols he uses. In vast three-dimensional design problems at the scale of the modern city, the traditional range of two-dimensional symbols has proved to be totally inadequate for the task at hand.

In the medieval era (see pages 53 to 57) perception and apprehension were often indivisible, and the representation or communication problem was greatly simplified because the designer and the builder were often the same man. In the Renaissance period the buildings and their mode of representation were very much in harmony because building design was largely an outgrowth of form produced by scientific perspective.

Today our design problems have expanded to a degree of complexity that is beyond the capacity of perspective to represent. Thus traditional representation breaks down as a means of communication, and, even more important, it fails to provide the range of symbols that the modern designer needs for the formulation of his concepts.

In the chart below an attempt has been made to summarize the interaction of apprehension, representation, and realization over four periods of history. I have put question marks in the last two sections of the modern period because the questions raised in these areas are still unresolved.

	APPREHENSION	REPRESENTATION	REALIZATION
MEDIEVAL Intuitive Design	Awareness of total environment	Simultaneously several objects from various viewpoints	Construction closely integrated to its environment
RENAISSANCE Individual-Centered Design	The precise observation of one individual at one specific moment	Rational, rigid, one-point perspective of a single object in space	Single, self-sufficient buildings, detached from surroundings
BAROQUE Single Movement System	Experience as simple continuity in time	Simultaneously multiple planes receding in space to single vanishing-point	Structures related to movement along a single axis
MODERN Simultaneous Movement Systems	Space-time relativity	?	?

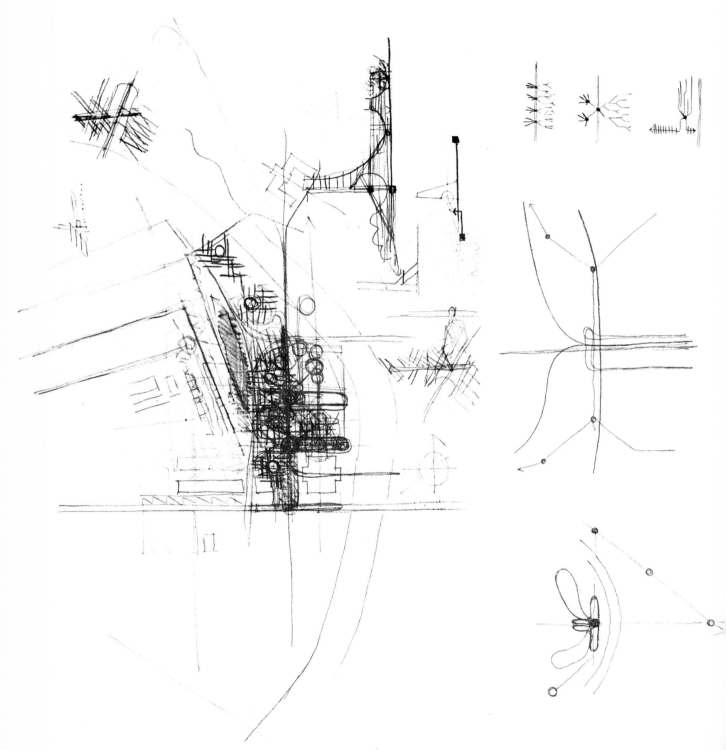

THINKING IN TERMS OF MOVEMENT SYSTEMS

drawings by Romaldo Giurgola

THE NATURE OF DESIGN

To influence the growth of cities, the designer must have a clear concept of the underlying design structure that must be produced to set in motion the involved processes of city-building. The methods of design used in single buildings or in a group of buildings are ineffectual on a city scale for two major reasons. First, the geographic extent of the city is so vast that the human mind is incapable of developing concurrently explicit three-dimensional plans for the entire area. And second, the city is of such a scale that its various sections are built and rebuilt over a long span of time. Therefore, any design used for part of the city should be able to be modified and extended into an ever-widening area.

From our work in Philadelphia we have come to believe that a clear representation of "simultaneous movement systems" in three-dimensional terms has the quality necessary to meet the two city requirements. What is involved is demonstrated on pages 264-307. By clarifying what is essential and what is nonessential, this method enables the designer to establish a central design structure without attempting to cover the entire area. Furthermore, this system of three-dimensional planning is capable of extension, refinement, and enrichment throughout the years. The system used in Philadelphia has proved to be a strong cohesive force in organizing the designs of a series of individual architects into a whole, and in generating the loyalties necessary to establish it as a political force in its own right.

The nature of simultaneous movement systems is described on the following pages, and the remainder of the book demonstrates how these movement systems can influence growth of city form.

THE NATURE OF SIMULTANEOUS MOVEMENT SYSTEMS

To understand the significance of "simultaneous movement systems" or paths along which city-dwellers move or are transported, three concepts must be considered:

1. Relationship of mass and space
2. Continuity of experience
3. Simultaneous continuities

RELATIONSHIP OF MASS AND SPACE

The first step is to orient one's mind as fully as possible to the concept of space as a dominating force, to respond to space as a basic element in itself, and to conceive designs abstractly within it. Scientific thought in recent years has continuously led us further into the realization of the dominance of space and movement and to the notion that matter is really the product of movement in space.

CONTINUITY OF EXPERIENCE

The role of design in the city should be to create a harmonious environment for each individual who resides in it from the moment he rises in the morning until he retires at night. Movement through space creates a continuity of experiences derived from the nature and form of the spaces through which the movement occurs. This gives the key to the concept of a movement system as a dominant organizing force in architectural design. If one can establish a track through space which becomes the actual path of movement of large numbers of people, or participators, and can design the area adjacent to it to produce a continuous flow of harmonic experience as one moves over that track in space, successful designs in cities will be created.

In other words, to the extent that the designer can project himself into the mind and feelings of the participator and so perceive his design as it is to be experienced by those for whom it was created, to that extent will the design achieve its original purpose.

SIMULTANEOUS CONTINUITIES

One must attempt to see the continuity of space experience in terms of a series of movement systems based on different rates of speed and different modes of movement, each of these inter-related with the others and each contributing its part to the total living experience in the city.

There will be sequences of simultaneous experiences for people who move about the city in automobiles, on expressways and local streets, in buses, on commuter railroads, and in subway tubes. The designer also is concerned with the impressions gained at the moment of transfer from a vehicle to the ground, and movement on foot to one or another destination in the city. It is possible to conceive the essential form of these simultaneous movement systems in three dimensions in space as an abstract design, from which the design structure of the city begins to emerge.

RELATIONSHIP OF MOVEMENT SYSTEMS TO NATURAL PHENOMENA

The ordered, geometrical forms associated with crystals, symmetrical patterns radiating from a center, were suited to the early Renaissance concept of the individual-centered world, expressing the experience of a single individual at a single moment in time. But where we are concerned with the experience of the total city and its interrelationships over a long span of time and growth, these forms are not suitable.

As we look at a tree we see in its basic design a form which is capable of growth and which is a direct physical expression of a series of basic movement systems. The seed of the tree contains the initial impulse for growth, a directive which results in a series of tubes possessing a common quality: unity of direction or parallelism, and, in relation to the environment in which they are located, a purposeful vertical direction.

The wonderful thing is that this original directive includes within it the allowance for divergence. If it did not, the indefinite continuation of exact parallelism of the food-carrying tubes would result in death, because the area of exposure to light would be insufficient to nourish growth. On the other hand, the divergence is within controlled limits and is always related to the original directional impulse.

So the strength of the city plan should lie not in authority but in the ability to influence growth, just as the seed has within it a force which causes the cells to group themselves according to an order necessary for the organism to develop.

The trunk of the tree, which establishes the path of movement of thousands of tubes, diverging in the branches and delivering the chemicals necessary for growth to the leaves, can be likened to a city's movement systems. Water acts as the vehicle to propel the chemicals to the leaves, and in turn it evaporates into the air. The point of change from water to vapor is the place where the flowers and fruit develop. So in cities the points of connection between systems should be places of special emphasis and design enrichment.

As the movement systems of a city become clearly defined and are used by more and more people over a span of time, they establish themselves deeply in the collective psychology of the community. As a natural outgrowth of this, logical extensions, increased continuities, variations, and enrichments begin to occur.

RHYTHMS IN TIME

As soon as we are able to think simultaneously about a range of systems and our thoughts relate one to the other, we are able to create a feeling of continuity and harmony in architectural designs. This simultaneous development of various themes is parallel in music, where themes are played against sub-themes, giving continuity and total form to a composition.

The parallel in literature is expressed in a sentence by John Ciardi written for the *Saturday Review:* "The words of a poem, when spoken most meaningfully, must not only speak themselves dramatically, but answer lovingly to the rhythms from which they have emerged, and anticipate as lovingly the rhythms into which they are flowing."

RELATION OF SIMULTANEOUS MOVEMENT SYSTEMS TO CITY DESIGN

Because it is organic, this system can be effectively applied to parts of the city at the beginning, leaving room for growth over an indefinite period of time.

When faced with the problem of producing a design for the development of a large city area, it is wise to study the basic movement patterns very carefully and, at the outset, to establish the beginnings of positive and purposeful movement systems on a fairly modest scale. Then, if one remains on the job continuously and observes and creates designs in relation to this central phenomenon, the concept of simultaneous movement systems inter-

acting upon one another will become increasingly clear. The idea itself must grow organically over time. It cannot and should not be produced in all its manifestations at a single moment. Only when a three-dimensional design is reducible to explicit positioning in space in terms of feet and inches can it be said to have arrived as a concept.

This approach to the problem prevents the confusion and fatigue that occur when the attempt is made to cover enormous areas at once. It leaves the designer free to move about a vast area with a fresh eye to determine what needs to be redesigned and what is best left alone.

The creative process of establishing a movement system is as difficult as, and perhaps even more difficult than, the process of composing a piece of music, writing a poem, or designing a building. It is not my intention, nor would it be possible, to explain exactly what this creative process is. It is something that can be felt only by those who have in themselves the qualities of being an artist. All I can do is suggest how the artistic genius of a designer can be directly related to the city problem.

Movement systems must be related to natural or manmade topography: they must take into account the nature of terrain and the natural features or structures that are a part of it. They can serve to emphasize, dignify, or give new meaning to churches and spires, to public buildings, and to historic monuments that have special significance in the community.

The actual design of each system must relate to the tempo of the movement it is to accommodate as well as to the general nature of the surroundings. Expressway systems require free-flowing forms and curves and widely spaced articulation to accord with the rhythm of fast vehicular movement. At the other extreme, pedestrian movement systems require interest, variety, and impressions of rapid change. This can be achieved through the frequent use of focal points and symbolic objectives — perhaps a series of short sections at different angles with definite visual termini. The problem of the city designer is to deal simultaneously with the different speeds of movement and different rates of perception, to create forms which are as satisfying to those in an automobile as they are to those who travel on foot.

It is astonishing how much power the concept of simultaneous movement systems has in organizing the designs of many architects into a coherent whole and in providing the ingredient of continuity which is so essential when building on the vast scale of a city. The concept provides a basic design structure to which each architect can relate his individual work. For example, it will influence the positioning of an architect's most significant buildings and strengthen the significance of existing landmarks, while allowing him increasing freedom to develop his design in depth as he moves away from the center or spine of the system.

I have perhaps been inclined to represent the design structure or movement system directive as self-fulfilling by some magical or mystic power. This, of course, is quite wrong. The way in which it fulfills itself is through the impact it makes on the minds and sensibilities of the participators who move over it, including designers, developers, administrators, politicians, and the public in general. The reactions experienced by large numbers of people finally produce areas of consensus which, in turn, result in agreement to move ahead on extensions or enrichments of an idea which many people have shared. Of course, this works only if there are clear central channels over which common movement occurs. If the movements are formless, multitudinous, or confused, no consensus or growth can result.

A clearly expressed movement system is a powerful influence, capable of seizing men's minds and developing loyalties around it. Of itself it becomes a major political force. This is essential if we are to achieve a continuity of underlying design order over the period of time that is necessary to rebuild any significant portion of the city. Such a system can provide the basic direction needed to liberate the creative capacities of the designers and to inspire the citizens with the will to see that the agreed changes are made.

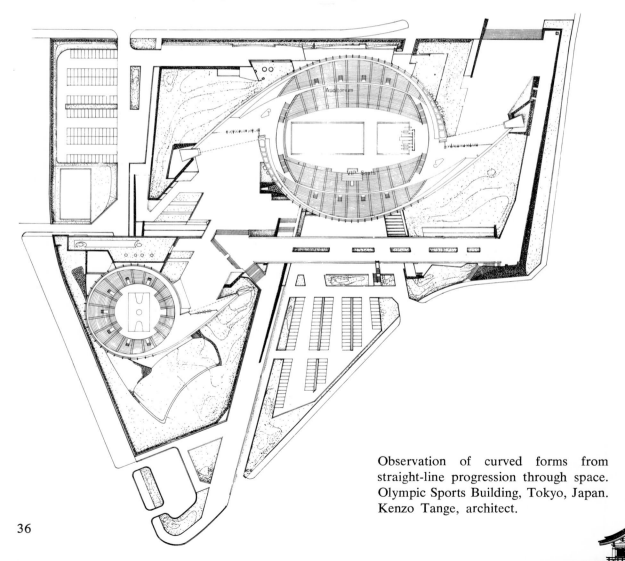

Observation of curved forms from straight-line progression through space. Olympic Sports Building, Tokyo, Japan. Kenzo Tange, architect.

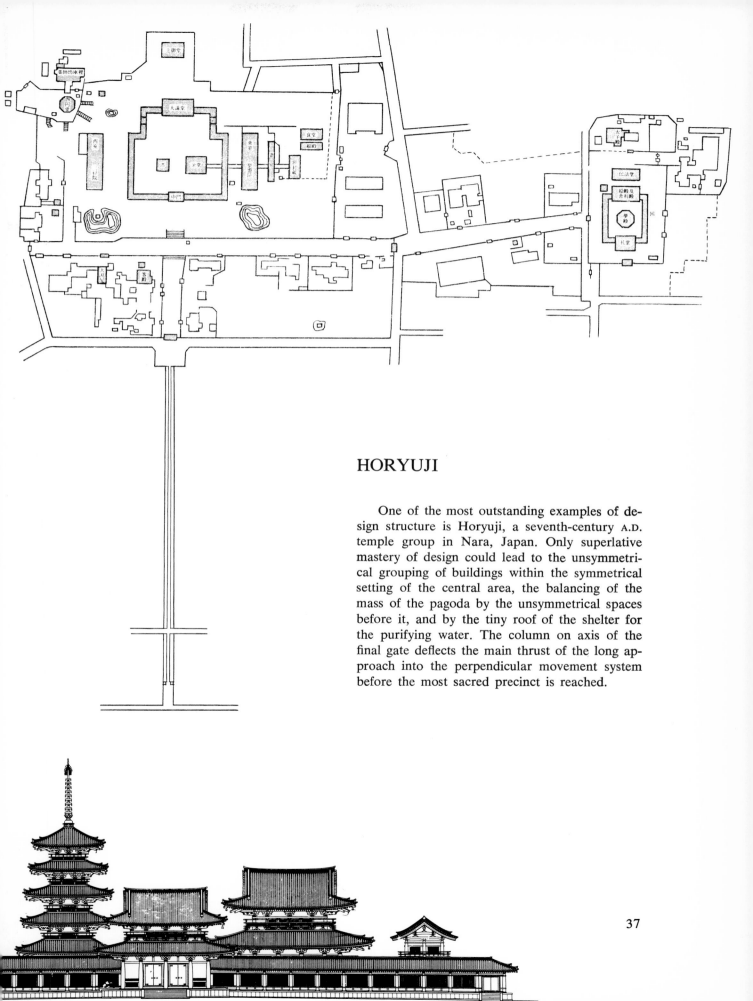

HORYUJI

One of the most outstanding examples of design structure is Horyuji, a seventh-century A.D. temple group in Nara, Japan. Only superlative mastery of design could lead to the unsymmetrical grouping of buildings within the symmetrical setting of the central area, the balancing of the mass of the pagoda by the unsymmetrical spaces before it, and by the tiny roof of the shelter for the purifying water. The column on axis of the final gate deflects the main thrust of the long approach into the perpendicular movement system before the most sacred precinct is reached.

37

OUTGOING

In the two drawings on this page Klee presents two kinds of people. Here is the outgoing man, ebullient, involved, exposed in both his strengths and his frailities. He reaches for more than he has or knows; he leaps into space aware of the possible consequences of a fall; a man with the courage to be vulnerable.

INGROWN

Here is the opposite type of man, inward-looking, self-concerned, and safe, reducing contact with the outside to an absolute minimum, avoiding exposure and involvement. One's self-image of one's function in relation to one's environment will surely determine the form of one's self and one's work, whether the "one" be a person or an institution.

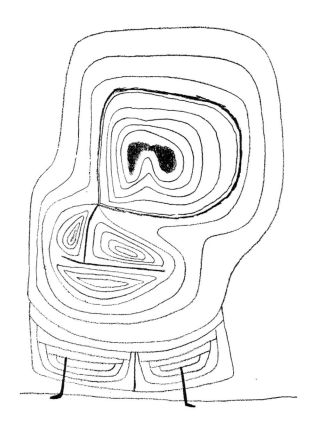

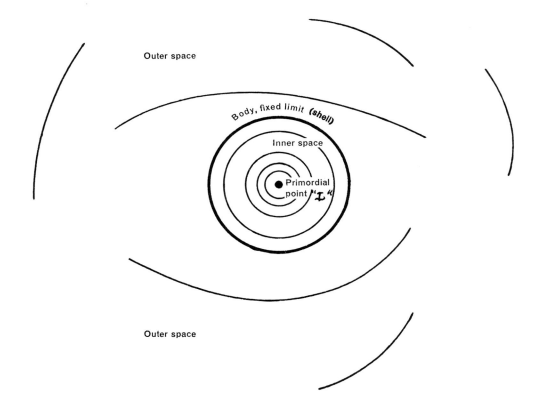

Outer space

Body, *fixed limit* **(shell)**

Inner space

Primordial
point "I"

Outer space

WAYS OF PERCEIVING ONE'S SELF

The application of the design process previously discussed is greatly influenced by the way the designer and the client perceive themselves. The primordial point, the "I" in the Klee diagram above, may be thought of as the individual, the artist, the creator, the organizer, the planner. It may also be an institution, a university, a building proposal, an innovative concept. In each case, the "I" has a definite view of its own identity, its own function and purpose, and its own aspirations. These, in turn, will influence the form that its physical extensions will take, the influence it exerts on the space immediately around it, the "inner space" in the diagram above.

The primordial point, the "I," also has its "outer space," the broader milieu within which its inner, more intimately related spaces function. While in this diagram Klee has designated the divider between the two as a fixed limit, a shell, it can also be seen in more abstract terms as the fluid division between the inner, the intimate, the familiar, the inherited, the customary, and the outer, the unfamiliar, the untried, the challenging, the dangerous, the painful, and the potentially disastrous. Each person, social group, each institution has these inner and outer spaces. The dress and folkways of the newer generation provide a protective inner space for that group just as surely as do the country clubs and social registers of the older: Each has its area outside, repugnant and terrifying. The way in which one's self relates to these two determines the nature of one's life and one's contribution to society, and, in physical terms, the nature and form of an institution.

WAYS OF PERCEIVING ENVIRONMENT

FROM A BOAT

Key to the form of one's self-image of one's projection into the space around one is whether one views his immediate and his more distant environment as hostile or favorable.

To demonstrate how the same thing may look to different people, these drawings were prepared showing favorable and hostile environments on the same terrain as seen by the boatman and the motorist. In the drawing on the left, the "I" on the boat sees danger as the land, the hazard increasing in intensity as the land rises in the bottom of the bay, and as it approaches laterally.

FAVORABLE ENVIRONMENT

HOSTILE ENVIRONMENT

FROM AN AUTOMOBILE

The hostile environment for the motorist is the very environment that is safe for the boatman and vice versa (drawing on the right). This obvious definition of environmental hostility is paralleled by a much more subtle and insidious feeling of environmental hostility which bears great influence on architecture. Its impact is recorded in the forms of buildings at various points in history. When viewed in this light, these buildings become remarkably sensitive barometers of changes in degree of hostility or harmony between the structure and the environment in which it is located.

40

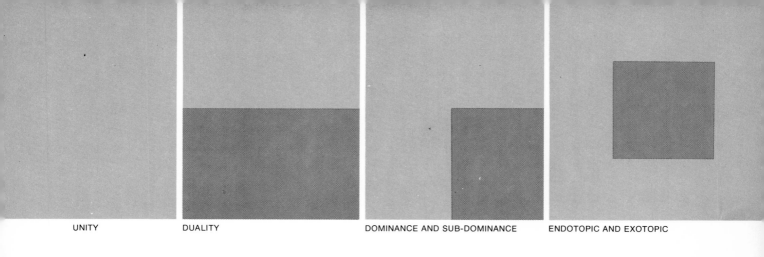

UNITY   DUALITY   DOMINANCE AND SUB-DOMINANCE   ENDOTOPIC AND EXOTOPIC

WAYS OF PERCEIVING SPACE

Key to the whole concept is the way in which one perceives the continuity of space within which the inner and outer spaces operate. The four squares above illustrate different ways in which such perception can take place. They should be thought of as planes of indefinite size, extending in all directions to the horizon and beyond.

The square to the left represents space as a boundless unit, the continuous interaction of opposites represented by black and white producing an unbroken extent of gray, as in systems of nature.

In the second square man enters and draws a line, whether physical or conceptual, dividing the system into two elements: love-hate, good-evil, indissolubly establishing duality.

In the third square the line is bent, creating an inequivalence. By the act of bending the line, the designer establishes the dominance of one element and the subdominance of the other.

In the fourth square the line is closed, creating a duality of a new sort: one (the darker square) a discrete object clearly defined which detaches itself from the other, the lighter gray plane of indefinite extent which surrounds it. The question then becomes whether because of exotopic blindness the designer sees only the discrete object, as he has been taught to do from infancy in the Western world, or whether he sees the situation as a plane of indefinite extent with a hole in it.

Paul Klee defines the inner square in relation to the line as endotopic, and the outer plane as exotopic, and illustrates ways in which these two intermesh when controlled by lines of differing character.

ENDOTOPIC

SHAPE—When viewed in endotopic terms the design process becomes that of making shapes. Architecture becomes the imposition of capricious shapes into the environment.

MASS—The third dimension is seen as the vertical projection of capricious shapes, and architecture becomes preoccupied with mass as geometrical form.

OBJECT—This approach culminates in thinking of the building as a discrete object, created independently of its background, arbitrarily placed in anonymous space. The negative aspects are stressed because so many designers are heavily endotopic, but true design involves an interplay of endotopic and exotopic thinking.

EXOTOPIC

SPACE—When viewed in exotopic terms the design process becomes that of articulating for human purposes some portion of a space of indefinite extent.

MOVEMENT—Since the articulations of space can be experienced only through movement, the designer's function becomes that of providing channels of movement related to larger movement systems.

FORM—In this approach form emerges naturally from the movement systems so that the step of creating capricious shapes doesn't exist in the design process.

A key test of design is whether the shapes are arbitrary or are derived from movement systems.

41

FAVORABLE ENVIRONMENT

In the medieval period, because of the limited effectiveness of the military missiles of the time, the degree of hostility of the environment varied markedly within horizontal layers. In this drawing of the Castle of Saumur from the Book of Hours of the Duke of Berry, the architectural forms respond to this variation as it rises vertically. Here, in the upper air, the architecture leaps outward into space, exposing itself in all directions, involving itself with the atmosphere to the point that the turrets, foliate projections, spires, and pinnacles seem almost to dissolve into space.

INTERMEDIATE ENVIRONMENT

In this intermediate section of the castle, partly but not completely removed from the threat of military missiles, the architecture involves itself in space beyond the minimum. The vertical ridges deliberately extend the area, and so the vulnerability of the wall. The architectural expression is of a single direction of thrust, up and away from the hostile environment of the ground.

HOSTILE ENVIRONMENT

Here the architectural forms are completely dominated by the need to resist the hostile environment outside. The inward-looking convex forms produce the minimum surface exposure for the maximum interior volume, and the curved mass tended to deflect such missiles as the military mind could produce.

The Klee diagrams in the center suggest the response of the primordial point to the three conditions of environment.

OUTREACH

In these three plans we see the struggle of the medieval structure to free itself from the oppressive demands of an environment seen as totally hostile.

In the upper plan, a late castle is beginning to break out of the rigid circular form of earlier fortifications, and to involve itself more richly in its environment, reaching out to significant points around it, even at the cost and dangers of greater exposure.

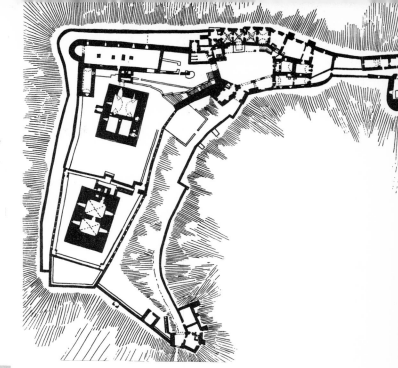

INTERMEDIATE

In this plan the internal structural discipline of the groin vault demands rectangular over-all form. The need for protection from a hostile environment in turn suggests minimum exposure and so a circular form. In this design, created within the tension of these two conflicting demands, military considerations clearly outweighed structural logic.

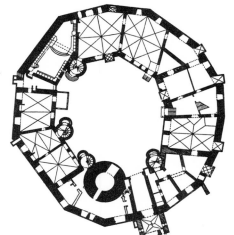

INWARD LOOKING

This medieval tower is the most efficient possible structure when protection from a hostile environment is seen as the dominant consideration. The resemblance between this plan and the Klee drawing on page 39 is striking. Here the "inner space" is that space around the tower which is controlled by armaments within it. The divider between this and the darker, uncontrolled "outer space" is not a "fixed shell" but an intangible line determined by the efficiency of the armaments.

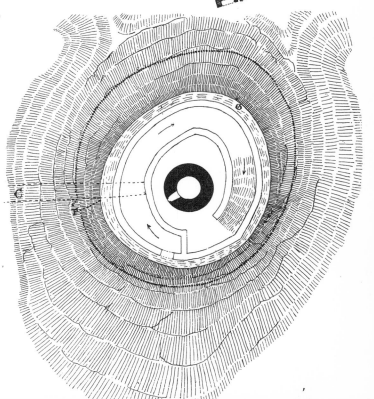

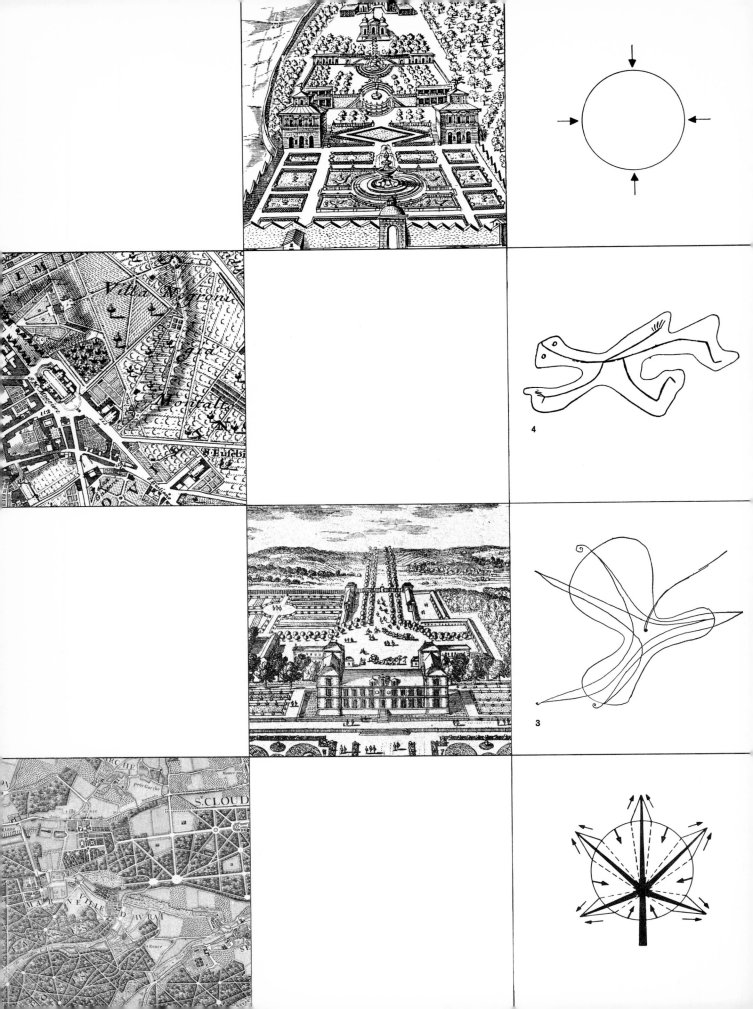

4

3

INWARD LOOKING

As we move into the Renaissance, we observe the outpush of architecture into an environment gradually freed of the most oppressive elements of medieval hostility. The fully developed Italian villa, such as the 1560 Villa Lante at Bagnaja shown on the left, contained the seeds of later work in their thrusts and counterthrusts, but all of these were totally contained within clearly defined bounding walls in the endotopic sense. The diagrams in the center are from Paul Klee's *The Thinking Eye.*

OUTREACH

In 1585 Pope Sixtus V introduced a new design dimension into Italian thought by his plans for Rome. These burst the bounds of any clearly defined building project and utilized the entire city of Rome as the design field. While the thrusts and counterthrusts of his movement systems extended over great distances, they always reached out to definite objects, and finally came to rest at some terminal point, such as a church, a gate, or a square.

OUTGOING

An entirely new dimension of design was introduced into France in the eighteenth century in the form of design thrusts that had no clear termination, that penetrated the boundaries of the inner space, that extended outward indefinitely, over the horizon seemingly to infinity. These concepts were developed at the time of the Encyclopedists and the mathematical explorations of infinity, and establish the idea of a design structure capable of indefinite extension over time.

INVOLVEMENT

The fourth design element, suggested by the Klee diagram to the left, involves not only the penetration of the inner space by an outward push, but concurrently a counter-movement of outer space influences penetrating inwardly toward the source. While this is illustrated here by the remarkable interaction of design thrust in the Paris region, it might better be illustrated in the institutional sense by the kind of involvement that is tending to come about today when wide sectors of people invade what the professional designer previously had thought was his private inner space of design.

PSYCHOLOGY OF SPACE

Erik H. Erikson, psychoanalyst and educator, in discussing the essence of play and interplay, said, "Play needs firm limits, then free movement within these limits. Without firm limits there is no play." He introduced the German word *Spielraum* to present the concept of the extension of the room of interplay which he related to the life cycle as depicted in his chart on the right. He developed the idea of "forbidding environment" in contrast to "facilitating environment," and showed how the balance between these two may affect one's response to the various turning points in one's life, strengthening or inhibiting the full realization of one's potential.

In simple terms, if the environment of a small child has so many forbidding elements, perhaps dangers or perhaps just breakable objects within the child's reach, that the mother is compelled constantly to say "no," a sense of guilt may be aggravated in the child and become disproportionate in relation to his confidence and initiative, and so the course of his development is affected. In much more complex terms the elements of "forbidding environment" and "facilitating environment" continue to exist as influences in adolescent and adult life. In relation to the chart opposite they affect the radius of significant relations and the quality of these relations, the nature and extent of interplay. Each of the psychological crises mediates between the inner life and the total environment and its counterpart in the dimensions of the radius of significant-relations.

Viewed in this light, much of city design is concerned with the establishment of firm limits within which there can be free movement, and extending these limits outward as the radius of significant relations expands. The change of concept from the term previously used, "favorable environment," to Erikson's "facilitating environment" adds an important dimension to the urban designer's task.

LIFE
CYCLE

Old Age

Adulthood

Young
Parenthood

Adolescence

School Age

Play Age

Early
Childhood

Infancy

PSYCHOLOGICAL CRISES		RADIUS OF SIGNIFICANT RELATIONS
Integrity vs Despair	**WISDOM**	My Kind Mankind
Generativity vs Stagnation	**CARE**	Divided Labor and Shared Household
Intimacy vs Isolation	**LOVE**	Partners in Friendship Sexuality, Competition Cooperation
Identity vs Confusion	**FIDELITY**	Peer Groups and Out Groups Models of Leadership
Industry vs Inferiority	**COMPETENCE**	Neighborhood and School
Initiative vs Guilt	**PURPOSE**	Basic Family
Autonomy vs Shame, Doubt	**WILL**	Parental Persons
Trust vs Mistrust	**HOPE**	Maternal Person

INVOLVEMENT TODAY

As I propose to indicate on the following pages, involvement encompasses much more than cerebral comprehension. It is a necessary ingredient for the creation of competent design.

Sigfried Giedion in his great book *Space, Time and Architecture* stresses the importance of moving beyond the purely cerebral into the realm of feeling, of involving one's sensibilities and emotions. Rudolph Arnheim, in Gyorgy Kepes's *Education of Vision*, quotes Albert Einstein's letter to Jacques Hadamard, "The words or the language as they are written or spoken do not seem to play any role in my mechanism of thought. The psychical entities which seem to serve as elements in thought are certain signs and more or less clear images which can be 'voluntarily' reproduced and combined." And further: "The above-mentioned elements are, in my case, of visual and some of muscular type. Conventional words or other signs have to be sought for laboriously only in a secondary stage, when the mentioned associative play is sufficiently established and can be reproduced at will." He adds his own comment "If Einstein's procedure is representative of intelligent reasoning, we may be strangling the potential of our brainpower systematically by forcing our youth to think primarily with verbal and numerical signs."

Leonard K. Eaton in his book *Two Chicago Architects and Their Clients* says, "As long ago as 1919 Carl Seashore noted that musically talented students possessed high auditory imagery (the ability to recreate a tone image), and that this faculty was closely related to motor imagery and motor tendencies: *These motor images are perceived in terms of feelings, of effort and strain in the body. This kinesthetic response plays a large part in the enjoyment derived from active participation in music, architecture and sport.*" (Italics mine.)

The point here is not bodily movement as "exercise" or "recreation," separate and divorced from the act of design, but rather bodily response as a built-in ingredient of the design process. It relates to the range of the images or models that are used in design. Thus, if one is bodily inert or incompetent, one tends to sit and contemplate. The forms that associate with this kind of bodily condition are crystalline shapes, spheres, cubes, or pyramids, discrete forms which can be comprehended without the need for bestirring oneself, for putting forth the muscular effort required for moving about. If one is physically and muscularly in such condition that it is a joy to move about, that one is impelled by an inner drive to leap forward to the next and the next experience, a very different range of perception of space and time is brought into play, and one is inclined to think in terms of linkages rather than discrete elements.

This may be illustrated by the problem of perceiving the basic design idea of two national capital cities: Washington, D.C., and Peking. If one stands at the foot of the Washington Monument at the intersection of the two main axes of the United States Capital, one has only to move around the base, a matter of a few feet, to perceive all of the basic elements of monumental Washington. In Peking there just is no way to perceive the design except by making the effort to move through the spaces over a two-mile track. One can't see from one part to another because each part is totally enclosed, yet it is not any individual part, but rather the linkage, which is the design.

In the education of small children we have systematically suppressed the motor tendency by forcing them to sit still for long hours at a time. In advanced education we have systematically denigrated sensory, sensual, and muscular perception, and fostered the dichotomy between body and thought. A reintegration is called for, not to make the student "healthy," but to equip him with the basic faculties needed for his work. Training in muscular skill and muscular and sensory perception should be part of every architectural and planning school. I believe that anyone intending to practice architecture or planning should be able to run up three flights of stairs without noticeable loss of breath and take joy in doing it.

INWARD LOOKING

THE INVOLVEMENT OF
THE SQUARE

Above stands the square, the paradigm of architectural thought, compact, self-contained, the minimum exterior exposure for the maximum interior area if a minimum number of perpendicular straight lines is also an objective. The form was developed in earliest times when protection from a hostile environment was building's main purpose. While still efficient as an enclosure of space, and still relevant to parts of a larger whole, it remains all too often as the paradigm for the whole itself. Here the residual effect can be damaging indeed. If it is used by an institution, a university in a low-income area, for example, and each extension is designed as nearly as possible to reconstruct a square of larger dimension, the impression will be given that the institution regards the environment into which it is projecting itself as hostile. The physical form will have a minimum of exposure and so of environmental involvement. The shape of the edge and the nature of the edge are both important because of the way in which they communicate the institution's message to its neighbors, of favorableness or hostility, as when a neighborhood rose up in protest because a university put a chain link fence along one portion of its boundary.

What follows is a geometrical development of the square in an attempt to present a countermodel for the growth and extension of an entity, be it an institution or an idea. At the top of the following page the square projects itself into a cross, shown in yellow, substantially increasing its length of exposure to the environment while retaining its original area. This increases the degree of involvement, but the form continues to be an aggressive one.

In the lower diagram on that page the red line designates the form produced when this same principle of exposure is applied to each of the nine sub-squares produced by the cross form. The two diagrams on the following page show, first in blue and then in black, the forms produced by extending this principle in two more stages. The drawing on page 52 shows the form taken to still one more stage of development.

It will be seen that the length of the line bounding the entity can be increased indefinitely while holding the diagram within definite bounds. As the bounding line approaches infinity, the degree of environmental involvement becomes greater and greater.

49

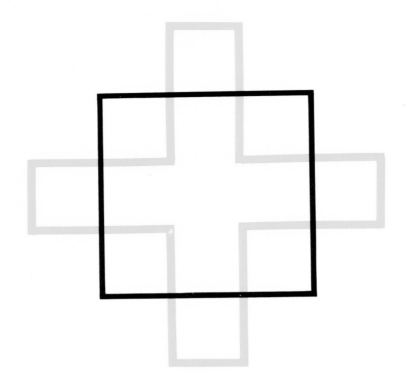

OUTREACH

OUTGOING

50

INVOLVEMENT A

INVOLVEMENT B

51

TOWARD TOTAL INVOLVEMENT

We have now come full cycle from the simple circle of Paul Klee defining the limit between inner space and outer space through the square which, orthogonally, most nearly approximates Klee's circle, through the square extension on the two previous pages, to the diagram above. The systematic application of the principle produced a form with elements approaching the circle, related to each other in definite groupings and sub-groupings. Yet the figure above is just as surely a single area with a single bounding line as is the Klee circle. It demonstrates that involvement tends to dissolve the distinction between the inner and the outer, and produces forms implicit in the first step of outreach, but difficult to anticipate in their entirety.

Of course this form is only a stage in a continuous progression to infinity. The line of exposure becomes longer and longer and the levels of foci become greater and greater with each stage of development, each of these approaching infinity. The point at which a form comes to rest along this progression is the point of equilibrium between the inner and environmental forces in terms of hostility and favorableness.

It should be restated that the geometrical form of this diagram has no symbolic significance beyond the principle it embodies. It should also be restated that, while this illustration was deliberately intended to suggest new ways to define the boundaries of institutional site plans in cities, the ideas it engenders relate to a much wider range of issues, the form of urban extension within a metropolitan region, (with maximum exposure to open space), the form of implantation of a new idea in a social group or indeed of a new institution within society. It relates wherever there is an inner and an outer, and that is nearly everywhere.

COLOR AS A DIMENSION OF PROGRESSION THROUGH SPACE

One of the elements which can be used to give continuity and form to the experience of moving through spaces is color. The purposeful use of color in a sequential sense is almost unknown in contemporary practice. That this was not always so is shown in the photograph above and in those on the four succeeding pages. Through the medium of the color camera we follow a woman delivering a load of straw to a destination on the other side of a little Italian hill town on the Mediterranean island of Ischia.

As our participator approaches her objective, the town of Panza, the heat and glare and the predominance of green in the orchards, vineyards, and olive groves begin to be modified by gray adobe walls and fresh white paint — pointers to the urban experience that is to come.

Before her she sees the beginnings of the actual form of the town as it emerges from among the trees, but the path is still tortuous, and the form is merely suggested, except for the bell tower of the church, which will shortly emerge as a powerful architectural statement, suggesting the character of the experience which lies ahead.

ANTICIPATION

In the photographs to the left we observe the unfolding of the architecture of Panza. The straw carrier has turned the bend, which was perfectly placed for the first viewpoint of the architecture of the square. The first flash of impression she receives includes a strong architectural impact through the rhythmic punctuation of the shadowy arches. An entirely new dimension of experience is added by the startling pink walls seen through the gray framework.

As she continues to move along the path, she becomes more and more aware of the predominance of pink until she has reached the town center, the lower portion of the central hourglass-shaped piazza. Here she is encompassed by the sensation of pinkness. In the sense of Léger, she has entered a "colored space."

Turning to her right and looking southward, she is now subjected to an even more intense sensation. Her eye takes in the orange-colored chapel with its circular window, which terminates the square and sparkles in the sunlight against the deep blue of the distant olive-clad hills.

In the picture on the opposite page, she is passing through the central constriction of the hourglass. The colors here are gray and white, counteracting the impression of bright pink and orange, and once more she is prepared for the new color impact ahead.

FULFILLMENT

The picture on the left shows the final impression the straw-carrier is to receive on her journey. The view which bursts upon her is that of the little church crowning the square, a gleaming form of yellow and white with a green door, resplendent against the intensity of the blue sky. Turning to her right, she arrives at the bell tower with its clock that was her first sign of the town, and her anticipation is fulfilled.

How did it happen that such a work of art was created?

The man who designed the second house from the corner (or the designers of any of the other houses for that matter) was a man who, like the straw-carrier, had, thousands of times since childhood, experienced the sequence of sensations just described. Because of the size and scale of the design organism, his apprehension of the town and its setting was complete and simultaneous; all parts of it and all its details were at one instant a part of his mental equipment.

As he decided where the door and the windows were to be, and what color to paint them, these and other details naturally and inevitably fitted in with the forms and the sequence of sensations surrounding them.

And so, in representation, the designer-builder made no drawings of his house. He represented his design in his mind, and finally it took form on the ground exactly as it was seen in the designer's mind. The final product was a perfect link in a total aesthetic experience, all of which existed within himself.

This phenomenon, often disparagingly referred to as "intuitive," actually represents a process so complex — simultaneously employing such a range of factors brought into mutual interaction — that no computer yet conceived by man, or ever to be conceived by man, can come close to duplicating it.

Sadly, a revisit to Panza revealed that everything represented here has been ruined by subsequent "improvements," showing how fragile is a work of this sort, and how remarkable that it could have existed at all.

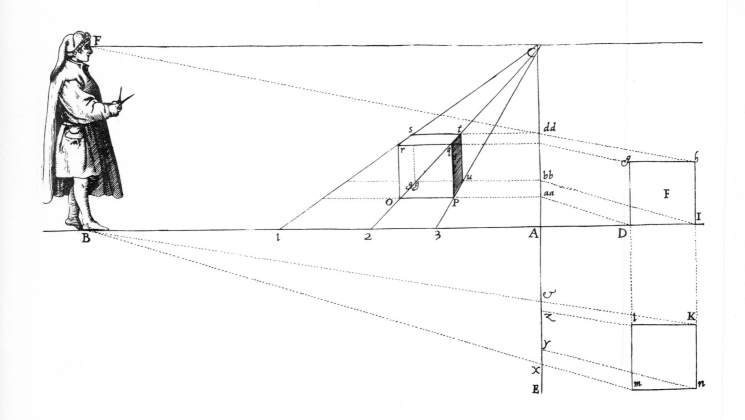

TIME IS ARRESTED — PERSPECTIVE

Giorgio Vasari, in his account of the life of architect Filippo Brunelleschi, has this to say: "He gave much attention to perspective, which was then [the early fifteenth century] in a very evil plight by reason of many errors that were made therein; and in this he spent much time, until he found himself a method whereby it might become true and perfect — namely, that of tracing it with the ground plan and profile and by means of intersecting lines, which was something truly most ingenious and useful to the art of design." Whatever the actual source, the discovery of the method of accurate projection of an object on a picture plane had a profound effect on the process of design, shattering the marvelously complex interaction of forces just described, and tending to arrest the intuitive flow of experience over time.

In the drawing on the opposite page, from Vignola's book on perspective, we see medieval man, emerging into Renaissance consciousness, observing a cube by perspective — something not possible before. The calipers he holds are symbolic of his new desire to view the world in precise measure, by numbers, an objective he can achieve only at great sacrifice. Here he has captured his cube and has imprisoned it precisely for all time

on his picture plane. But this is a cube seen by one man at one point in space at one instant in time; never again will it be seen in this precise and highly individualistic way.

The change from a collective to an individual experience, from a harmonic flow of sensations to a separate, precisely defined, but fragmented sensation, set the stage for the Renaissance and the age of science which followed. This mode of seeing was perpetuated by the camera's eye. Every photograph taken today is essentially the same method of representation as that of the sixteenth-century engraving. For hundreds of years we have been imprisoned within the confines of the perspective picture plane, and are only now beginning to free ourselves from the restrictions imposed.

The drawing by Paul Klee at the bottom of this page, reproduced from *The Thinking Eye*, can be considered as a bridge between the rigidities of perspective and the new freedom of simultaneity. Here we see the cube just beginning to dissolve as a rigid form; we see the struggle to depict it as it might be seen by several men simultaneously or by one man over time. In its ambiguity it conveys the spirit of free form in space and heralds the resumption of the flow of time.

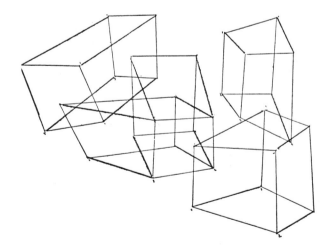

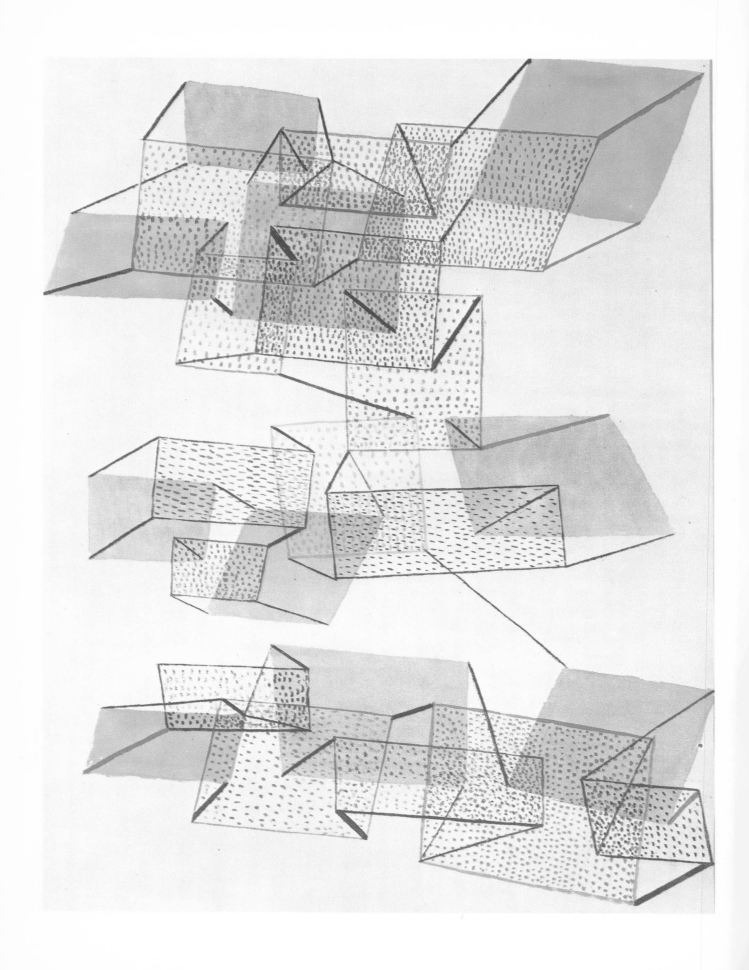

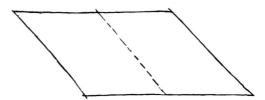

One pair of lines in like direction
lineally expressed

Another pair of lines in like
direction lineally expressed

TIME FLOWS AGAIN
—SIMULTANEITY

"Now I shall proceed so as to have all essentials brought to the fore, including that essential which optical perspectives conceal; and thus I shall have staked out a small but uncontested territory of my own: I shall have created the beginnings of a style." These words, written by Paul Klee in 1902, preceded by twenty-eight years his water-color "Sailing City," reproduced on the opposite page. In this painting we have a full expression of free form in space, a construction in three dimensions altogether freed of the limitations imposed by perspective. Klee's design recaptures the range of simultaneous sensations that produced the intuitive development of Panza, but there is also the added dimension of an awareness of space, movement, and time which science has provided. The colored volumes are firmly positioned in space and precisely related to one another, and they set in motion a series of interactions that move outward from their source. In terms of design, it is this kind of thinking that we need as a base for the development of concepts relating to our evolving present-day city forms.

The painting is not the product of capricious willfulness. It is the result of years of painstaking and disciplined work of an artist-philosopher-scientist who tried to capture, on a picture plane, the new forces that science had unleashed.

The diagrams on the right, derived from Klee's notebook, are but a few of a whole range of studies which led to the composition of his "Sailing City." Through the study of such analyses we may find the key to bring apprehension, representation, and realization into harmony again, and so conceive and build city designs that are worthy of the age we live in.

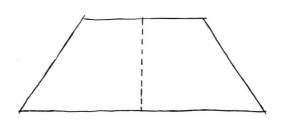

One pair of lines in different
direction lineally expressed

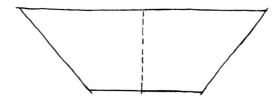

Another pair of lines in different
direction lineally expressed

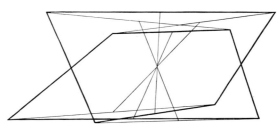

The four operations
combined

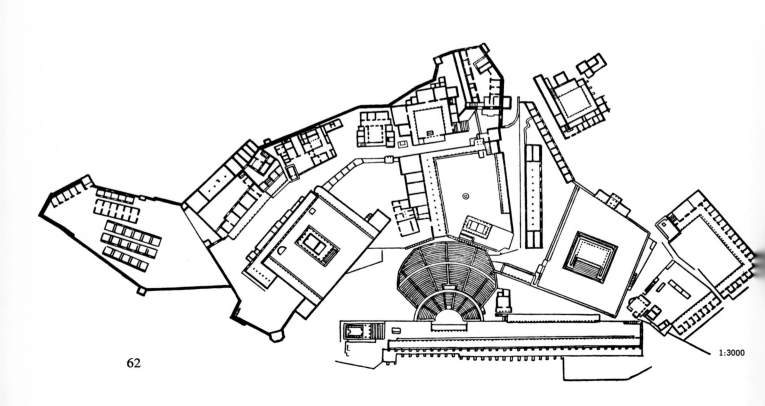

62

1:3000

THE INNER FORCES AT WORK

On the opposite page is a drawing by Paul Klee, and under it a plan of the Hellenistic and Roman work on the acropolis of Pergamon in Asia Minor. The similarities between the two drawings are coincidental, except insofar as all organic things are related, for it is most unlikely that Klee had Pergamon in mind when he made his diagram.

The purpose in bringing these drawings together is to demonstrate how, through the eyes of artists like Klee, the work of the ancients can be seen in a new light. By penetrating the surface manifestations of stylism, we can better comprehend today the inner forces that were at work in the creation of great compositions of the past. These are as fresh today as at the instant they were conceived.

Paul Klee states that the laboratory of the artist is to be found "where the primal law feeds growth . . . where the central organ of motion in space and time — be it called the heart or the head — inspires all functions of creation." The drawing he made is an expression of this law. The central lines of movement curve and interpenetrate space. The lines of growth which extend perpendicularly outward from them form areas of fluctuating intensity and nodal points where many lines intersect within the embrace of curves. Looking again at the plan of Pergamon, sinuously wound into the curving hills, we see similar central lines of movement, from which the perpendicular submovements extend to form focal subcenters, nodal points, and areas of differing character.

Below is a drawing by a student of mine, Sarantis Zafiropoulos of Greece, done in response to a walking trip through central Philadelphia, showing simultaneously movement, rhythm, symbol, texture, volume, time, hegemony, as they exist within the realities of the city, adumbrating a new approach to design structure.

A CONCEPT OF MOVEMENT SYSTEMS

The energies put out by the design structure are ineffectual unless they are received by an instrument that is attuned to them. That instrument, of course, is the sensibilities of the people of the city.

The capacity to respond to design stimuli differs greatly with each individual; furthermore, the level of public response has varied in different countries and at different times in history. Thus the red walls of the Forbidden City of Peking are unthinkable without the pageant of color which, in an ever-changing symphony of dress, flags, and equipment, moves before it. The way people clothe themselves, and their awareness of the changing role of the color of their garments in relation to the background, is a phenomenon unparalleled in the West today.

I think few of us can stand before the Parthenon without being painfully aware of the wide range of responsive sensitivity which the Greek citizen must have possessed and which we in the twentieth century have lost.

In the long run the designer can stimulate in individuals new areas of awareness by the force of his product, but this is a slow and uncertain direction of effort. Alternately, through the architectural form of his structure, he can channel the movement of people through purposeful routes of movement and points of pause, influencing the nature of their responses.

One of the most brilliant historic examples of a human channel of movement is the Panathenaic procession in ancient Greece. It occurred every year — and in an especially rich manner every four years — as a major event in the civic life of Athens. This procession (the subject of the Parthenon frieze illustrated above) took place along a clearly marked route extending from the Dipylon Gate at the city wall across Athens and up the slopes of the Acropolis to the culminating point,

the statue of the goddess Athena. While this route was used by the citizens of Athens every day of their lives for a multiplicity of purposes, its use must always have raised association with the brilliant and beautiful procession all of them had witnessed since childhood. The degree to which this procession was in the collective consciousness of Athens is shown by the end of the Oresteian Trilogy of Aeschylus. Here, jointly, both the actors and the audience created the last scene, moving out of the theater and down into the city of Athens along the Panathenaic Way.

This procession was not primarily to provide a spectacle for the onlooker, but rather to create an event in which many could take part. Thus the citizen became both actor and audience, affecting and being affected by the collective event.

From the time of its first beginning in archaic days, the Panathenaic procession and the sensations of those taking part in it gave the central theme to the development of Athens. From that time on, much of the architectural effort was directed toward providing punctuating points in the experience of its movement, toward adding a note to the rhythm set by previous generations. But the conceiver, the promoter, the architect, and the builder of these injections into a sequence of sensation were themselves the product of the cumulative effect of moving over the Panathenaic Way, and so were automatically attuned to the demands of its accumulated rhythms.

With these basic points once established — the simplicity of the single central movement system through the city, the understanding of the value of memory and of response to forms, — we can now view the Panathenaic procession not merely as a spectacle of humans and animals in harmonic movement, but as the central organizing force in the architectural and planning development of Athens.

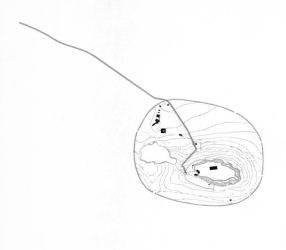

600–479 B.C.

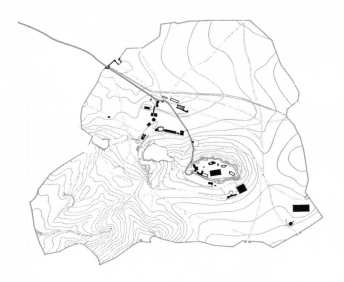

478–339 B.C.

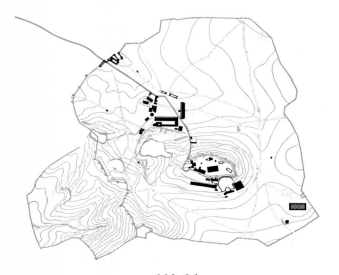

338–86 B.C.

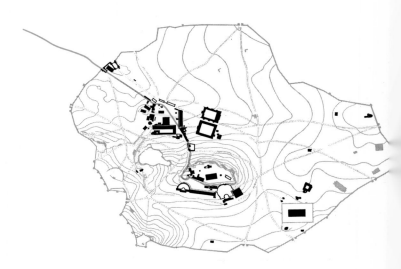

86 B.C.–287 A.D.

1:25000

66

THE GROWTH OF GREEK CITIES

ATHENS

As we have just seen, the Panathenaic Way was far more than a city street; it was part of a system of regional movement which linked some of the most sacred places in Greece. From earliest times it joined the route which led from the mystic grottoes of Eleusis across the Greek countryside, through the Daphnae pass to the Dipylon Gate of Athens. As it continued diagonally across the originally amorphous space of the agora or market-place, and on up the slopes of the Acropolis through the Propylaea to the statue of Athena, it served both as the sacred way and also as the main street of Athens. It was the central spine along which occurred the principal mercantile, industrial, and political activities which made up the life of the city. Indeed the position and size of the Parthenon are comprehensible only when it is viewed in relation to the entire Panathenaic sequence.

The drawings opposite demonstrate the evolution of the form of Athens. The route of the Panathenaic Way is indicated in blue, the thrust of shaft of space from the Temple of Hephaestos (the Hephaisteion) is shown in yellow, and the principal buildings as they developed are indicated in black. Here we see the evolution of the form of the agora integrated with the design and development of Athens as a whole.

The superb placing of the Hephaisteion, the product of a deliberate act of will, part of the way up, but not at the highest point of, the long ridge adjacent to the Panathenaic Way, set into motion a shaft of space which, by its intersection of the movement along the Panathenaic Way, establishes a point in space. This became a significant design element in the subsequent development of the agora.

The design of the Hephaisteion itself is perfectly conceived to generate force of sufficient intensity to animate all the events that happened around it. The patch of sky between the columns on the left emphasizes the interlock between the structure of the temple and the shaft of space perpendicular to the ridge.

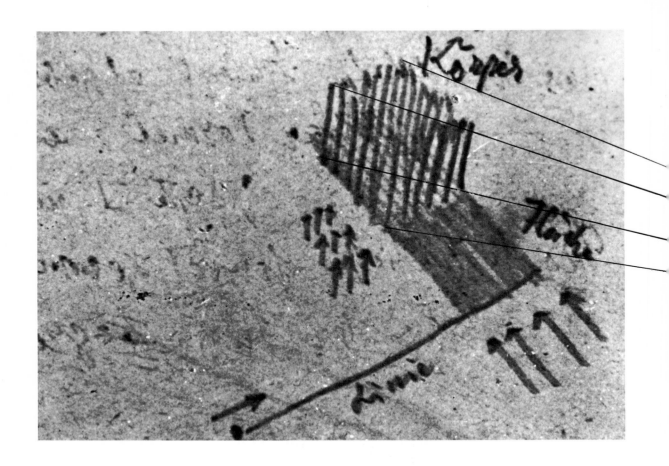

DYNAMICS OF DESIGN EXTENDED INTO THE NEXT DIMENSION

In approaching the first elements of design, Paul Klee says,

"I begin where all pictorial form begins: with the point that sets itself into motion.

"The point (as agent) moves off and the line comes into being — the first dimension (1). If the line shifts to form a plane, we obtain a two-dimensional element (2).

"In the movement from plane to spaces, the clash of planes gives rise to a body (three dimensional) (3).

"Summary of the kinetic energies which move the point into a line, the line into a plane, and the plane into a spatial dimension."

The essence of architectural design, when reviewed on the scale of a city, consists in large measure of a skillful interplay of dynamic forces that are as simple as those portrayed by Klee's drawing above and by the gist of the words just quoted.

Design on the scale of a single building, or indeed of a few related buildings, has been developed to such a high degree that there is a vast, complex, but generally understood vocabulary concerning the interplay of such forces. However, when the field shifts to the relatively uncharted territory between individual building design and city-wide planning abstractions, a review of first principles and a liberal use of simple analogies and elemental concepts are, I think, essential. For a long time we have been blind to the elements of design at this level, and have assumed that large-scale problems can be solved by mechanical repetition of small-scale ideas. If progress is to be made, it must be re-established that design does exist at this level and, indeed, that it is a most important phase in architecture and city-planning.

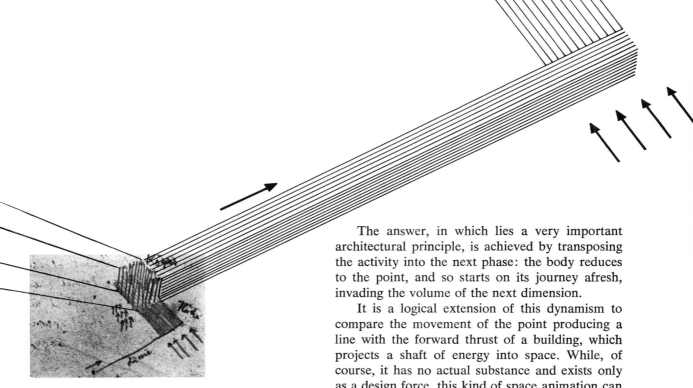

The answer, in which lies a very important architectural principle, is achieved by transposing the activity into the next phase: the body reduces to the point, and so starts on its journey afresh, invading the volume of the next dimension.

It is a logical extension of this dynamism to compare the movement of the point producing a line with the forward thrust of a building, which projects a shaft of energy into space. While, of course, it has no actual substance and exists only as a design force, this kind of space animation can become a major influence in architectural composition, as in the development of Athens.

Moreover, in the finest work the shaft of space is precisely defined, thus setting up a demanding discipline for the design and placement of all forms that are to relate to it and at the same time putting into motion powerful forces which impinge on the sensibilities of the people who move about in the areas or the spaces it affects.

"The line moves and produces the plane: the plane moves and the body comes into being."

In these words Paul Klee restated the principles shown and discussed on the opposite page. The reader may well ask, "And when the body moves, what then?"

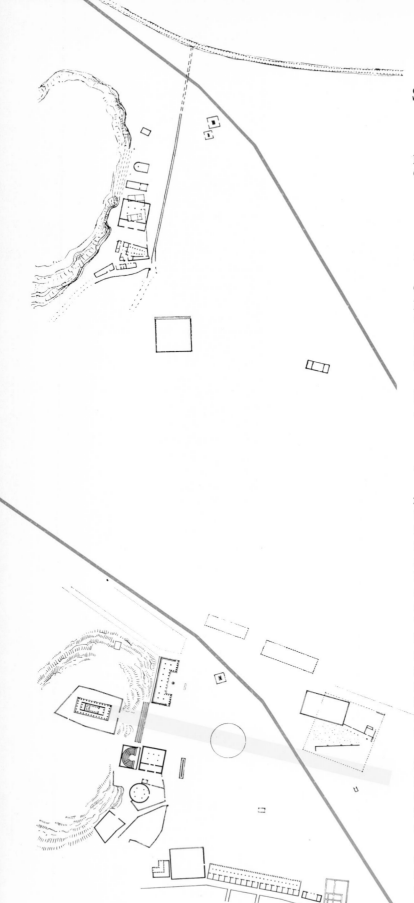

SHAFT OF SPACE IN ACTION

We now observe the effect of the shaft of space projected by the Hephaisteion on the development of the Athens agora.

500 B.C.

The Panathenaic Way, shown in blue, passes diagonally across the somewhat amorphous marketplace, and past the government buildings strung out along the base of the ridge to the west. To the south was the old *bouleuterion,* or Council House, a square structure with five interior columns. And to the north were three small temples.

The marginal drawings on these pages are based on John Travlos's work on the growth of Athens from the earliest times to the present.

420 B.C.

The second illustration shows the development of the agora soon after the Hephaisteion had been built. Here, the shaft of space (in yellow) set into motion by the Hephaisteion begins to make its influence felt as an ordering element. The new *bouleuterion* with its semi-circular stepped seats is built into the hillside behind the old one, and the cylindrical *tholos* sets into motion a vertical influence which counterfoils the horizontal shaft. The Stoa of Zeus sets a long horizontal line at the base of the hill, and the broad flight of steps furnishes a fine visual base for the temple. These steps served as spectators' seats for activities in the agora. The circle represents the orchestra for the theatrical performances which took place in this area up to the time the theater was built on the slopes of the Acropolis.

Since the movement of the Panathenaic Way is directional, it seems natural that the first major architectural work defining the space of the agora, the south stoa, should be built where it was, facing the line of march and powerfully punctuating the experience of movement along it.

The definition of the edges of the space of the agora remained amorphous, but the influence of the now clearly established design structure continues its work.

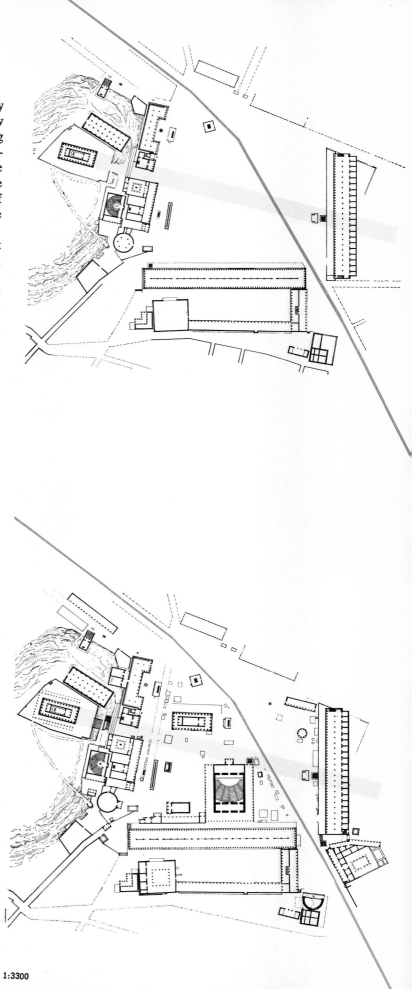

HELLENISTIC PERIOD

In this plan the agora is in the full maturity of its development. The old *bouleuterion* is now replaced by the *metroon,* which provides a long horizontal base line of a colonnade complementary to the earlier Stoa of Zeus to the north. The area before the Hephaisteion is crowded by the new Temple of Apollo Patroos, but the shaft of space projecting from it is still respected. (See page 69.)

The south stoa has been rebuilt at a different angle and the new middle stoa has been added, so that the space of the agora is better contained. The Stoa of Attalos, built perpendicular to it across the Panathenaic Way, defines the east side of the square. These two buildings provided a powerful architectural enframement for the heart of the civic life of Athens, and together they set the visual interrelationship across the space of the square shown in the photographs on pages 72 and 73. Through their design, the rhythm of highlights and rectangular shadows, they infuse the space with spirit and texture.

SECOND CENTURY A.D.

As shown here, the space of the agora was modified as the pressures of the growing civic life pressed in upon it. The new Temple of Ares injected itself in the space in front of the Stoa of Zeus, and many fountains and statues were added to the plan. The clean open quality of uncluttered space of the earlier periods is gone, and in its place confusion has set in.

Symptomatic of the architectural disaster to come is the huge, clumsy structure of the Odeion, an indoor meeting hall designed to hold a large number of people. Its ungainly mass throws the sensitive and delicate buildings of the earlier periods out of scale. Affected also is the space relationship of the Odeion with the Hephaisteion, whose dominance as a design force is seen to be on the wane.

From this time on, the agora deteriorated until it was destroyed in 267 A.D. by the Herulians. However, the form of the agora as an idea was so powerful, so fresh, that today, some two thousand years after its creation, men have been motivated once more to clear its spaces and to rebuild at least one of the defining structures so that the ancient buildings that remain can reach out across the historic spaces and find a response.

1:3300

ARCHITECTURE
WHICH INTERLOCKS

The forces projected by mass into space, which act upon the participators as they move about in that space, cannot achieve full effectiveness unless the architecture is related to the special demands imposed by them. This is demonstrated in these photographs, which were taken within the Hephaisteion. Directly above, the view is across the agora to the Stoa of Attalos. The stoa was built in about 140 B.C., some three hundred years after the Hephaisteion, as a protected meeting place for the citizens of Athens. Some distance to the left of this picture lies the Dipylon Gate. The Panathenaic procession moved across the agora between the Hephaisteion and the Stoa of Attalos, winding its way up the slopes of the Acropolis. The Parthenon is seen on the right in the picture

above. These pictures demonstrate how an architecture which has a discipline developed over a long period of time can relate to a specific city problem. Here is architecture which interlocks, buildings which reach out across space to other buildings, each one firmly implanted in the space in which it is located and creating interrelations and tensions between. Rhythms in the foreground are repeated in the background. The temple on the Acropolis contains the same kind of rhythmic pattern as the covered colonnades of the marketplace.

This serves to remind us of the contemporary problem we face of bland buildings that lack the necessary elements for interaction. The development of each building as an entity in itself, often in an attempt to establish a new stylistic mode, tends to repel rather than attract interaction with other buildings. Worse still is the development of buildings that are devoid of any character at all, curtain-wall buildings which neither reach out into space nor receive space into themselves, buildings whose sterile qualities stimulate no desire and evoke no response.

What we need today is a new policy for design, not one that is dependent on stylistic imitation, but one that incorporates the qualities displayed here. If we are to establish tensions across movements in our urban spaces, how much more careful we must be when we compare the demands of the fast movement on the expressway with that which was needed to create harmony along the Panathenaic Way.

73

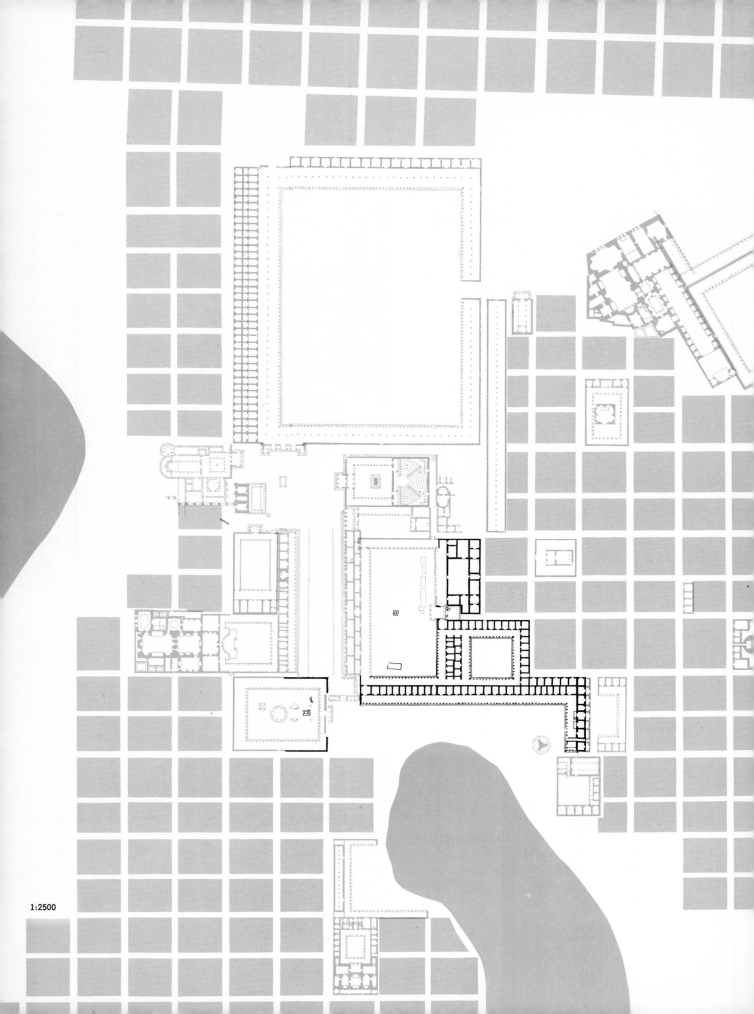

1:2500

DEVELOPMENT OF MILETUS

Miletus, influenced by the great Greek city-planner Hippodamus, is one of the most splendid city plans ever made. It shows how it is possible to develop forms of tremendously dynamic quality as counterpoint to the rigid discipline of the grid-iron plan. The repetitive module of the regular rectangular blocks which constitute the residential part of the city sets up a rhythm which is the basis for the composition of the public parts of the city, the temples, the gymnasia, and the stoas facing inward onto the agoras and out toward the harbors. Furthermore, within this rhythm it was possible to compose in three widely separated periods according to the three very different approaches to design: the Greek work of the end of the fourth century B.C., shown in black on the map on the opposite page; the Hellenistic remodeling in the middle of the second century B.C., shown in blue; and the Roman work from the second century A.D., shown in yellow (north point down).

To the right are three models made by students at the University of Pennsylvania showing central Miletus in the Greek period, top; Hellenistic, center; Roman, bottom.

The difference in philosophy of each of these periods is strikingly expressed in the different form of the masses and the open space. The Greek work involves the minimum of construction necessary to articulate the space for man's use, to bind the free-flowing space of the agora with the shore of the harbor, to set up a rhythm of columns and bays, but not to enclose or confine the spaces. The Hellenistic work is more extensive than the Greek; emphasis is placed on symmetrical arrangement of architecture, giving a more formal character to the civic open spaces. Architectural forms project into the spaces, defining but not enclosing them; angular forms in different directions set up dynamic interactions. During the Roman period all the projecting arms were incorporated into colonnades completely surrounding courts. The spaces were divided into separate units, each of a formal rectangular shape, reflective of the Roman philosophy of dividing life into different rituals, each with its own special space and architectural expression. The work of five centuries all stemmed from the basic design of Hippodamus's rhythmic square.

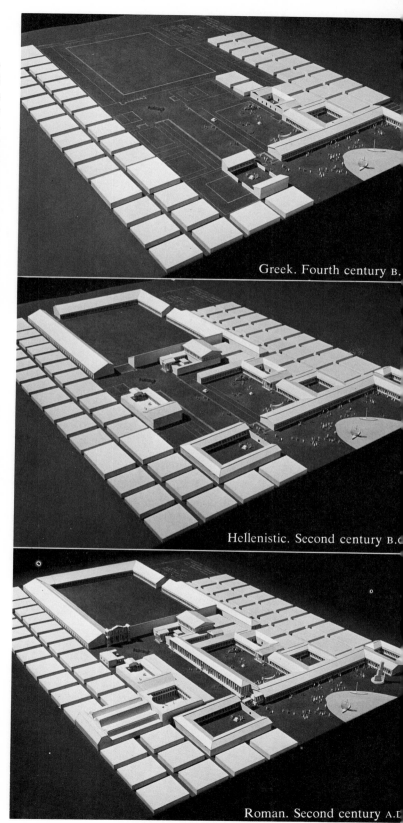

Greek. Fourth century B.

Hellenistic. Second century B.

Roman. Second century A.

DELOS

Delos, the Greek-built city on an island of the same name in the Aegean Sea, consisted of a large number of internally ordered forms which relate to one another and to the natural terrain in an extraordinarily free yet orderly way. Much of the excitement of the interrelationships cannot be conveyed on a two-dimensional map, but must be experienced on the ground.

The heart of the city, with agoras and temples, clamps firmly onto the bay, but its spaces are inward-looking and self-contained. An angled street leads up to the theater on the side of a hill away from the city center, relating to a different part of the region. The street continues to a higher series of terraces and temples overlooking the central agoras, the formality of their shapes recalling the design of the city's heart, culminating in a shrine on the top of the highest hill.

The free-positioned but formal geometry of the stadium and athletic area, on a different side of the island, establishes man-made order with a minimum of effort and provides a fine vantage point for experiencing the whole of the natural space.

The plan of Delos has characteristics in common with the plan of Hadrian's villa (pages 90-91) and the regional plan of Paris under Louis XV (pages 194-195), but in Delos the connection between the rectangular sections, with linear thrusts in different directions, is made not by curved mass, as in Hadrian's villa, nor by direct visual connection as in Paris, but in the mind's eye, the various sections being totally disconnected from one another by the stretches of countryside.

All the architectural forms are based on simple geometric shapes. There is no attempt to ape nature in the man-made forms, nor is there any blurring of the boundaries between what is man-made and what is natural. Yet there is utmost sensitivity in the placing of each element in relation to other elements in their natural setting. It is through such clarity of expression that the Greeks achieved harmony between man and nature.

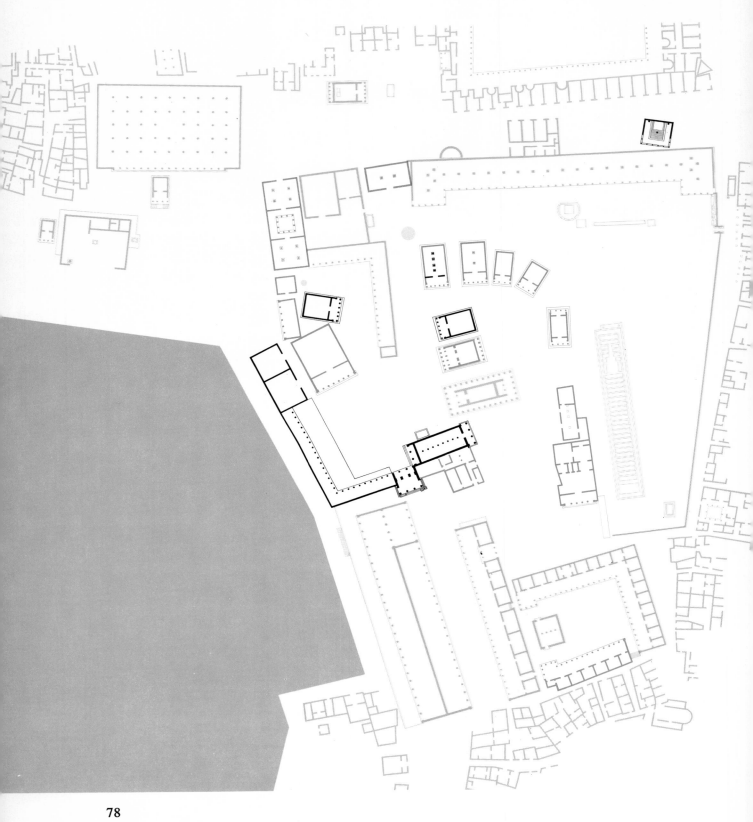

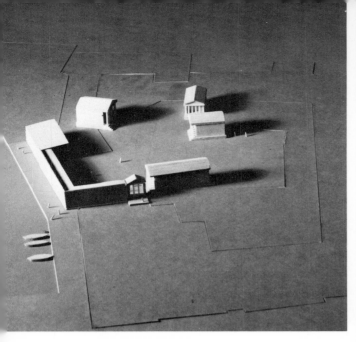

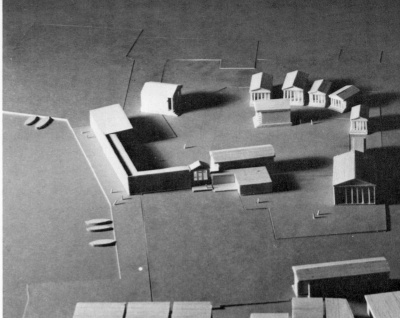

The heart of Delos, shown in plan opposite and in growth models on this page, demonstrates the evolution of the forms. In black is shown the Greek construction of the sixth century B.C., in blue the construction from 417 to 314 B.C., and in yellow all later work. This plan demonstrates the way in which the city responded to the pressures of population growth. Here we have a method of design which is capable of expansion by increments, which can grow and extend and, as it does so, reorient and reintegrate itself on an ever-increasing scale. The L-shaped architectural forms angled in relation to one another to produce dynamic residual spaces have provided a city center of extraordinary richness. Under this scheme ancient shrines have been preserved and have retained their identity although encompassed by new forms. There is no lack of boldness or breadth in the expanded plan, yet the intimacy of inherited tradition is maintained.

Along the quay, the two buildings, subtly angled and positioned in relation to each other, provide a powerful statement of man-made order and give impetus to the city forms that progress up the hillsides. The entrance into the central area of the agora is through the series of controlled and architecturally defined spaces leading off the broad paved areas along the quay. The plan adapts itself over the years to the expanding scale of the structures and the spaces culminating in the vast scale of the Italian Agora, at the top of the drawing, which still sits comfortably alongside the older work.

MODELS BY STUDENTS AT THE UNIVERSITY OF PENNSYLVANIA

CITY OF ONE DESIGNER
— PRIENE

When a society decides that it will base its social and political order, not on the despotic control of one individual or small group, but rather on the Greek system of *demokratia,* the members of that society are forced to consider whether or not a strong enough leadership can be provided to develop order within the system of individual freedom.

Presented on these pages are the two contrasting towns developed by Greek colonists on the shores of Asia Minor. It was in Greece's colonial cities that its democratic ideas received their purest expression. The city of Priene represents perhaps as fine an example as can be found of a single design idea dominating an entire city. The central movement system, the main street, moves up the slope from the city's west gate (indicated by the white arrow) to a sharp change of grade where it meets the agora, a level widening along the route of a disciplined and geometrically defined space. The activities of the marketplace were dominated by the Temple of Athena, which stood on a prominence northwest of the agora. The north stoa, adjacent to the marketplace, with its forty-nine uniform columns and immensely long terrace and steps, provided a firm base for the spectacular cliffs which rise above the town.

The temple itself was approached by a movement system parallel to, but higher than, the main street, passing adjacent to the theater. These two levels of systems were connected by stone stairways, part of a series of minor ways extending perpendicularly from the central spine.

The most remarkable thing about Priene is the total harmony of architecture and planning, extending from the over-all form of the city down to the last detail. As one sits on the stone seat of the Assembly Hall one senses a strong, direct relationship between the shape and placing of each individual block of stone and the design of the city as a whole.

CITY OF MANY DESIGNERS
— CAMIROS

Sharply contrasting with Priene, yet architecturally almost as beautiful, is the city of Camiros on Rhodes. The pure rectangular and lucid geometrical order are replaced by a complex interaction of rectangular forms in angular relation to one another. Here the development of a single concept is replaced by a gradual accumulation of buildings over many years — far too long a time span to be under the direct control of any one individual.

The site of the city is a bowl-shaped form on a mountain overlooking the sea, and at the bottom of the site a broad space was originally hollowed out for the agora and sacred precincts. Temples and public buildings were built there, based on a system of orthogonals, with projection, recessions, and interlocks. The retaining walls and a great stairway led up to the lower part of the main street, whose angular position to the agora created a continuously variable series of relationships. The street moved up the hill in changing directions, each of which established a new view of the agora.

In the second century B.C. the citizens of Camiros added a long colonnaded stoa at the top of the hill. Built over the cisterns that provided the city with water, this new element contributed a dramatic climax to the movement upward. Besides crowning the hill with a disciplined architectural form, the stoa provided a place for a promenade overlooking the city and the sea. At each end the stoa led to a spectacular view of the mountain valleys of the hinterland, thus visually joining the city with the countryside which sustained it.

When there is one unified design idea to synthesize the work of many, a city like Priene can result. Where there is no single dominant idea at the beginning, the city form being determined by the cumulative effect of the work of individual designers, as in Camiros, a great work can also be produced if each individual is sensitive to the special discipline which this method imposes.

Air photograph taken by the Royal Hellenic Air Force and supplied by the General Hellenic Air Force Staff

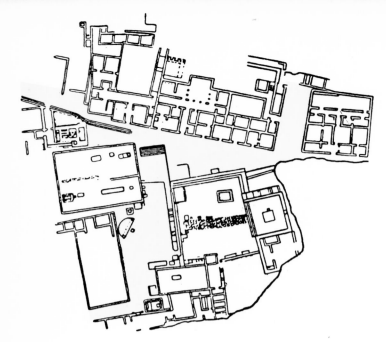

METHODS OF DESIGN GROWTH

GROWTH BY ACCRETION — SPACE AS CONNECTOR

This is a method used by Greek designers with superlative skill. Each new building, internally ordered around one axis, is so placed in relation to existing buildings that an angular volume of space is created which binds the two together. Coherence is maintained by the tension between buildings across the angular space. The elegance and beauty of the spaces created, as here in Camiros, and the endless variety of interrelationships between the internally disciplined buildings provide a principle for city design applicable to problems today.

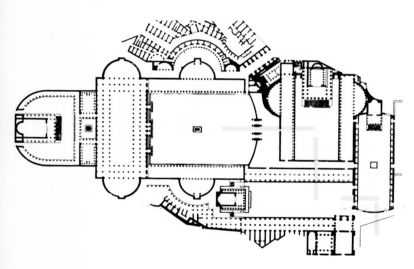

AXES AS CONNECTORS

When the Greek sensitivity gave way to the Roman love of order and logic, a new element was introduced in large-scale design, that of interlocking axes. Thus the five "new" fora of Rome, built one after the other by emperors, lie next to one another, with little or no space between. The central axis of each building was made exactly perpendicular to that of the one before, producing a system of cross axes that unified the whole. Because of their interrelationship, designs which in themselves are very formal and perhaps rather sterile create a dynamic over-all result.

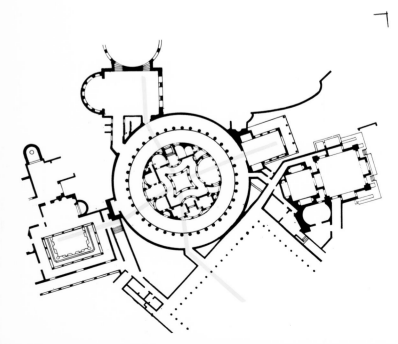

MASS AS CONNECTOR

In the later period of the Roman Empire, notably under Hadrian, a new freedom of design crept in, a return to large-scale site-planning based on a variety of angular relationships. The Romans developed a far greater variety of architectural forms than did the Greeks. Curved structures such as exedras, rotundas, and cylindrical colonnades offered a wide range of angular sub-axes which could interlock various parts of the composition. Thus, in Roman work, such as Hadrian's villa, at left, it was curved building mass which bound together the various parts of a many-angled composition.

GROWTH BY ACCRETION — INTERLOCKING SPACES AS CONNECTORS

During the medieval period, up to the fifteenth century, cities often grew around rectangular spaces. These gradually took form as individual buildings were built around their periphery. In Todi, Italy, an extraordinary result came about through the conception of two interlocking prisms whose corners overlapped to create a single intensive volume of space. The latter was strengthened and emphasized by the construction of two tall towers which contributed a vertical force at the point of juncture. This principle is seen in many forms in medieval cities.

GROWTH BY TENSION

At the beginning of the Baroque period the ordering principle in the growth of the city of Rome was the establishment of lines of force which defined the tension between various landmarks in the old city. The interrelationship of these lines and their interaction with the old structures set into play a series of design forces which became the dominating element in the architectural work along them. Here the cohesive element is a line of force rather than a volumetric form.

GROWTH BY EXTENSION

Still a different concept is a line of force extending outward from the point of origin in the city and establishing an ordering principle that penetrates the adjacent land area. The Champs Elysées in Paris dramatically illustrates this. There, in the extension of the medievally conceived garden of the Tuileries Palace, we can trace the line of propulsion which thrusts farther and farther into the surrounding countryside. This first thrust was joined by a series of similar ones which set up a network of design systems that were capable of indefinite extension.

While there are many other modes of city growth, the six concepts just discussed are basic themes which occur again and again.

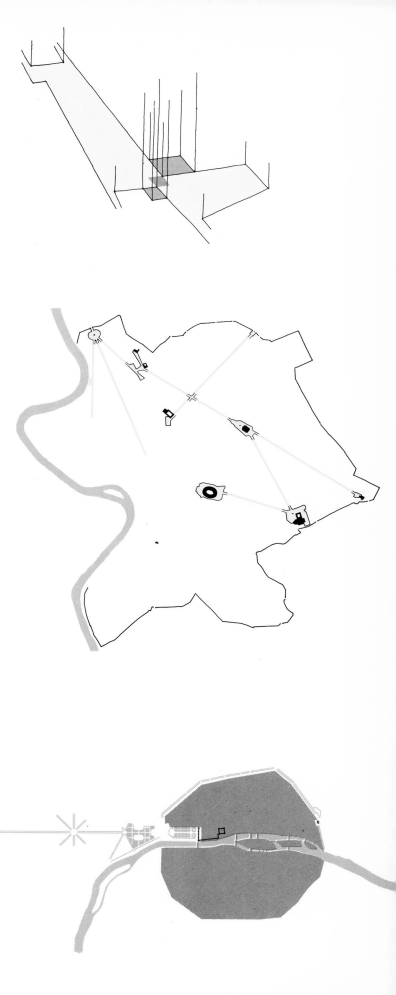

DESIGN ORDER OF ANCIENT ROME

Whereas the Greeks developed the highest expression in Western civilization of the flow of life as total organic unity, and built their cities accordingly, the Romans achieved and sustained a rational order which was made possible only by the fragmentation of functions into separate units. The Greek principle, based on the interaction of tension in a delicately balanced equilibrium, was highly unstable and, indeed, lasted only a few short years. Just as the vast Roman Empire, headed by one of the most stable governments the world has ever known, was based on separate, individually governed cities and provinces, so classical Rome itself was based not on an over-all design structure, but on the gradual accumulation of self-contained building complexes. Each of these was designed to serve a discrete function, and each was interrelated to its neighbors. The whole design was held together by the sheer mass of its individual elements, each bound to another by the friction of compression caused by the ever-growing city.

Perhaps insight into the essential differences can best be obtained by comparing the Panathenaic Way of Athens with the route of the Triumphal Procession in Rome. Here one might say that the movement system, instead of being extended the length of the city, was coiled into a single self-contained, self-completing circuit in a space specially set aside for the purpose—the Circus Maximus, at the extreme left of the photograph below. True, after many times around the Circus, the procession, according to ancient tradition, proceeded to the Capitoline Hill, where the victor laid down his arms in the Temple of Jupiter. This, however, was the secondary rather than the primary expression of the victory parade.

The method of growth by accumulation of massive, self-contained units of building, each cheek by jowl with ones built before, each held firmly in place by the powerful force of compression, proved to be adaptable to the change in scale of a growing city. The purity of geometry, the use of cylinders, half-cylinders, half-spheres, and elliptical prisms, contrasting with rectangular forms, produced areas of great architectural excitement. These were held together by the rhythm of the unifying post-and-lintel colonnades and similarly scaled rows of arches. Even where high vaults were used, entirely different in dimension from the older trabeated temples, the spaces within the vaults were penetrated by screens of a post-and-lintel columnar construction which brought the scale down to one consonant with the rhythm of the rest of Rome's architecture. Without the modular unity of this kind of architectural expression, the massive forms of ancient Rome would have canceled one another out and ended in chaos.

1:40000

CLASSICAL ROME — COMPRESSION

It is revealing to compare the underlying design approach to the city of Rome during two periods of development. The design structure of classical Rome, shown here as it existed in the third century A.D., was built up of massive monumental buildings of formal geometrical design, laid against one another and related to one another by sheer inertia of their mass. The forms grew in vastness and achieved sufficient size to give texture and richness to the total extent of the topography. But no underlying design element in scale with the total space existed. The early city is an example of the accumulation of harmonious elements which produced an effect of unity because of their similar theme. The Via Sacra constituted a

movement system punctuated by triumphal arches and characterized by a series of elegant views, but of itself this did not impose the basic form of the design pattern. The section of the ancient Via Flaminia (now the Via del Corso) leading from the Flaminian Gate was also a central and important way of movement in Rome, with a series of arches erected in different periods, but this could not be counted as a major influence in the development of the over-all design. The forms of the buildings, dominating the city by their very massiveness, influenced great areas around them. They were placed closely enough together to allow the rhythms of their order to project themselves across the spaces of confusion between them.

86

BAROQUE ROME — TENSION

Baroque Rome of some thirteen hundred years later represents the opposite extreme. Here the buildings themselves are generally much smaller in scale than the great baths, stadia, amphitheaters and fora of classical Rome, yet the total design impact is great indeed. We can see an entirely different concept at work: the establishment of points in space pinned down by the vertical mass of the obelisks, and the definition of lines of tension between these points. The articulation along the lines of movement is not arbitrary, as it was in the placing of arches in the Via Sacra and the Via Flaminia in classical Rome; instead it is determined by the crossing points of the forces of tension derived from the location of the ancient buildings, churches, gates, and public squares.

As we look at the basic design ideas of the third century A.D. and compare them with those expressed in the plan of Sixtus V for Rome thirteen hundred years later, we are challenged to consider exactly what is the underlying idea for design at a city-wide scale today. The nearly four hundred years that have elapsed since the time. of Sixtus V have seen a completely different scale of metropolitan growth, with greater complexity and speed of movement. While this twentieth-century idea will include some elements of both the classical and Baroque methods of design growth, it must contain some completely new ingredients if it is to be effective.

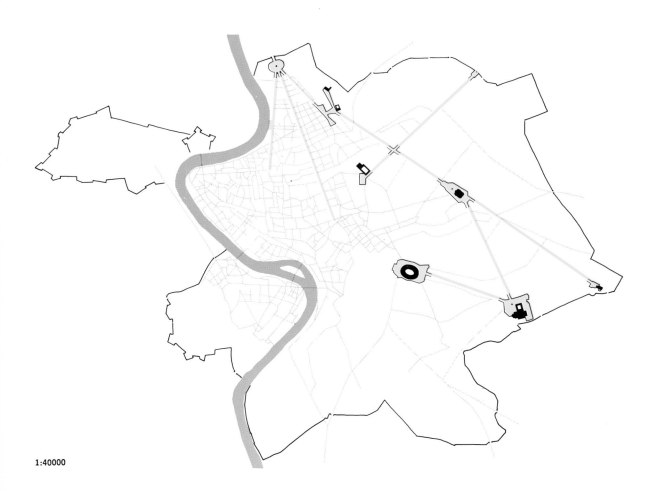

1:40000

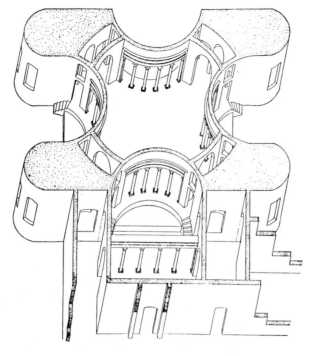

The Pavilion of the Accademia, at left, from a drawing by Heinz Kähler in his book on Hadrian's villa, demonstrates the tremendous range of architectural expression available to the designer of the day. The interior, symmetrical on four axes, consists of a subtle interpenetration of positive and negative expressions of cylindrical forms in space. The exterior, in contrast, presents three completely different kinds of architectural impact. The façade with its concave curve behind the flat plane, at the top of the drawing but not actually seen here, expresses passive reception of space. The two adjacent façades, with their two outward-pushing curved masses, express the dominance of mass and the aggressive movement of the building into the space before it. This building can, and does, play a complex, aggressive, and unifying role in the organization of the spaces which converge on it. Because of the variety of architectural forms that were developed as a result of this kind of inventiveness, a range of possibilities in the organization of the larger spaces was extended and enriched far beyond anything that had existed previously.

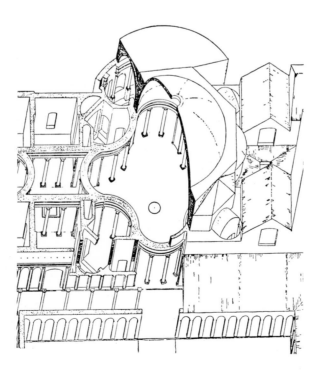

The Pavilion of the Piazzo d'Oro, at left, also from Kähler's book, illustrates the mastery of the plastic design of space existing in Rome at the time. A plan of the building, drawn at the level of the columns, would present a complex, sinuous form interlocking the rectangular corridors and the curved chamber. This would look very different from one drawn through the dome above the columns, where the dominant form would be a perfect circle. The extremely rich forms throughout the villa are strikingly similar to some of the most inventive forms of architecture today. For instance, there is a marked similarity between the curved apse which terminates the Canopus and the forms at Ronchamp by Le Corbusier. The forms of the villa continue to provide a storehouse of ideas, both for the design of buildings themselves and for their relationship to exterior spaces.

HADRIAN'S VILLA

The reintegration of separate elements into a larger design structure on a city-wide scale was foreshadowed in the design of the great villa of Emperor Hadrian in Tivoli, shown in the plan on the following two pages. The construction of the villa began in A.D. 117 and was completed in A.D. 138, during the latter period of the great Roman Empire. The solution of an ever-expanding problem by the fragmentation of its parts into units which are treated separately is possible only up to a certain point. Beyond this the demands of scale require reintegration. This is what happened in the building of Hadrian's villa: the first elements of the villa consisted of relatively small, rational, inward-looking geometrical forms, and the terrain could easily be changed to accommodate them. (See the photograph above.) As the elements grew in size and were extended over the uneven ground, it became necessary to institute some ordering principles if any degree of unity was to be achieved.

During the development of the Roman Empire the rigid application of elementary geometrical forms was replaced by an ever-growing inventiveness and subtlety of architectural shapes. Under Emperor Hadrian's leadership this enrichment of architectural form burst forth in a tremendous flowering of creativity. The two architectural works illustrated on the opposite page, selected from the many in Hadrian's villa, indicate the assurance with which designers employed new forms. The architectural freedom that was made possible by this mastery of curvilinear form provided the essential element in the order that was established at Hadrian's villa.

89

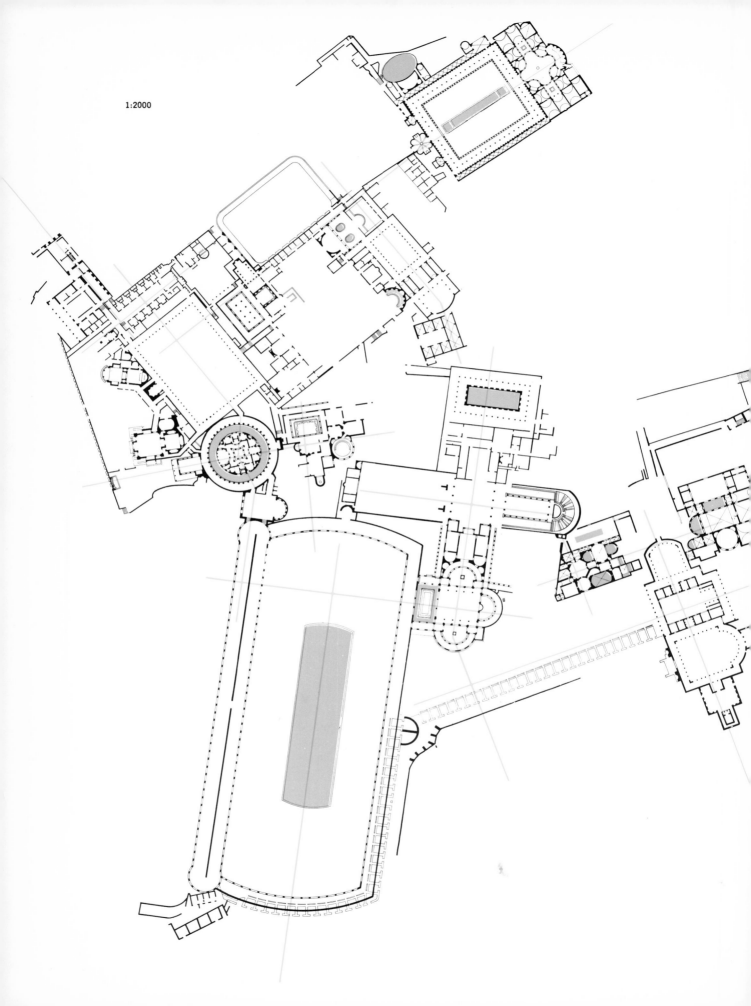

1:2000

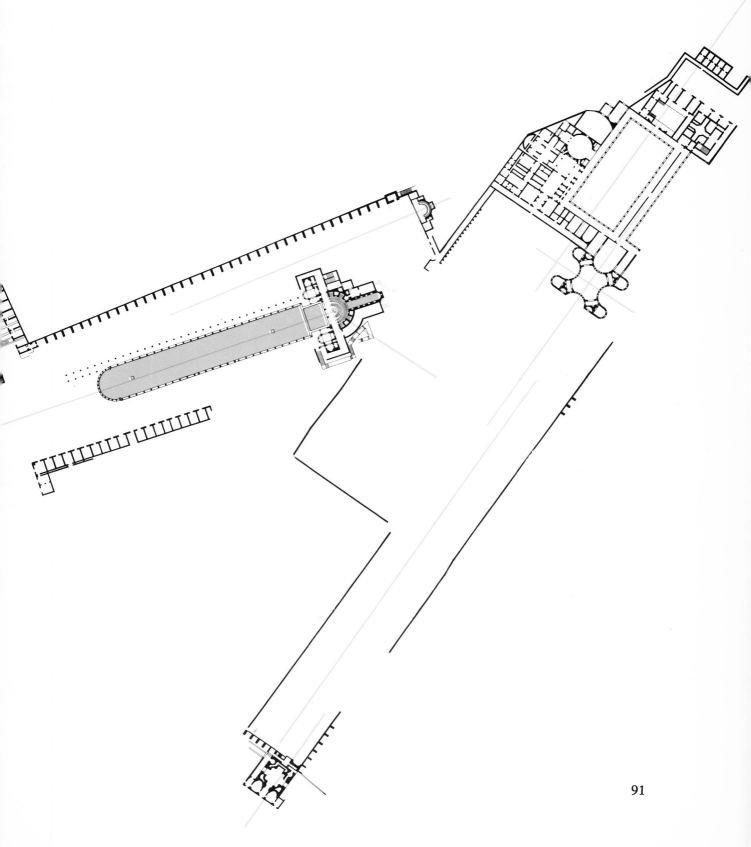

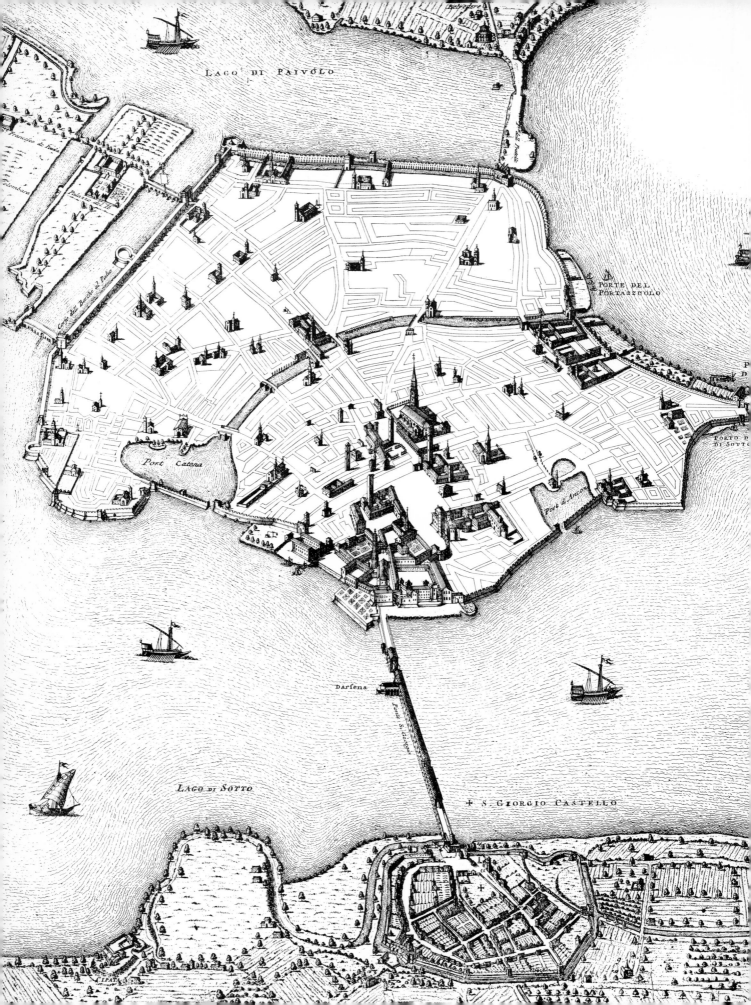

LAGO DI PAIVOLO

PORTE DEL
PORTAZZUOLO

Port Catena

Port d'Ancon

PORTO D
DI SOTTO

Darsena

LAGO DI SOTTO

☩ S. GIORGIO CASTELLO

MEDIEVAL DESIGN

With the fall of the Roman Empire, building on the scale used in classical Rome and at Hadrian's villa disappeared from the Western European scene. Gradually a new integration of design took place, which culminated hundreds of years later in the small medieval cities which produced city design based on rational principles.

The painting above, of a hill town in Tuscany, made by Ambrogio Lorenzetti about 1340, shows the artist's awareness of the city as an organic entity. Technically this painting shows a major advance in visual representation because of the artist's ability to project the image of the entire city on a picture plane from a bird's-eye point of view. In it we see the voids and masses of the city in their interrelation to one another, presented by isometric projection which preceded scientific per-

spective by many years. Most important, this town is seen as an entity, as indeed the cities of this period were seen by their citizens, including the builders who changed and enlarged them. It is this image of the totality that is one of the most important contributions of medieval design.

The engraving of Mantua on the opposite page shows how this image is held together as the city expands outward. Here the symbolic image of the city as a whole, expressed in the cathedral spire, is recalled in the spires of the parochial churches and civic buildings spread throughout the town. By this method of design dispersal, unity between the scale of the neighborhood and the scale of the city is achieved, and a kind of design reverberation is set up which gives great richness to a city, and which is brilliantly exemplified in Venice.

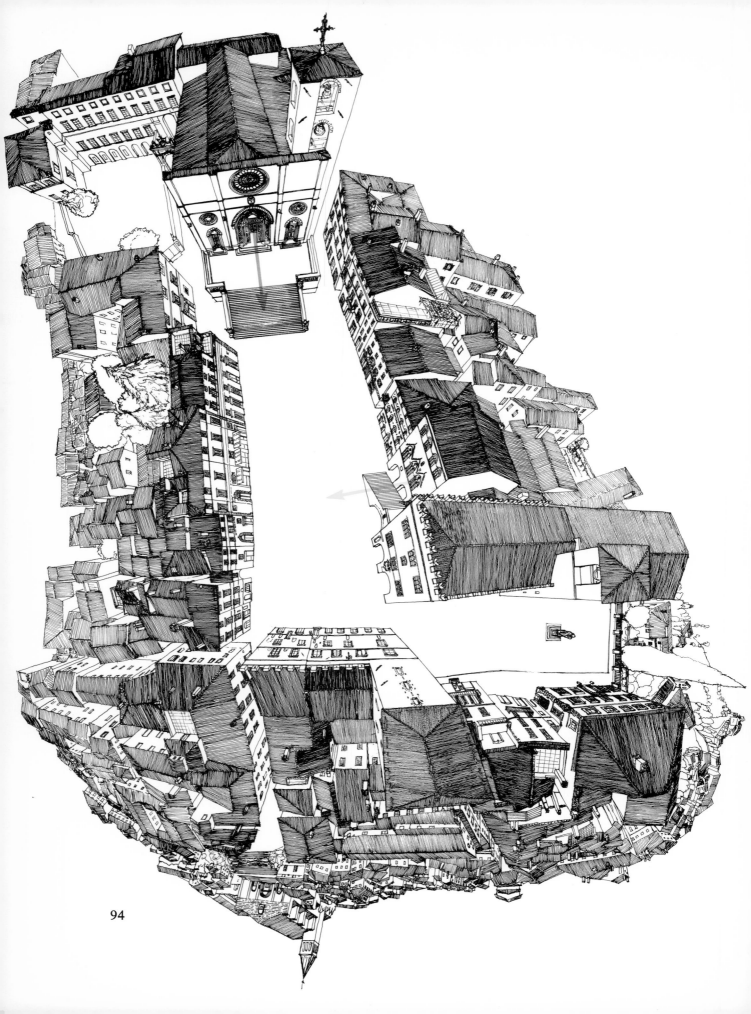

94

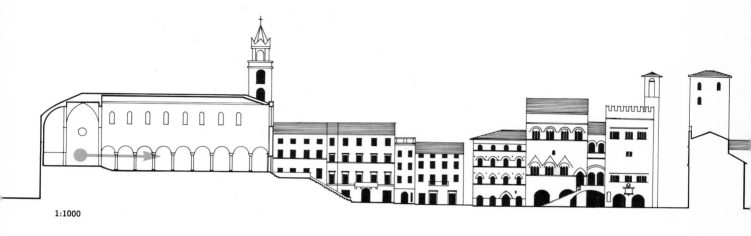

1:1000

THE STRUCTURE OF THE SQUARE

Spectacular among the architectural works of medieval cities is the design of the two interlocking squares in Todi. The smaller of the squares (at the extreme right of the drawing opposite), with a statue of Garibaldi at its center, overlooks the rolling Umbrian plains and draws the spirit of the countryside into the town. It was conceived as a space, with one corner overlapping the area of the principal center square, the Piazza del Popolo, thus establishing a small volume of space common to the two squares, of special intensity and impact. The towers of the Palazzo del Popolo and the Palazzo dei Priori, shown on the extreme right of the drawing above, flank this abstractly defined space and provide vertical forces that hold down the two corner points at the position of greatest intensity of design.

The positions of the buildings representing the two principal functions of communal life (symbolized in yellow for the mayor and blue for the archbishop) are precisely determined in the design both in plan and in a vertical relationship. The entrances to both the Palazzo del Popolo and to the cathedral are raised above the plane of the public square onto a level of their own, accessible by a large flight of steps. The simplicity of this over-all design is such that the citizen never loses his feeling of relationship with the city as a design entity while he is participating in his function as a member of the church or as a member of the political community.

In a process somewhat the reverse of Michelangelo's idea of cutting away the superfluous marble to liberate the mass of the statue which, in his mind, was contained there, the collective mind of the citizens of Todi must have conceived the space volumes of the two squares as abstract entities, and then brought them into being by the construction of individual buildings over many years, which gradually defined their edges.

The remarkable drawing of J. H. Aronson opposite, influenced by modern technology but utilizing multiple vanishing points, attempts in a way quite different from that of Lorenzetti to present the picture of the city as a totality. You may intensify your pleasure in this drawing by slowly revolving the book through 360 degrees.

THE APPROACH

In the city of Todi, as in many other cities of the Middle Ages, the design energy does not expire with the completion of the central squares, but it extends outward to the limits of the city at the walls, or, conversely, it penetrates inward from the walls, thus relating the heart of the city with the surrounding countryside.

In Todi there is great clarity to the form of the total city, and, as in Athens, it is easy to visualize the sequence of space experiences as one moves from the gate to the square.

Particularly subtle is the series of views and sensations provided by the approach from the southeast. The street is bent, so that one sees first a narrow shaft of space focused on the central bay of the cathedral (photograph above). The view shifts to the right bay, and, as the space widens, shifts back again (photograph below). At the point of entry into the space of the smaller square with its spectacular view across the countryside, the space of the arcaded loggia under the Palazzo del Popolo becomes dominant and strengthens the feeling of the downward thrust of the mass of the tower above.

THE ARRIVAL

As one moves into the square (the vista being completely enclosed so that there is no distraction from the civic functions which take place there), the great flight of steps along the north side of the square leading up to the cathedral looms as the dominant element in the composition. When going up these steps, one can catch a glimpse over the countryside to the left. The experience of the square is complemented by the experiences of the interior space of the cathedral with its great apse at the end, which deflects the design force back into the square.

As one comes out of the cathedral, the square presents a totally different aspect. From here the two towers emerge as dominant elements, and the great flight of steps up to the plane of the Palazzo del Popolo only now makes itself felt, drawing our attention down into the central square, then up again.

Here is an example, developed over time, of the full interplay of the many necessary elements of design — recession planes, penetration in depth, meeting the sky and the ground, ascent and descent — which were shown in the Guardi drawing.

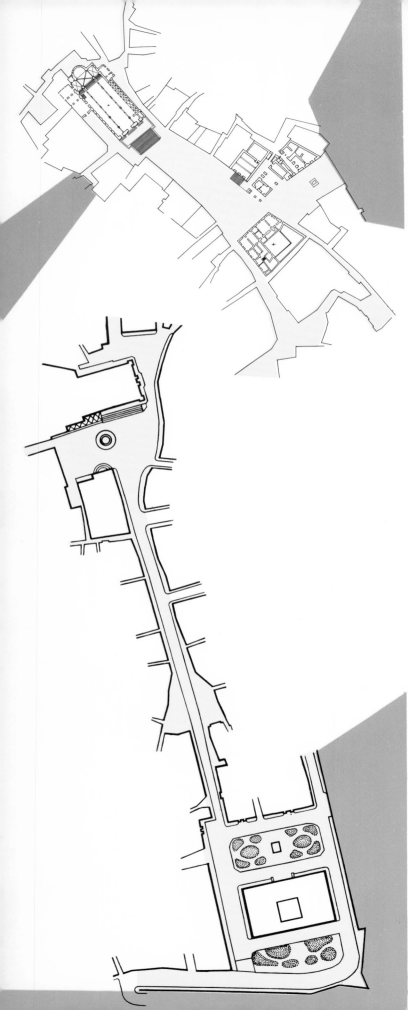

BASIC DESIGN STRUCTURE

Within the range of cities built in Italy during the medieval and Renaissance periods there emerges a recurring theme in which there is a direct and purposeful design extension from the central square to an outward point where it clamps onto an expression of the forces of the region. Presented on these pages are four examples, drawn to a common scale, all strikingly similar in their basic concept.

TODI

The diagram emphasizes that the interlocking squares are firmly positioned between vistas, one in each direction, across the Umbrian hills. The architecturally contained center square, affording glimpses of nothing but overlapping façades of buildings, establishes unequivocally the urban character of the city core, and makes more dramatic the inrush of the countryside (shown in green), in a narrow, sharply focused channel on the upper platform before the cathedral, and in a broad expanse at the end of the smaller square. The identities of the town and countryside are kept separate and are sharply defined within the individual parts of the composition.

PERUGIA

Perugia, another Umbrian medieval hill town, expresses the same design principles as does Todi. The central square, with its ancient and beloved fountain (shown by the circle), so skillfully interrelated with the design of the cathedral on one side and that of the city hall on the other, receives the thrust of space defined by the street leading in from the square overlooking the countryside. The cathedral is turned so that it receives the impact of the space movement broadside, which is unusual for Gothic cathedrals.

At the other end of the connecting street two squares are developed on each side of a public building, and promenades extend along the angled city wall, allowing wide vistas of the surrounding terrain.

1:3000

FLORENCE

The medieval square of Florence, Piazza della Signoria, was originally conceived as an entirely self-contained urban center, with no thought of including in its design an expression of the forces of the region which sustains the city. It was a purposeful act of Cosimo de' Medici to cut through a jumbled area to the River Arno, and to commission Giorgio Vasari to design the Uffizi Palace as both a practical and an architecturally symbolic link between the town center and the River Arno. (The palace is positioned on either side of the street extension, drawn in yellow, leading to the river.) With superlative mastery Vasari fulfilled the hopes of his client. The palace visually interrelates the ancient monuments, the Palazzo Vecchio, the dome of the cathedral, and the sculpture in the Piazza della Signoria, and fuses the perpendicular movement from the square onto the movement along the course of the Arno, thus dramatizing the river's existence.

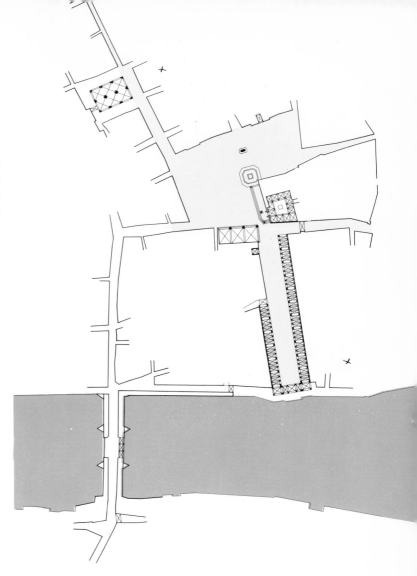

VENICE

The basic form of Piazza San Marco in Venice is similar to that of Piazza della Signoria in Florence, but the history of its development is different. In the port-oriented city of Venice, the open space which is now the Piazzetta was part of the original design, leading to an only slightly larger space before the Cathedral of Saint Mark. Here the open space was principally an extension of the maritime space of the Grand Canal. Piazza San Marco, as we know it today, was a much later enlargement of the central open space, the formalized expression of the urban entity.

In all these examples the underlying design theme is the establishment of a clear and powerful expression of civic unity connected to some feature expressive of the natural forces of the region.

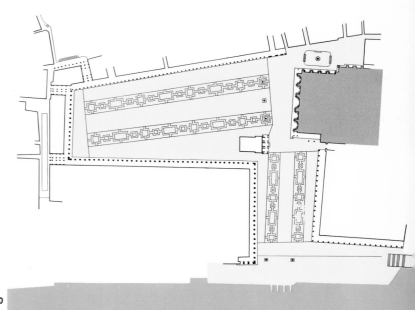

1:3000

Canaregio

Casino de Spiriti

Sacca della Misericordia

Le Fondamenta Nove

Sacca di S.ta Chiara

Isola di S.ta Chiara

Riva di Biasio

Canal Grande

Canal Grande

Canal Grande

Piazza di S. Marco

Il Broglio

Riva delli Schiavoni

Dogana da Mare

Riva delle Zattere

Canal della Giudeca

Redentore

Canal di S. Giorgio

Redentore

100

VENICE — DOMINANT AND SUBDOMINANT THEMES

The engraving of Venice below shows the basic design movement in the heart of the city. The intersection of the flow of commerce along the Grand Canal, with the perpendicular thrust of the space past the façade of Saint Mark's and the Doge's Palace, firmly positions the city center in the region.

Venice is the clearest example of a principle expressed in the engraving of Mantua on page 92 —that of establishing a primary center of the city, and a system of subcenters which recall the dominant center. The citizen feels the pride of belonging. His identification with Piazza San Marco is an expression of the total civic life of his city, and with his daily life centering around the local square with its church, café, wellhead, and perhaps monument, he feels a reflection of the total civic magnificence in his own neighborhood. Or, conversely, as he identifies with the intimate square where his children play in his own community, he is able to move from this personal experience to an identification with the more difficult concept of the common life of the city as a whole.

The principle of the dominant center and dispersed subcenters, also discussed in contemporary terms on page 319, was expressed in the organization of the city, as shown in the map opposite, and in the detailed arrangement of buildings, squares, and monuments shown in the drawing on the next two pages. It was also expressed in the three-dimensional architectural forms shown in the engraving below. The many church towers and spires recall but never dominate the Campanile of Saint Mark's.

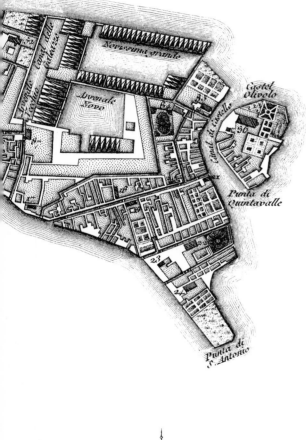

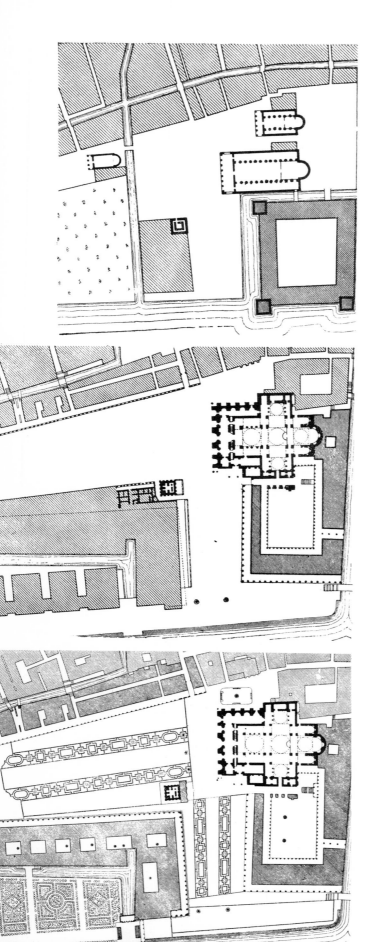

DEVELOPMENT OF PIAZZA SAN MARCO

The drawing on preceding pages 102-103 was intended to show the series of squares and Piazza San Marco as a concatenation of linked spaces, each comprehensible only in relation to the others. This drawing demonstrates specifically how the paving pattern, the placing of steps, bridges, enriched façades of churches (shown in gray), wellheads, monuments, and flagpoles, and indeed the very placing of the tables in the cafés (blue) and accompanying potted plants (green), all contribute to the unity of the experience, and frequently link one part with another.

The evolution of the form of Piazza San Marco itself is shown in the three plans to the left, demonstrating that the space design over this period was a self-conscious process and was the result of a long series of "agonizing decisions" constantly aimed at perfecting the squares. The transformation between drawings two and three, in which the whole south wall of the square has been torn down and replaced a few feet farther south (thus disengaging the old campanile from the buildings at its base and allowing it to rise free from the space around it), shows the degree to which public action was geared to purely aesthetic ends.

The drawing reproduced below by architect Louis Kahn emphasizes a fact about the square which is often overlooked: the way in which the plane established by the two free-standing columns at the center of the picture receives the thrust of the movement along the Grand Canal (at this point contained and directed by the balustrade of the bridge) and deflects this thrust deep into Piazza San Marco as it butts against the projecting mass of Saint Mark's library. Here an architect of rare insight helps us to understand the primary forces at work in a composition which is often viewed only in its superficial, romantic aspect.

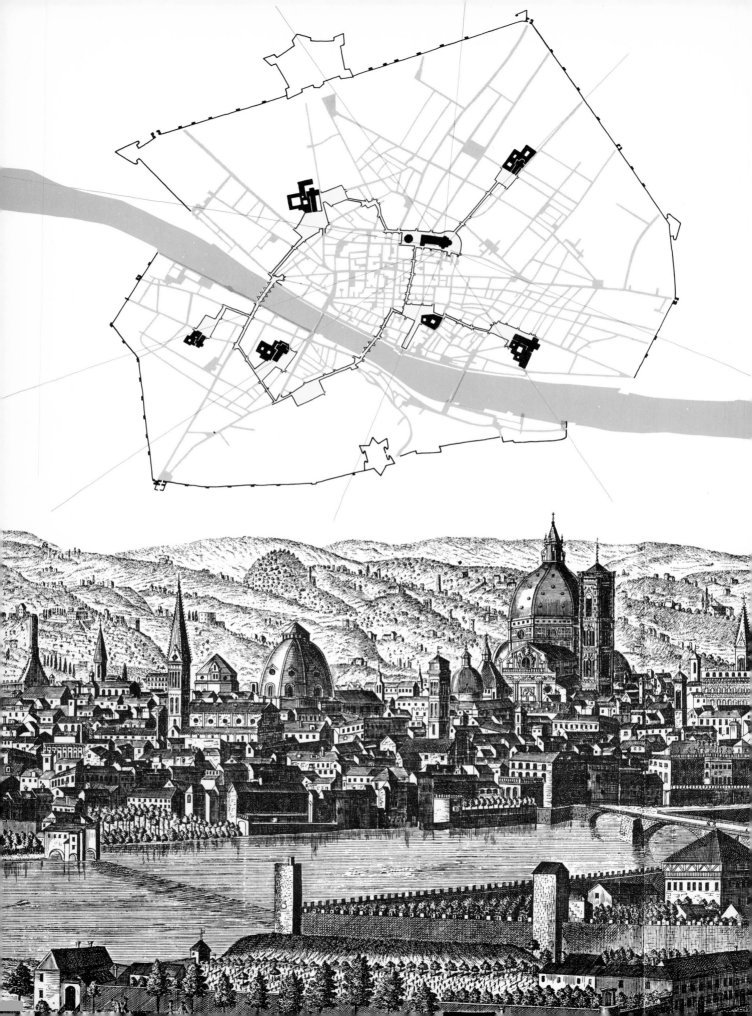

UPSURGE OF THE RENAISSANCE

The coming of the Renaissance brought new energy, new ideas, and a new rational basis for city extension in accord with the new scale of city growth. It was in Florence that the Renaissance first found full expression.

In 1420 the building of the dome over the octagonal walls at the crossing of the cathedral of Florence, designed by the architect Brunelleschi, was far more than a brilliant achievement of building technology. It provided Florence with a psychological and visual center which became the orientation point for much of the later work.

When the Servite monks decided to lay out a new street through property they owned, from the cathedral to their church of Santissima Annunziata, probably during the second half of the thirteenth century, they set into motion a process of orderly city extension which culminated in the great expression of the emerging ideas of the Renaissance, Piazza della Santissima Annunziata. The design of Brunelleschi for the arcade of the Foundling Hospital set a level of architectural excellence that was continued around the square by later designers, so creating a spectacular architectural termination for the much earlier plan of movement from the cathedral.

The map on the opposite page, showing the cathedral dome as the center of converging blue lines which radiate outward from it, also illustrates the direct physical relationship to it of both the Piazza della Santissima Annunziata and the Uffizi extension from Piazza della Signoria to the Arno River. This map, showing in yellow the network of interconnecting streets and squares and the principal church buildings in black, suggests the beginning of a city-wide design structure on a new scale, an idea that reached full magnificence in the later development of Rome.

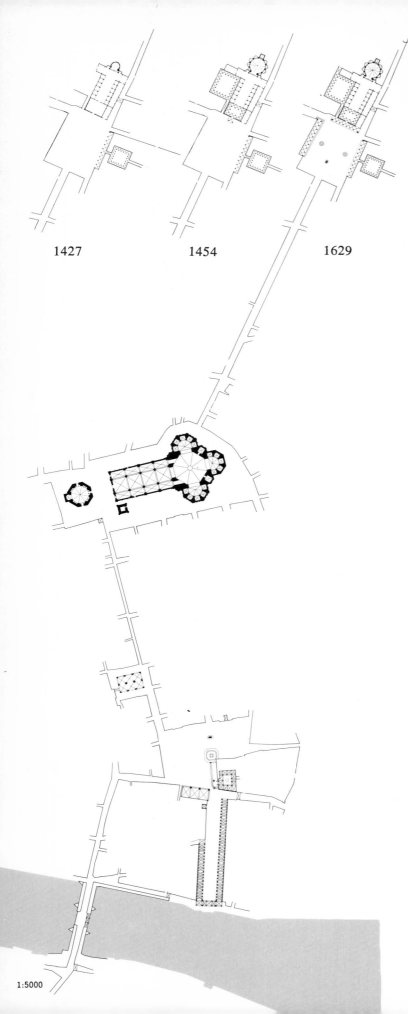

1427   1454   1629

1:5000

PRINCIPLE OF
THE SECOND MAN

Any really great work has within it seminal forces capable of influencing subsequent development around it, and often in ways unconceived of by its creator. The great beauty and elegance of Brunelleschi's arcade of the Foundling Hospital, shown on the right of the engraving above, found expression elsewhere in the Piazza della Santissima Annunziata, whether or not Brunelleschi intended this to be so.

The first significant change in the square, following the completion of the arcade in 1427, was the construction of a central bay of the Santissima Annunziata church. This was designed by Michelozzo in 1454 and is harmonious with Brunelleschi's work. However, the form of the square remained in doubt until 1516, when architects Antonio da Sangallo the Elder and Baccio d'Agnolo were commissioned to design the building opposite to Brunelleschi's arcade. It was the great

decision of Sangallo to overcome his urge toward self-expression and follow, almost to the letter, the design of the then eighty-nine-year-old building of Brunelleschi. This design set the form of Piazza della Santissima Annunziata and established, in the Renaissance train of thought, the concept of a space created by several buildings designed in relation to one another. From this the "principle of the second man" can be formulated: it is the second man who determines whether the creation of the first man will be carried forward or destroyed. (The same principle can be seen at work in Stockholm, page 314.)

Sangallo was well prepared for the decision he faced, having worked as a pupil of Bramante, possibly on the plan for the Vatican Cortile, which was the first great effort of the Renaissance in space-planning. The effect of his decision is shown in the engraving above. Sangallo's arcade is at the left, and in the center are the fountains and the equestrian statue of Grand Duke Ferdinand I sculptured by Giambologna (placed there as a directional accent in imitation of Michelanglo's siting of Marcus Aurelius in the Campidoglio). Behind these are the architect Caccini's extensions of Michelozzo's central bay, forming the arcade of Santissima Annunziata, which was completed about 1600.

The drawing to the left shows three stages of the development of this piazza in relation to the design structure of Florence.

The quality of Piazza della Santissima Annunziata is largely derived from the consummate architectural expression that Brunelleschi gave the first work, the Innocenti arcade, but it is really to Sangallo that we owe the piazza in its present form. He set the course of continuity that has been followed by the designers there ever since.

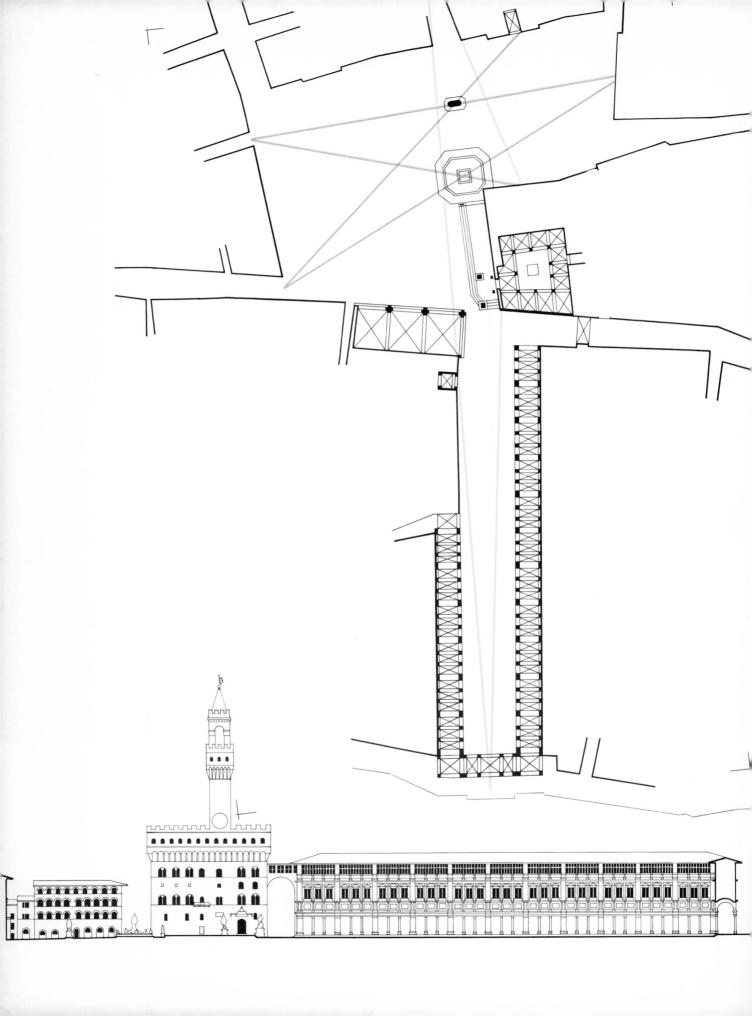

IMPOSITION OF ORDER

It is impossible to enter Piazza della Signoria at any point without being confronted with a complete and organized design composition. The powerful impression received is largely due to the interplay of points in space defined by the sculpture with the formal façades of the medieval and Renaissance buildings behind them, a Renaissance ordering of the space of a medieval square.

If one enters by Via Calimaruzza in the northwest corner of the square, looking east, one sees the view shown in the upper photograph. (Green lines on the diagram on the opposite page.) Bartolommeo Ammanati's massive white statue of Neptune is silhouetted against the shadowed north wall of the Palazzo Vecchio, and the dark equestrian figure of Cosimo I by Giambologna stands sharply outlined in the center of the sun-bathed Palazzo della Tribunale di Mercanzia. The view from the northeast shows the buildings on each side of the narrow street framing the steeply vertical composition of the Palazzo Vecchio and its tower (upper yellow lines on opposite page). The equestrian figure and the figure of Neptune almost overlap, forming a plane in space, which reinforces the direction of movement of this approach to the square.

The lower photograph shows the view which suddenly opens up at the entry point of the Via Vacchereccia in the southwest corner (blue lines). Neptune now appears at the center of the Palazzo della Tribunale di Mercanzia's façade, and Cosimo I has moved to the center of the richly rusticated façade of the palazzo on the north side of the square. The Loggia dei Lanzi, on the south side of the square, acts as a fulcrum at the point of juncture with the Uffizi. The view at the foot of the opposite page shows the Palazzi della Tribunale di Mercanzia and Vecchio, and one side of the Uffizi Palace.

As one walks about the square, the variously placed sculptural groups appear to move in different directions in relation to their backgrounds and to one another, involving the onlooker in continual orientation, disorientation, and reorientation to a new set of relationships.

DESIGN IN DEPTH

One function of architecture is to create spaces to intensify the drama of living. The superb engraving by Giuseppe Zocchi opposite presents the Uffizi in its full dramatic aspect, in terms both of its own design and of its relationship with the whole of Florence. Not shown in the engraving is the continuing drama of the view that lies in the other direction — the River Arno framed by the central arch. The plan on page 110 shows the way in which the pavilion of the Uffizi projects out into the street by the Arno, giving the effect of seizing the flow of space along the river's course, and pulling it into the Piazza della Signoria.

The principle of the recession plane and of design in depth is illustrated by the Klee drawings below, the right one being a side view and the left one a view along the axis of a few simple objects in space. If these are compared with the Florentine example in the engraving opposite, the large dot suggests the River Arno, the heavy square the Uffizi arch, and the small dot in the background the lantern on the dome of the Florence cathedral. The other squares suggest the various planes in between. The shaft of space contained by the Uffizi walls and framed by the arch at the end links the planes together and focuses on the cathedral dome, with the result that its importance is drawn into the space of the square.

This engraving effectively represents one of the most remarkable aspects of the Piazza della Signoria. The plane in space established by the line of sculpture from Hercules and Cacus to the right of the Palazzo Vecchio's entrance, on to the copy of Michelangelo's David, to Ammanati's Neptune fountain, and ending in the figure of Cosimo I on horseback, starts and ends in the physical sense, but in spirit extends in each direction, exercising extraordinary influence in all parts of the square.

Internal volumes, two-dimensional. The broadening of the lines corresponds to gradations from far to near or: rear to front

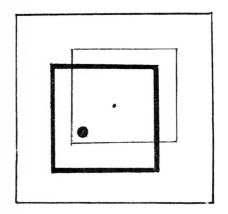

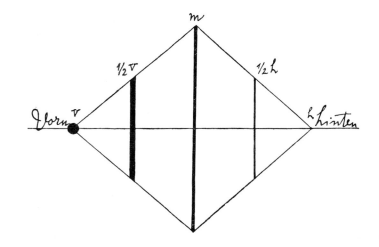

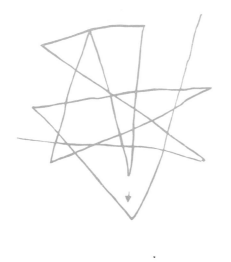

MICHELANGELO'S
ACT OF WILL

Only by reconstructing the Capitoline Hill as it existed before Michelangelo went to work on it can we comprehend the magnitude of this artist's genius in creating the Campidoglio. This master-work forms a link between the early Renaissance expressions of urban design in Florence and the great Baroque developments in Rome.

The drawing on the left, by J. H. Aronson, based on various sketches by artists of the period, is an attempt to reconstruct the area as it existed in 1538, when Michelangelo began work. It shows the Palazzo del Senatore at the top and the Palazzo dei Conservatori at the right. The sketch by Van Heemskerck (below), made at the same time, gives an authentic view of the confusion on the ground. The formless, unplanned relationship between the medieval Palazzo del Senatore (on the left below) and the Palazzo dei Conservatori (right) was complicated by mounds of earth, columns, and an obelisk. There were also the statues of the two Roman river gods, on each side of the entrance to the Palazzo dei Conservatori. This, then, was the physical situation with which Michelangelo was faced when he reluctantly acceded to Pope Paul III's orders to recreate the Campidoglio as the heart of Rome.

The approach Michelangelo took produced one of the great masterpieces of all time. The actual basis for the artist's design was an enormous intellectual achievement. By a single act of will he established a line of force on the axis of the Palazzo del Senatore, a line which in effect became the organizing element that pulled chaos into order (the line is shown in yellow on the drawing).

Similar in its basic form to the final Michelangelo plan for the Campidoglio (shown on page 119) is Paul Klee's drawing at left above. Here we see how pure directional force, indicated by the arrow, pulls order out of an angled diagram.

DEVELOPMENT OF ORDER

In their discussion of the angle between the two flanking buildings of the Campidoglio, and its significance in relation to perspective as diminishing or increasing apparent distance, antiquarians sometimes seem to lose sight of the fact that this angle was determined long before Michelangelo started work. What Michelangelo did was to repeat the angle already set by the Palazzo dei Conservatori, symmetrically on the other side of the axis of the Palazzo del Senatore. Accepting this angle as a point of departure, he set about to treat the space it created. The decision he made is remarkable because it contained elements of two violently contradictory points of view.

On one hand, Michelangelo saved the basic structure of the two old palaces which he found on the site by confining his efforts to the building of new façades. On the other hand, what he did was to create a totally new effect. One might have thought a man of such drive toward order and beauty would have swept away the old buildings in order to give free rein to his own creative efforts, or, conversely, that such modesty would have led to a hodgepodge compromise. Michelangelo has proved that humility and power can coexist in the same man, that it is possible to create a great work without destroying what is already there.

On orders of the Pope, and against the advice of Michelangelo, the statue of Marcus Aurelius was moved from San Giovanni in Laterano to the Campidoglio, and Michelangelo positioned the figure and designed a base for it. The drawing of the Campidoglio below, made in its earliest stage of development, shows that the first act was the setting of this figure, and by that single act the

integrity of the total idea was established. It shows, in the extremely disorganized front that the Palazzo del Senatore presents, the degree of imagination necessary to conceive the order that eventually would arise. The barest beginning of the new stairway has been constructed, and one of the reclining river gods, shown in its previous location in the Van Heemskerck drawing, has been moved to its final position in front of the stairway.

The drawing above shows a further progression. To the left, below the ancient church of Santa Maria in Aracoeli, is the retaining wall with the niche, now occupied by a statue of Marforio. The wall became the rear of the palace built according to Michelangelo's plans, primarily to complete his space composition for the square.

The drawing shows that, in this chaotic setting, the completion of the stairway of the Palazzo del Senatore and the positioning of the Marcus Au-

relius statue establish a relationship between two architectural elements in space. Each of these is modest in extent, yet of such power that the feeling of order is already present and the drive toward the larger order is irreversibly set in motion.

Michelangelo had designed a new tower to replace the unsymmetrical medieval one, but his design was only vaguely followed when the tower was finally, in 1578, replaced by another.

A comparison of this drawing with the engraving on the next page reveals the admirable skill with which Michelangelo introduced a totally new scale into this space. He modulated the façade of the Palazzo del Senatore by establishing a firm line defining the basement, and above this he placed a monumental order of Corinthian pilasters. These interact effectively with the colossal two-story order of the flanking palaces which sweep from the base to the cornice in one mighty surge.

ORDER ARRIVES ON THE CAPITOL

One of the greatest attributes of the Campidoglio composition is the modulation of the land. Without the shape of the oval, and its two-dimensional star-shaped paving pattern, as well as its three-dimensional projection in the subtly designed steps that surround it, the unity and coherence of the design would not have been achieved. The paved area stands as an element in its own right, in effect creating a vertical oval shaft of space which greatly reinforces the value of the larger space defined by the three buildings.

The engraving above, made after Michelangelo's death, shows the incomplete state of the Campidoglio at that time. It emphasizes further the remarkable power of the idea, which was sufficient to motivate later builders and architects to construct the palace needed to complete it. The product is a space which, apart from its beauty, still serves as the symbolic heart of Rome.

The Campidoglio was designed some thirty-five years after Bramante made his great plan for the Vatican Cortile, and it followed by just over twenty years Sangallo's plan for the second arcade in Piazza della Santissima Annunziata in Florence. While the Campidoglio incorporated ideas contained in each of these earlier works, it went far beyond them in the degree of integration between the architecture of the buildings, the placement of sculpture, and the modulation of the land. Furthermore, it established more powerfully than any previous example the fact that space itself could be the subject of design. In the richness of its forms, the Campidoglio heralded the arrival of the Baroque.

The Aronson drawings of the Campidoglio before and after Michelangelo's work may be seen simultaneously by lifting pages 115 to 118 to a vertical position.

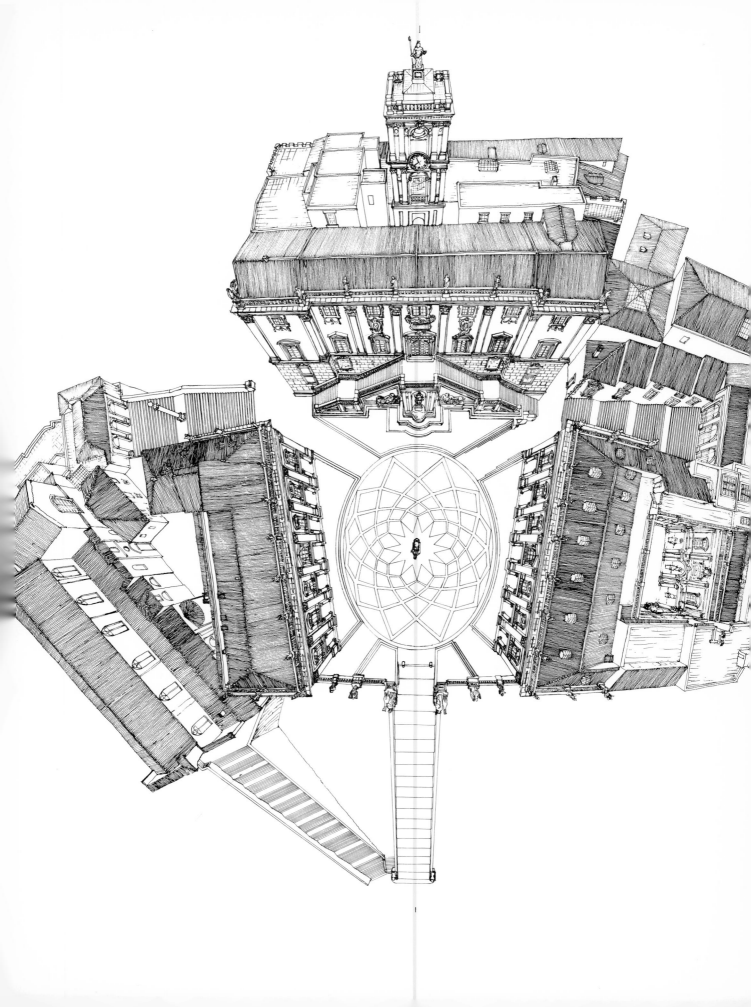

NEW CITY VISION

The painting on the opposite page, made by Neroccio di Bartolommeo in the latter half of the fifteenth century, clearly demonstrates the problem of design when old methods are replaced by a new technology which has not yet been entirely mastered. This is a situation I believe to be comparable to that of the present day. Through the science of perspective the artist has modulated the base plane by squares laid out with mathematical accuracy, and on this he has arbitrarily imposed his unrelated hexagonal structure, producing design confusion at the edges and creating residual spaces that are at the same time shapeless and accidental.

Above and below are details from the predella of this painting. Bartolommeo was struggling to make order out of the great new riches that the rediscovered classical model had provided — a model already proved to be a unifying force in the design of individual buildings. As far as the city as a whole is concerned, the classical remains of Rome produced in the mind of this artist a vision of a city (above) of dissonant forms, each conceived separately, each arbitrarily placed within the whole, a city which rears its confused mass against the sky, while the beautifully articulated and organic medieval city stands below as a discarded lesson beneath the devil.

This wonderful effort of the artist to conceive of the city as a unity, in the light of the new Renaissance ideas, shows the incompleteness of the intellectual grasp of the total city problem at the time. Its close parallel to prevailing architectural ideas of today should give us confidence for our designs of the future as we follow the developments that led out of this morass into the broad and powerful city-design concepts which emerged with the Baroque.

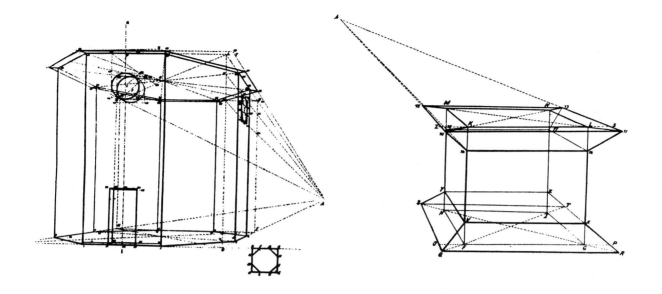

STIRRINGS OF THE NEW ORDER

The first hint of the system that would lead to the new order came from the artists using the new and glittering tools of scientific perspective. We have already seen how these stemmed the intuitive flow of experience which led to the organic design of cities in the medieval period, and, on the page before, how they led to positive advocacy of organized confusion.

On the opposite page, in the drawing of Antonio Pisanello, who lived in the first half of the fifteenth century, we see the beginning of a new idea of design. As applied in the drawings of Piero della Francesca shown above, the science of perspective was used to delineate mass. The space between the object and the vanishing point was merely a convenience for determining how the angles of the mass should be directed. In Pisanello's drawing, however, he is fascinated, not with the shape of mass, but with the shape of space. He has created a tunnel of space articulated by the series of recession planes, through which his figures move in depth toward the pull of the vanishing point.

This sets into motion the idea of architectural design, not as the manipulation of mass but as articulation of experience along an axis of movement through space. This is a totally different way of thinking from that represented by Francesca's drawings above. It was provided by exactly the same basic scientific technology, but this was employed in a different way, which led to a liberation of the designer's thinking, and set into motion a new ordering principle in city design. Over the next two hundred years, one can observe a continuous growth and development of the seminal idea contained here, in its acceptance by designers and its application on a vast scale in actual construction on the ground.

SINGLE MOVEMENT SYSTEM

We now observe the working of the axial movement idea through the four stages of the Renaissance, in which the experiments of the artist, especially in stage design, provided the basis for city-building.

EARLY RENAISSANCE   CA. 1470

The detail at left, taken from the Baltimore painting, "The Ideal City," influenced by the writings of Alberti, shows the beginning of the artist's fascination with the representation of space. The preoccupation with the representation of mass, which dominates most of the painting, is here replaced by the overlapping of two recession planes. There is no systematic shaft of space or sense of movement, but there is space in depth.

HIGH RENAISSANCE   CA. 1500

Here Bramante, the master mind of the High Renaissance, picks up and develops the idea expressed in "The Ideal City." Two arches recede deeply, and the perpendicular shaft of space is clearly defined, creating a thrust of movement deep into the picture. The building program, however, is that of a single institution, an academy or a monastery, perhaps; the city has not yet emerged as the designer's sphere.

MANNERISM   CA. 1530

Some thirty years later, the mannerist Baldassare Peruzzi intensifies the movement and views the design in relation to the city as a whole. Here, however, the great new forces unleashed receive expression in a tumultuous confusion. The idea is set, but not maturity of design.

(Note that Peruzzi copied the Bramante drawing above to provide the central element for his work.)

PREVIEW OF BAROQUE   CA. 1560

In the detail of his drawing above, Francesco Salviati, the mannerist architect, painter, and theatrical designer, brings the concept to full maturity in his abstract vision of the ideal city, which previsions the ideas of the Baroque. The inward thrust of the shaft of space, firmly defined, moves deep into the picture. The circular buildings suggest cross movements and an extension of a movement-system network, not just a single axial path. The architecture of the building at the end takes on the function of dominating and illuminating the space before it, giving character to this section of the city and an articulate experience to the citizen who moves toward this building and beyond.

INSIDE-OUTSIDE RELATIONSHIPS

Until the beginning of the seventeenth century, the energy of designers was absorbed in the problem of applying new-found Renaissance principles to the solution of the interior form of the building, and then to the façade. In the seventeenth century, after almost two hundred years of experimentation, the flow of energy was reversed. The design vitality began to spill out of the building into the streets of the city around it. The designer, having mastered the internal building problem, now cast his eye on the building's environment, and expended his extra energy in a euphoric flow of design activity to create a setting for his structure. This was the opposite of the principle shown in the Salviati drawing on the previous page, in which the designer of a building met the requirements of a setting created by somebody else.

In Paul Klee's drawing here, the lines of energy radiate outward from a central source in a manner similar to that of Baroque design. The energies of the design expired in the depths of the city, the points of expiration themselves creating a form — as, for example, a piazza connected with a Baroque church. Out of this grew the deliberate planning of a network of lines of design energy on a city-wide basis, providing channels for the transmission of the design energy of buildings already built and at the same time creating locations calling for a new design energy in buildings yet to come.

It was the extra energy of the Baroque period, resulting from the confidence inspired by the mastery of design technique, which produced the great interaction between structure and setting. This is demonstrated in Pietro da Cortona's work on the church and square of Santa Maria della Pace in Rome, shown opposite. Raguzzini's Roman Square, Piazza Sant' Ignazio, seen in plan on page 161, with its three contiguous oval prisms of space reflecting the aisles and nave of the church of Sant' Ignazio, also expresses this interplay. Similar exuberance was expressed in the Roman plan of Sixtus V for a city design structure binding the points of design energy into a total system.

The drawing by Theodore J. Musho below is from inside Sant' Ignazio looking into the Piazza outside. It displays a new kind of awareness of transparency, continuity and simultaneity.

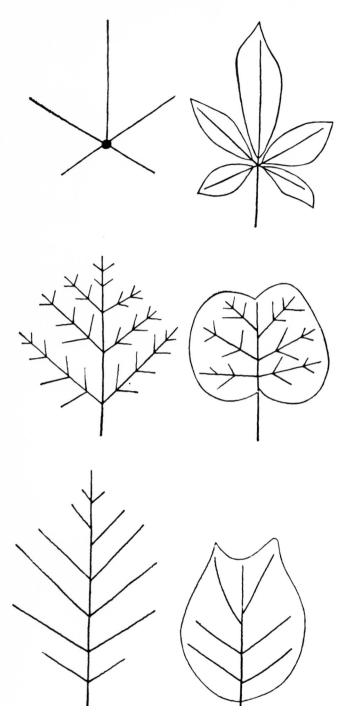

KLEE ON MOVEMENT SYSTEMS

As in nature, the life forces of design must flow freely before rich flowering and fruitful forms can be produced. The diagrams based on Paul Klee's work, on this page, illustrate the flow of lines of energy along the veins and sub-veins radiating outward from the stem of the leaf, and from them, the outward flow of the flesh of the leaf. This flow of energy expires in space, the points of expiration determining the form of the leaf.

With the tree itself, a more complex expression of precisely the same principle is manifest: the form is determined by the location of expiration of the energy of growth in relation to the point where the seed was planted in the earth. This was explained to me by my great teacher Eliel Saarinen as the point of equilibrium between the creative impulse of growth and the restrictive requirements of correlation: the necessity of conducting the nourishing chemicals of the soil to the outermost leaf.

The Klee water-color on the opposite page adds another dimension to the structural movement of energy within the city: the creation of fields of quality at the points of convergence of movement systems. Since the veins of a leaf or the branches of a tree are comparable to the channels of movement of people and goods within a city (as noted on p. 34), we see the parallel between organic structural forms and the city movement system, their sequential effect on the sensibilities of the people who move over them, and the resulting effect on the appearance and character of the city adjacent to them.

In this painting we see that it is the movement systems which determine the shape of the fields of influence. These vary in intensity with the degree of movement, overlapping one another as they radiate outward.

DESIGN STRUCTURE OF BAROQUE ROME

Sixtus V, in his effort to recreate the city of Rome into a city worthy of the Church, saw clearly the need to establish a basic over-all design structure in the form of a movement system as an idea, and at the same time the need to tie down its critical parts in positive physical forms which could not easily be removed. He hit upon the happy notion of using Egyptian obelisks, of which Rome had a substantial number, and erected these at important points within the structure of his design.

The power of this idea is demonstrated on the next six pages. Here can be seen what actually happened to the Basilica of Saint Peter in various stages between the erection of the obelisk by Sixtus in 1586 and the completion of the Bernini colonnade. The design influence of the deliberate act of Sixtus was realized eighty years after his death, so it did not stem from any direct power he exercised during his lifetime. The point in space demarcated by the obelisk became the determinant in later construction because of the power of the idea in men's minds, transmitted over generations by the physical fact of the obelisk's existence. The continual criticism about the inapplicability of Sixtus's ideas in the present day, because his success was due to his despotic powers, which do not now exist, is absurd. Sixtus achieved far fewer actual architectural changes during the five years of his reign than any democratic city government could achieve today. It was the inherent power to his idea, not his political influence, that caused the chain of events which followed.

That the actual physical accomplishment at the time of Sixtus's death was quite pathetic is shown by the two paintings on the opposite page, from the Sistine Library in the Vatican (see also pages 144 and 154). The upper fresco shows the confused and chaotic west façade of the venerable Saint Peter's Basilica before Sixtus started work, and the lower painting shows the appearance of the square at the time of his death, with the obelisk in place. This is hardly an impressive civic achievement, but the idea of order has been implanted. As in the Klee drawings to the right, the single point in space can become a powerful design force, bringing order out of chaos.

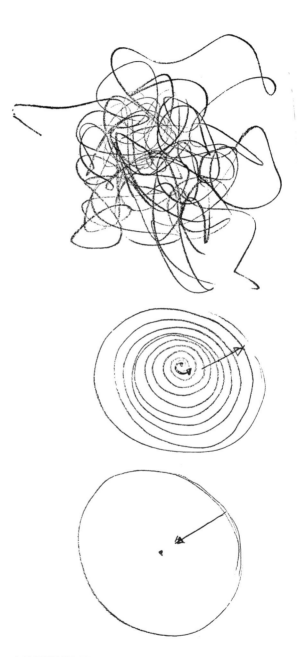

A POINT IN SPACE AS AN ORGANIZING FORCE

THE ORGANIZING FORCE AT WORK

The engraving above, made by Israel Henriet about 1640, shows the changes in Saint Peter's and the square around it after the placing of the obelisk. The dome on Michelangelo's drum has been completed. The nave and façade of Saint Peter's have also been built, not, however, according to Michelangelo's or Bramante's ideas, but according to the new Baroque concepts expressed by the architect Carlo Maderna, who rejected the grandeur of the four-sided symmetry on the central dome. Considerable new work was carried out on the Vatican, shown to the right of the picture, but the palace still presents a rather raw appearance to the square. In the center is the two-story Bernini tower proposed by the architect to be one of the two symmetrical structures to rise above the Maderna façade. After its completion, cracks developed in the lower structure because of faulty engineering calculations and, when it became clear that the stability of the structure of a major part of Saint Peter's was threatened, the vast tower had to be torn down. The columns from

this tower were transferred to the Piazza del Popolo to complete the great Baroque composition shown on page 155. They are now in place on the façades of the twin churches there.

A comment on the attitude toward professional practice of the day is the fact that the Roman Catholic Church, which commissioned Bernini to design the disastrous and costly Saint Peter's tower, recommissioned the same architect to design the great piazza before Saint Peter's some twenty years later, despite the display of engineering incompetence in the design of the defective tower. The world is the beneficiary of that remarkable decision.

The water-color to the right, made in 1642 by Israel Silvestre, of the view from the top of Saint Peter's dome, shows that, despite the ordering of Saint Peter's façade, the open space in the foreground was still chaotic and formless. The old fountain, the obelisk, and the square were unrelated, and the total effect was unimpressive, as it would continue to be for another twenty years.

THE IMPULSE IS FULFILLED

In this superb engraving by Giambattista Piranesi, a portion of which has been removed, we see the obelisk on the site created for it by the great oval colonnade of Bernini. Yet it was the pre-existing obelisk that determined Bernini's design. The old fountain was moved to a new location, a new one was built to balance it, the columnar screen gave shape and definition to a magnificent extent of space, and order was achieved. In terms of mass the obelisk is only a tiny part of the whole; in terms of the idea, it dominates.

Throughout this book the theme is stressed that we may look to the artist to help us see what is going on about us and to understand the essential nature of events. An excellent example is this engraving by Piranesi, in which, with superlative skill, the artist conveys the feeling of the obelisk as the organizing center of the entire complex. He shows it not simply as a static mass, but as a life force in the same sense that Klee conveys the feeling with a dot in the drawings on page 131.

The influence of the point of space established here by the obelisk covers a small area, as it properly should do, in relation to the dominant basilica of Saint Peter. Its energies expire at the border of Bernini's oval, and it seems to me that Mussolini was mistaken in trying to extend them through his vulgar and ill-advised Via della Conciliazione. Bernini's original plan provided for an additional columned section defining the oval between the two end pavilions. It was his idea to complete, quite firmly, the self-contained character of this space and to preclude the very type of axial extension which Mussolini built.

In the rest of Rome, a chaotic, tangled area with the other six votive churches scattered about, Sixtus V saw the need for an entirely new design approach. During his five-year reign he placed the three remaining obelisks as points in space, determining the termini of the sections of his movement system and establishing the ends of the lines of force stretched taut between them. In this way the obelisks not only influenced the architecture in their immediate vicinity, but also extended their influence along the length of the connecting highways.

MOVEMENT SYSTEMS AND DESIGN STRUCTURE

"At that time Vasari was with Michelangnolo [*sic*] every day: and one morning the Pope in his kindness gave them both leave that they might visit the Seven Churches on horseback (for it was Holy Year), and receive the Pardon in company. Whereupon, while going from one church to another, they had many useful and beautiful conversations on art and every industry." These words written in 1560 by Giorgio Vasari, chronicler of the lives of the painters, architect of the Uffizi Palace in Florence, and painter in his own right, convey with fresh lucidity the feelings of the pilgrims as they moved from one votive church to another. The famous Antoine Lafréry engraving of 1575, reproduced below, shows quite accurately the ancient walls of Rome and some of its monuments and, on an enlarged scale, the seven churches which were the object of the pilgrimage. This is a graphic representation of the program for the Sixtus plan, of the phenomenon of undirected, undifferentiated movement. Because it is meandering, it would induce in the pilgrims no clearly organized sequence of purposeful architectural impressions, but rather a series of blunted visions of scattered houses, churches, and rolling countryside.

Apart from the uncompleted Renaissance drum of Michelangelo's design for the crossing of Saint Peter's, the architecture is Romanesque or Byzantine, with classical ruins remaining from earlier periods.

OBELISKS AS POINTS IN MOVEMENT SYSTEMS

The remarkable engraving above, published in Rome in 1612, is evidently based on the one opposite made by Lafréry thirty-seven years before. In the later example we see the architectural alterations that had been made during the intervening period, and, most specifically, the four newly placed obelisks of Sixtus V. A comparison of the two engravings provides a visual experience involving both the maturing of architectural form under the influence of new ideas and the appearance of the obelisks as design elements. The movement system emerges as a total design idea, symbolized by the obelisks positioned at its terminal points.

The obelisk at the extreme left is the one which Sixtus put near the Porta del Popolo, adjacent to which is the church of Santa Maria del Popolo, shown in small size in both engravings. The older fountain appears only in the later print, its existence evidently called to the engraver's mind by the new obelisk. This obelisk did not relate to any of the seven churches: it was a kind of greeting which confronted the visitor at the moment he entered the city through the principal gate.

The next obelisk is that on the west end of Santa Maria Maggiore, about two kilometers from the Porta del Popolo, which marked the terminus of Strada Felice orginally intended to connect the two obelisks. Clearly visible are the twin domes, making a principal design interplay with the point of the obelisk. The dome on the right was built by Sixtus V.

The lower of the two central obelisks is, of course, in front of Saint Peter's, shown with the completed Maderna façade and the dome. The upper obelisk is the one erected by Sixtus V in front of San Giovanni in Laterano, now provided with a setting created by the newly built palace to the left of the church, and by the new two-tiered arcaded façade of the church itself. Both of these were the work of Domenico Fontana, Sixtus V's architect and adviser on building and city-planning projects.

On these two pages is portrayed the metamorphosis of form over a period of time in response to a design idea.

NODAL POINTS DISPERSED

Again with the help of artists we see here the evolution of the popular image of Rome as it was affected by the larger design idea. Taddeo di Bartolo's painting of Rome, (at left, above), was made in 1413, Giovanni Francesco Bordino's engraving, (below), was made in 1588, and Paul Klee's sketches from *The Thinking Eye*, (opposite), belong, of course, to the present century.

In the Bartolo painting, Rome is seen strongly articulated by a series of ancient and medieval symbols associated with the various parts of the city: the Antonine and Trajan columns, the domed Pantheon and the Colosseum, the Dioscuri (statues of Castor and Pollux with their horses) on the Quirinal Hill, and, in the upper right, the equestrian statue of Marcus Aurelius before its removal from the San Giovanni in Laterano area to the Capitoline Hill. Interspersed among these remnants of classical Rome are medieval churches and towers. An early form of the Trevi Fountain with its three basins can be seen just below the Dioscuri. All these monuments are distributed in a general way in the appropriate parts of the city, but without any specific positioning or hint of design interrelationship. They may be compared with Klee's upper drawing showing points in space apparently distributed at random and producing no shape at all.

The Bordino engraving below, made only three years after the accession of Sixtus V to the papal throne, shows the astonishing rapidity with which his spatial-organization idea became known and understood. Here are some of the same symbols shown in Bartolo's painting. The two columns are clearly identifiable, as is the Colosseum. Santa Maria Maggiore is represented by a drawing of the Virgin, and the Dioscuri on the Quirinal Hill appear above the words "Mons Caballus." But each nodal image is precisely positioned and related to every other image by the design system of straight connecting streets. Although some of the streets had not been finished at this time, the idea of the movement system as a design-orienting element was so strong in the mind of Bordino that this became the organizing feature in his engraving and, by its very existence, served as a transmission agent, implanting the seeds of this idea in the mind of others.

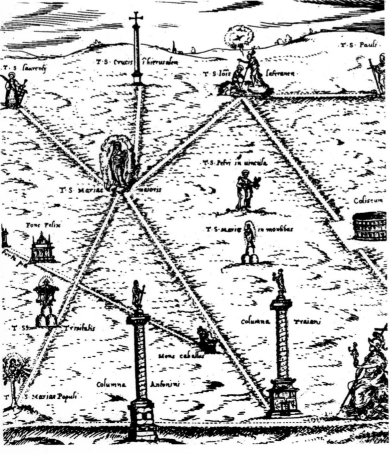

NODAL POINTS CONNECTED

When he developed the idea shown in the diagram on this page it is unlikely that Paul Klee knew of the plans of Sixtus V for Rome, let alone that he made any connection with it. It is pleasant to accompany the rich representational drawings on the opposite page with the simple diagrams of Klee, because the fundamental design forces at work in Sistine Rome are as applicable today as they were in the sixteenth century if we consider their essential nature rather than their stylistic manifestations.

The establishment of points in space may be for emotional or spiritual associations with pre-existing monuments or structures (as was the case in Rome). Equally they may be points of production in regional economy, or centers of social regeneration in blighted areas. The concept of connecting these points by channels of energy, or lines of force, as demonstrated in the lower Klee drawing, may not only create an aesthetic physical design entity as happened in Sixtus's Rome, but produce an awareness of the structural relation of functions in what appeared to be a chaotic distribution of independent functions (upper diagram).

Both the aesthetic design entity and the concept of a system of functional interrelationships are manifestations of the same underlying order, and the integration of the two is required if we are to solve contemporary problems on an urban scale. The fashion in contemporary architectural and planning thought of separating them by a "no-man's-land" to assure their continued individual identity — even to attach a whole professional vested interest separately to each one — has meant serious damage to efforts to solve the problems of the modern city.

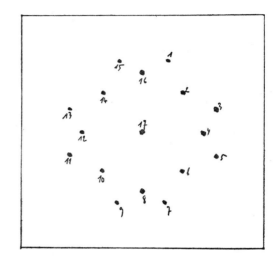

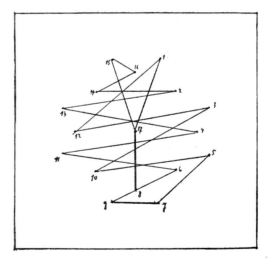

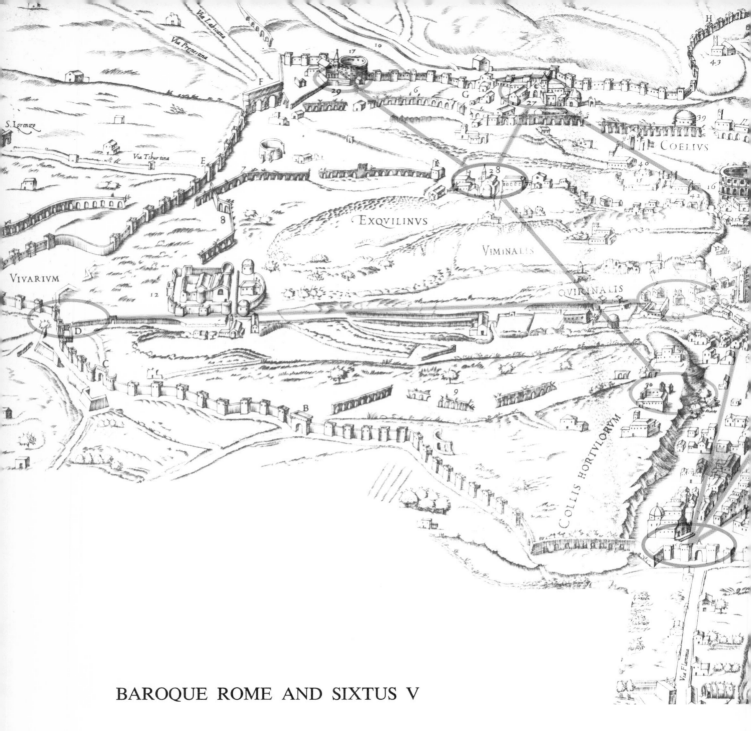

BAROQUE ROME AND SIXTUS V

As Sixtus V cast his eye over the city of Rome after his election as Pope in 1585, he considered how he could make the sprawling, disorderly city into a fitting capital of Christendom. The only example in the entire city of a contemporary effort to relate more than one building to another in a design sense was Michelangelo's three-building "Capitoli," shown in this 1561 engraving by Antonio Dosio. For the rest there was the crowded, jumbled medieval city, taking up about one-third of the space within the ancient Aurelian walls, the remainder being a few churches and ruined monuments scattered through vineyards and wasteland.

During the years of frustration which he spent in his villa near Santa Maria Maggiore as a neglected Cardinal ignored by hostile Popes, Sixtus formulated his ideas for the regeneration of Rome. Suddenly he was thrust into a position to do what he had so long desired, and his ideas took shape in the form of a clear plan for the city.

Extending from the Porta del Popolo in the northern wall of the city (circled in red and marked

"A") in the foreground are three converging streets, the right-hand one leading to Porto di Ripetta at the Tiber River (circled in green). To these streets Sixtus, in his mind's eye, added a fourth one, Strada Felice, extending directly to Santa Maria Maggiore (also circled in red and marked 28 on this plan). Only the portion from San Trinità dei Monti (circled in blue) was built and is here shown as a yellow line intersected by the old Strada Pia (also shown as a yellow line). This connects with the Dioscuri (circled in green), clearly visible on the Quirinal Hill, and with

Michelangelo's Porta Pia (circled in blue and marked "D").

From Santa Maria Maggiore one new road branched off to Santa Croce (circled in green and marked 29) and another one reached to San Giovanni in Laterano (circled in blue and marked 27) by a route indicated in yellow in this illustration. From here another route led to the Colosseum.

Here is demonstrated the seminal idea of the great plan for Rome, a colossal intellectual feat of an imposition of order on an environment of chaos.

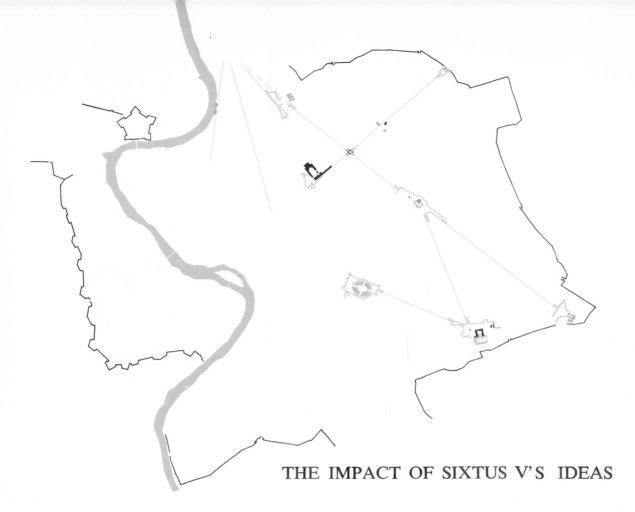

THE IMPACT OF SIXTUS V'S IDEAS

Demonstrated here is the unfolding of one of the most remarkable design processes in history, the impingement of the ideas of Sixtus V on the minds of clients and architects long after he was dead. The impact of his ideas is brought to light in the following series of diagrammatic plans especially prepared for this book. In them, time is shown by color, and various drawings and engravings of different periods are juxtaposed to portray the changing form of Rome over three centuries.

The plan above sets forth the system used in all the diagrams. The buildings indicated in red are the significant ones which existed before Sixtus V set to work and were influential in the development of his design ideas. The yellow lines represent the principal movement systems that constituted the network of Sixtus V. These include some pre-existing streets, as the three which converge on Piazza del Popolo at the top of the map: the central ancient Via Flaminia (the present-day Via del Corso) leading from the Porta del Popolo to the Forum and the Campidoglio, the Via Ripetta on the south (leading to the river), and the Via del Babuino on the north (right). The fourth street, indicated by a dashed yellow line to the north of Via del Babuino, is the never-to-be-built extension of Strada Felice from its actual northern terminus in the Napoleonic obelisk before San Trinità dei Monti at the head of the Spanish Steps.

The other pre-existing street was Strada Pia, the route from the Quirinal Hill to Porta Pia, which intersects the Strada Felice at right angles. But here Sixtus made his influence felt because he lowered the grade four feet in parts to establish a visual connection between the monuments at the two termini.

From Santa Maria Maggiore (at right center of the map), the Sixtus movement system extended in two branches of a *Y*. The northern branch (upper yellow line) led to Santa Croce, and the southern one (lower yellow line) terminated in the obelisk before San Giovanni in Laterano, where it connected with the projected highway back to the oval Colosseum shown here in red.

To the diagrams have been added (in black) the actual structures built by Sixtus V during his brief reign, all of which clearly relate to his movement system. This, in all its glorious simplicity, is the basic design structure of Sixtus V for Rome. What it did to Rome is complicated indeed.

CONTEMPORARY ROME

In the diagram above, the principal structures that were built after the death of Sixtus V in 1590 have been added in blue. These buildings were directly influenced by the over-all design structure he created and were complementary to it. While the total extent of this work may not seem very impressive, the impact it makes on the ground is very great indeed. This is because the buildings surround and dominate large open spaces. Since these spaces are part of a controlled sequential experience (provided by the movement-system design structure), the individual design impacts build up into a powerful force and the connecting framework dominates the visual image of a large part of Rome.

At the northern end of the city (at the top of the map), the black dot of Sixtus's obelisk in Piazza del Popolo becomes surrounded by structures defining its location, and eventually by a cross-movement connecting the Tiber River with the gardens of the Pincio high above. The church of San Girolamo degli Schiavoni at the Tiber River, with the Porta di Ripetta before it, becomes the terminus of one leg of a cross connection from the Via Fla-

minia, the Spanish Steps being the terminus of the other. The Spanish Steps also serve as the substitute for the projected extension of Strada Felice; they receive the northern thrust of the space of Strada Felice, direct it downward to the lower plane of Via del Babuino, which in turn conducts it to Piazza del Popolo, an objective of the Sixtus design. These steps are a splendid connector in three dimensions of a system which functions in two planes.

The Palazzo Barberini (in blue), with its Piazza Barberini and the Bernini Triton Fountain, is much influenced in its position and design by the Strada Felice, which it faces, and the piazza is a rhythmic element in the progression to the four fountains at the Strada Pia crossing. The formalization of Piazza Quirinale (center of map) and the resetting of the Dioscuri on each side of the obelisk (erected in the eighteenth century) carry forward the enrichment of the old Strada Pia. The rebuilding of Santa Maria Maggiore is another change directly influenced by the Sixtus plan, and together these works show what architecture and city-planning can do when these two elements are interrelated.

FROM FUNCTION TO DESIGN STRUCTURE

The plan of Sixtus V was not an arbitrary pattern, but a functional form in response to a specific need. The painting above, from the Sistine Library in the Vatican, shows a procession of pilgrims over the open terrain to Santa Maria Maggiore. The painting below, also from the Sistine Library, shows the plan of Sixtus V for the regularizing of this movement, for its containment and direction in a straight channel from his obelisk in Piazza del Popolo (seen in the lower left of the painting) to his obelisk at Santa Maria Maggiore (see upper right). This he called Strada Felice. The rebuilt, intersecting Strada Pia is clearly visible, and so too are the Palace and Dioscuri of the Quirinal (at extreme right), the four fountains at the crossing, and the three-arched fountains of Acqua Felice erected by Sixtus (upper center). Michelangelo's Porta Pia is visible in the Aurelian wall at the upper left of the same painting.

To the right is a plan extending from Santa Maria Maggiore to the Spanish Steps, with the four fountains halfway between. Above is a view of Santa Maria Maggiore as it appeared from the old Strada Felice (now Via Agostino Depretis) during Sixtus's lifetime. The covered horse-drawn cart heralds the new mode of transportation, the obelisk marks, symbolically, the movement system to serve it. The dome of Sixtus's chapel, quite different in scale and design from the medieval form of the apse of the old church, spells the emergence of the Renaissance spirit. The forces of the new design are in place, and the interaction is soon to begin.

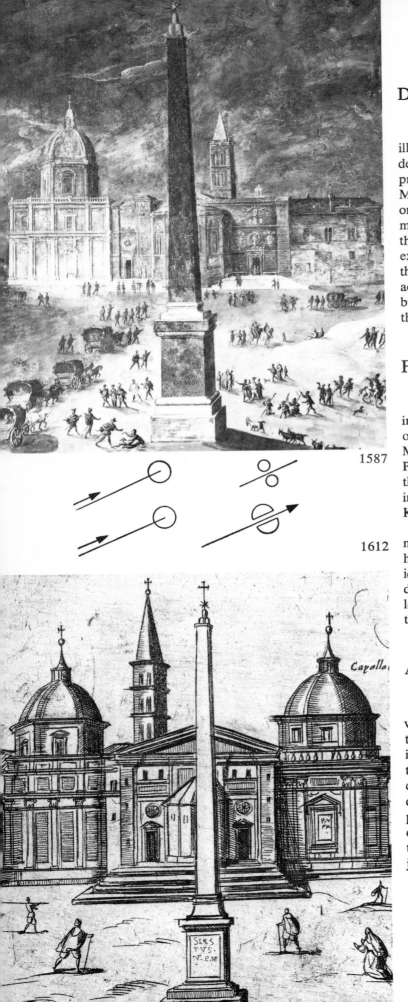

1587

1612

DESIGN STRUCTURE

By simple visual comparison of these three illustrations, we observe the flow of design from design structure through form to architectural expression. This is what actually happened to Santa Maria Maggiore after Sixtus directed his influence on it, an influence which dealt with all three elements: design structure in the Strada Felice, and the obelisk; form in the dome; and architectural expression in the façade below the dome. Although firmly rooted in each of these phases, the achievements under Sixtus V were fragmentary, but the later work was the logical completion of the formula which they established.

FORM

The diagram based on Paul Klee to the left indicates the kinetics of the impact of the thrust of Strada Felice on the mass of Santa Maria Maggiore. Twenty-one years after Sixtus's death Pope Paul V built the complementary dome on the other side of the Strada Felice axis, and so, in fact, completed in form the same forces that Klee sets forth in the upper right of the diagram.

While one may say this is obvious, it is remarkable that a Pope subjected his identity, and his architect his self-expression, in accepting an idea, a form, and an architectural design exactly dictated by a predecessor. The engraving at lower left, made in 1612, shows the form in place, but the architectural expression is still chaotic.

ARCHITECTURE

The engraving on the right shows the full development in architectural terms of the forces that had now been at play over eighty years. This is Carlo Rainaldi's 1673 design for regularizing the architecture and for building this part of the church into one total expression, thus fulfilling the demands that are placed upon it by reason of its position in a larger design structure. Only now does it serve as an adequate visual terminus of the old Strada Felice, and a symbolic node at a juncture in Sixtus's movement system.

1673

MEETING THE REQUIREMENTS
OF DESIGN STRUCTURE

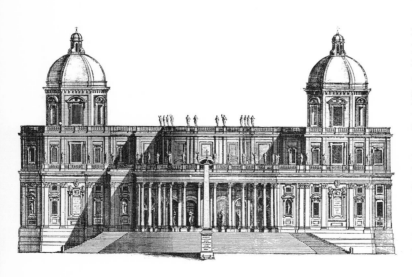

The processes described on the preceding pages, which may give the impression of a smooth flow of design along predetermined channels, were in fact fraught with dangers and potential disaster.

The drawing (top left) is the sketch made by Bernini of his proposal for the façade of Santa Maria Maggiore, and below is an engraving of the elevation with the obelisk shown. The genius of Bernini is not in question, but rather the suitability of his design to the site. A comparison of the drawings on this page with the rendering of Rainaldi's façade on the page before, establishes Rainaldi's as the better design, and it is fortunate that he was entrusted with the work.

Instead of creating a single unity above the all-embracing steps, as did Rainaldi, Bernini divided his façade into separate parts, each splendid in itself, but each claiming its own identity at the expense of the whole. Thus Bernini failed to create a mass of sufficient weight to counter the thrust of the old Strada Felice axis. The heavily articulated semicircular colonnade, in addition to detaching itself from the mass of the main façade, created vertical rectangles of deep shadow between the columns. This was the worst possible background for the obelisk, which would, in reality, have largely been obscured by it.

Here is the phenomenon of a good building in the wrong location. Why the powerful and respected Bernini did not get the job is obscured in history. While it would be pleasant to attribute the selection of Rainaldi to the astute vision of the client, we cannot authoritatively do so. But we can rejoice that history was on the side of the plan's unity.

The engraving to the right, copied by Rossi from an earlier sketch, shows a building in the process of transformation to meet the demands of new forces introduced into the environment. It shows the metamorphosis into a totally new scale at the point of impact of the thrust of the old Strada Felice just behind the obelisk, a scale that eventually would envelop the whole structure.

In the diagram opposite, the two black spots representing the obelisk and the chapel of Sixtus V, in conjunction with the thrust of the new roads (shown in yellow), acting upon the ancient basilica (in red), resulted in the magnificent construction shown in blue. Thus it was that the building assumed its final role as a focal point in the design structure of Rome.

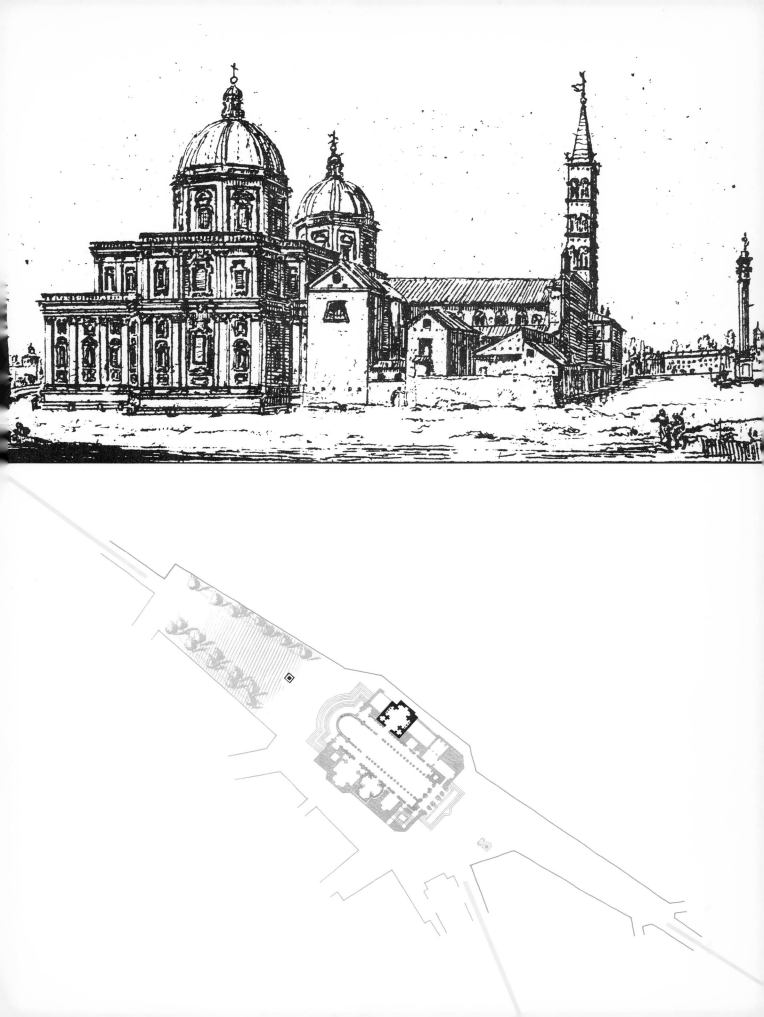

CREATIVE TENSION

During the Baroque period full architectural expression was given to the idea of placing two bodies in space so that a vital flow of forces from one to the other was set up, resulting in tension between them. This principle had been overlooked during the early Renaissance but re-emerged in this new period as a vital force in design.

There is a special pleasure in presenting here the hands of Adam and God as Michelangelo painted them on the ceiling of the Sistine Chapel,

together with the anonymous painting in the Lateran Palace (below left) which shows Michelangelo's Porta Pia communing across the space of Strada Pia to the ancient Roman Dioscuri, which are symbolic of classic art from which Michelangelo derived so much inspiration. The Lateran painting shows better than any photograph, and indeed better than any single experience on the ground, the visual juxtaposition of the symbolic termini of a great avenue, to create a connection which exists in the mind's eye but which cannot be presented visually by ordinary means. This relationship was unavailable by technical methods of representation until very recently, when similar effects have been produced by the telephoto lens on television, notably at the time of the funeral procession of President Kennedy. Only on the television screen was it possible to see, in proximity, the symbolic termini of the avenues of Washington, conveying the over-all design idea as the cortège moved through the shafts of space.

The Piranesi engraving to the right, of Acqua Felice, the fountain erected by Sixtus V to symbolize the bringing of water to this part of Rome by the repair of the aqueducts from the Alban hills, expresses the tension in space between Acqua Felice and the Baroque façade of Santa Maria della Vittoria, erected later than the fountain.

RHYTHMIC ARTICULATION

The diagram to the right shows the rhythmic articulation of the movement along Strada Pia (now the Via Quirinale and the Via Venti Settembre) which came about through the deliberate act of Sixtus. Halfway between Porta Pia and the Quirinal Palace, which Domenico Fontana designed for Sixtus (it is shown under construction in the painting in the Lateran), Sixtus placed the Acqua Felice. And it was halfway between here (in the Piazza San Bernardo) and the palace that he placed the four fountains, erected in his lifetime. These fountains, placed as free-standing walls at the corners where there were no buildings, marked the crossing of the old Strada Pia and the old Strada Felice (Via Quattro Fontane); they also acted as a symbolic foreground for four views, each of which was great in its own right.

Thus the art of urban design as practiced by Sixtus included not only the design structures, but also the determination of where new structures were needed to carry forward his larger design idea.

Veduta del Castello dell'Acqua Felice
presso le Terme Diocleziane. 1 Chiesa di S.Maria della Vittoria

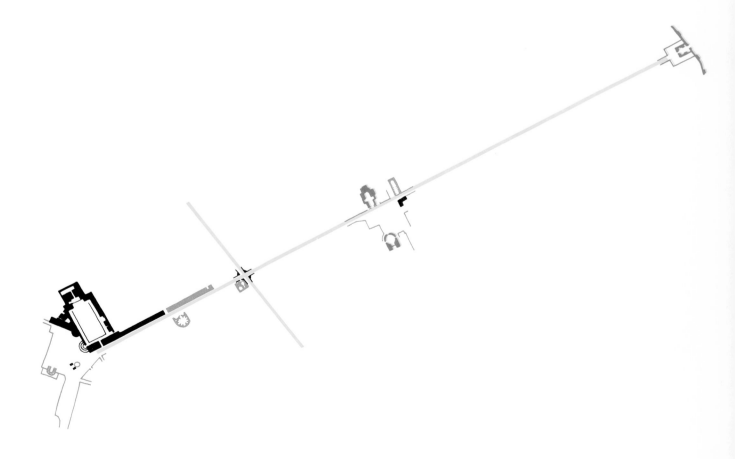

FOUR FOUNTAINS

The three engravings assembled here link together a wide range of Sixtus's symbolic elements along his movement systems. Above is a Rossi view from the four fountains at the crossing of Strada Felice and Strada Pia looking north to Santa Maria Maggiore. The obelisk before the church anchors the movement systems. Adjacent to one of the fountains is the curvaceous façade of San Carlino alle Quattro Fontane by Francesco Borromini, who adapted his plan to the requirements of this difficult diagonal.

In the Falda engraving below we revolve our viewpoint 180 degrees and look down Strada Felice in the other direction to the twin towers of San Trinità dei Monti. The barely visible fountain at the extreme left of the view above becomes the central feature of the view below.

The 1754 Piranesi engraving opposite shows Francesco de Sanctis and Alessandro Specchi's Spanish Steps ascending from Piazza d'Espagna to San Trinità dei Monti at the terminal of Strada Felice. These steps brilliantly tie together two elements of Sixtus's movement systems at different levels.

At the foot of the Spanish Steps is the boat fountain by the father of Giovanni Lorenzo Bernini, and to the left is a view down Via del Babuino to the obelisk that Sixtus raised in Piazza del Popolo. Here we see the economy of means Sixtus used to assure the future development of his plan. In terms of actual construction, the only works of Sixtus visible in these engravings are one of the domes of Santa Maria Maggiore, two obelisks and the four fountains. All of the rest of the architectural work done after his death profoundly reinforced his idea.

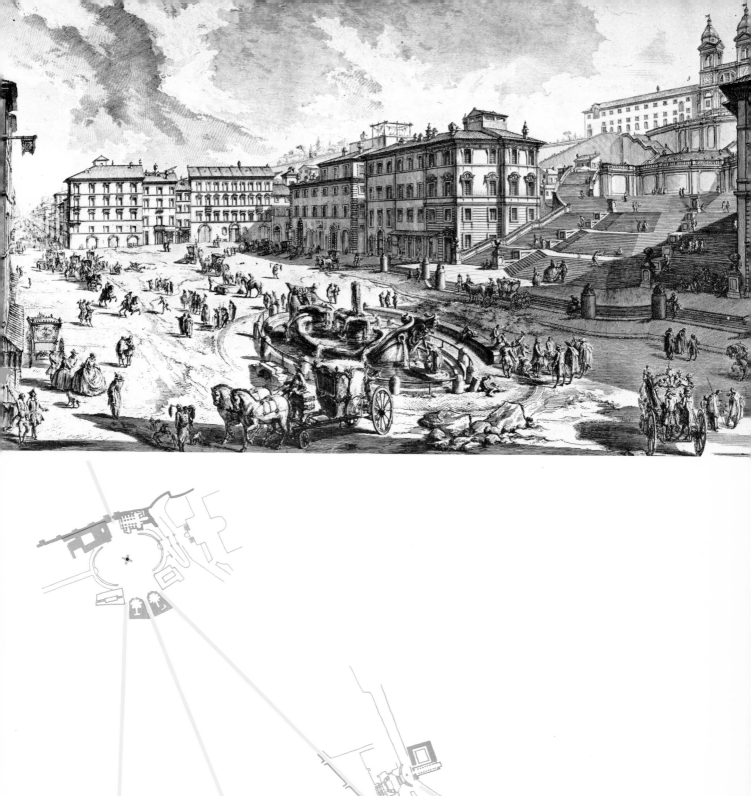

S Maria
de populo

Piatta populi

TIBER

DESIGN OVER TIME — PIAZZA DEL POPOLO

The development of Piazza del Popolo demonstrates more clearly than any other single work in Rome the power of an idea as an organizing force over time. We are indebted to Tempesta for the splendid representation of this part of Rome in his woodcut (left) made just after Sixtus V's death. The woodcut portrays the general squalor and confusion of the area, the mudbank before San Trinità dei Monti, and Piazza della Trinità without its fountain, and, at left, the undistinguished Piazza del Popolo.

It was the architect Rainaldi who saw the great possibilities of this site and who himself promoted the buildings which he felt to be necessary to carry forward its design potential. The building of two virtually identical churches (shown below) across the street from each other was most illogical, yet this is what Rainaldi wanted, and this is what was done. Rainaldi was commissioned in 1660 to design both of them, and Bernini and Fontana helped to complete them.

Here are two churches, Santa Maria dei Miracoli (right) and Santa Maria di Monte Santo (left), whose entire justification is the role they play in the larger structure of design. The buildings are neither totally of the square nor totally of the street, yet they link both and are related to both as well as to the obelisk of Sixtus V.

The churches were completed by 1679, and the Piazza del Popolo remained in this state until the early nineteenth century, rich at both ends but ragged and dull in between. In 1813 Giuseppe Valadier's plan was approved, providing for great sweeping exedras with the new buildings on either side of the twin churches, and repeating the basic form of Santa Maria del Popolo on the opposite side of the Porta del Popolo. This regularized the design of the piazza and brought it into closer relationship with the obelisk. To the east Valadier designed a great stairway, ramp, and cascade descending from the Pincio Gardens, which had the effect of binding this open space into the structure of the piazza. Eventually a street was cut through on this axis to connect the piazza with the Tiber River. The harmony and unity of the total work are the more remarkable in that its parts were created in such widely spaced periods of time, each having its own mode of architectural expression.

19TH AND 20TH CENTURY

This 1880 lithograph shows Rome in all its magnificence, a very different Rome from the one that Sixtus V knew when he became Pope three hundred years before (see page 140).

Piazza del Popolo, with its obelisk, twin-domed churches, and the two semicircular extensions of Valadier, is prominent in the foreground. The street to the river had not yet been cut. To the left rises the series of ramps, loggias, and stairways that tie the Pincio Gardens and the piazza together. The Porta di Ripetta, the curving Baroque stairway to the river before Sixtus's San Girolamo degli Schiavoni, can be seen just at the bend of the Tiber to the right. The obelisk and the top of the Spanish Steps are visible in front of the twin towers of San Trinità dei Monti, and directly above is the obelisk before the twin-domed Santa Maria Maggiore, with the old Strada Felice stretching between. Just to the left, invading the horizon, is San Giovanni in Laterano, with the obelisk of Sixtus V in front of it.

This is a city in all its complexity, a city with an entirely different technological, sociological, and economic base from that which existed when Sixtus was Pope. Yet it is a city in which the quality of living, the joy of being there, and indeed the function of getting around are far more deeply influenced today by the vision and conviction of Pope Sixtus V than they were in his lifetime.

The great American landscape architect Frederick Law Olmsted, Sr., wrote, "What artist so noble . . . as he who, with far-reaching conception of beauty and designing power, sketches the outlines, writes the colors, and directs the shadows of a picture so great that Nature shall be employed upon it for generations, before the work he has arranged for her shall realize his intentions."

Sixtus V succeeded in developing a similar kind of picture, employing the processes of city building rather than those of nature for the realization.

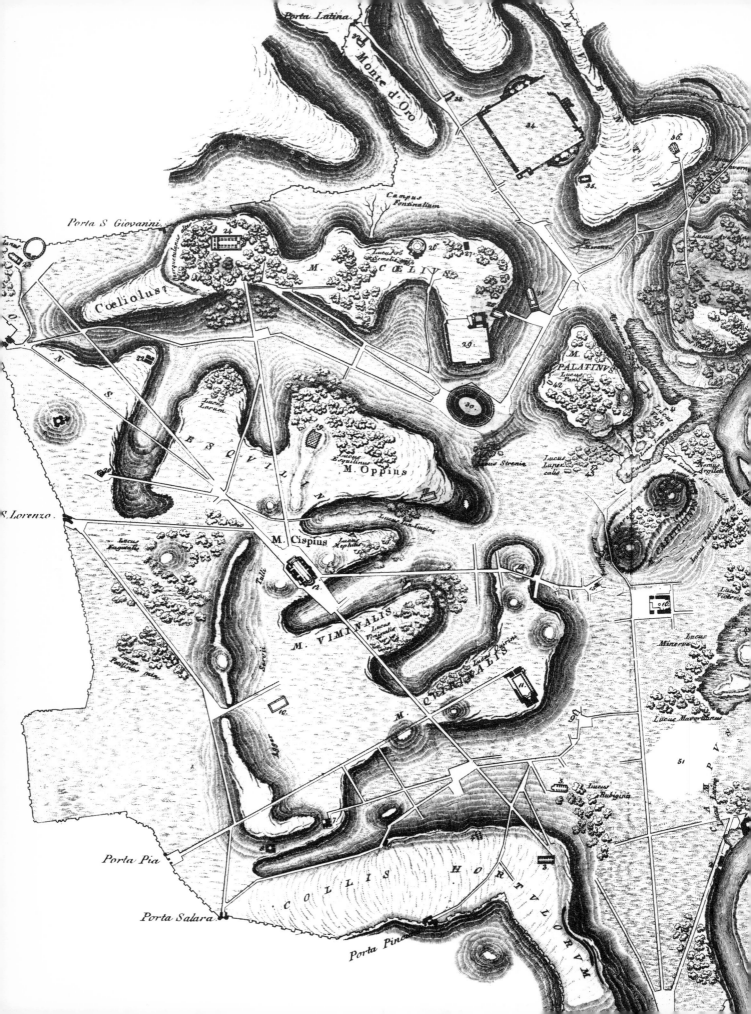

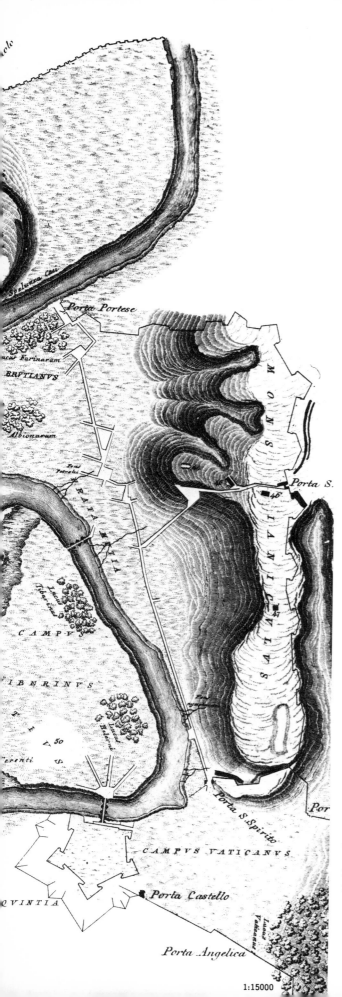

1:15000

FORM AND NATURE

There is more to the lesson of Rome than the interrelationship of planning and architecture. There is the lesson of the relationship of planning and terrain. In this city of seven hills the problem of imposing a rational design network on such a rugged countryside is a formidable one.

During the classical period in Rome, when design concentrated on the establishment of self-contained building complexes, the topographical problem was principally that of hollowing out hills or filling in valleys to create exact geometrical planes for the formal, symmetrical buildings.

The design concept of Sixtus created entirely new topographical problems because he was concerned about a straight line, not a few hundred feet long as in the classical Roman fora or baths, but a few thousand feet long, as required for his vistas and movement system. The interaction between his design, the key buildings, and the topography is lucidly displayed on the map at left, the work of Giovanni Battista Brocchi in 1820.

The movement system acts uncompromisingly across the countryside, tense and organic, moving directly to its goal but disturbing only what is necessary for the achievement of its purpose. We can clearly see the hillock on the old Strada Pia that Sixtus had to cut away in order to connect Porta Pia visually with Piazza Quirinale. We see how Strada Felice went up and down hill in its straight course from San Trinità dei Monti to Santa Maria Maggiore, and in the very process of this rising and falling created a rhythmic experience, the impact of which would have been lost had it not been straight in plan. The branching roads to Santa Croce and to San Giovanni in Laterano also descend the valleys and ascend the hills, and it is the very purity of this counterpoint, the tense network of ways overlaid on the soft, rounded contours of the land, that contributes so greatly to the quality of Rome.

The quality of the land, made articulate by movement systems, is or should be a generating force in all architecture.

159

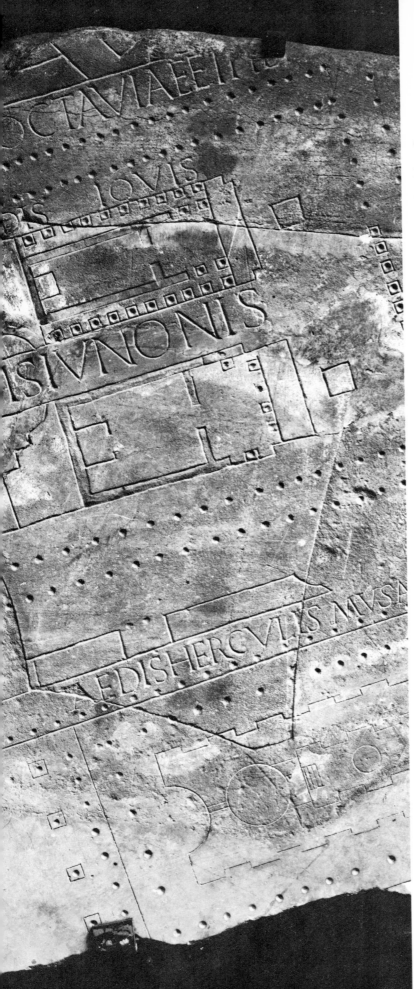

WAYS OF SEEING

CLASSICAL ROME

Illustrated on these pages are two remarkable city plans, both of Rome, but of two widely separated periods. On this page is a fragment of the "Forma Urbis," an incised marble map of the city set up by Septimius Severus early in the third century A.D. on the wall of a building in the Forum. This map demonstrates an approach to design in which the exterior and the interior are integrated. Space flows freely throughout the entire area. Modulating the space is a unified system of columns rhythmically placed in disciplined rows which give a sense of function and order.

The various fragments of this map present a great variety of forms, some rectangular, some semicircular, some circular, and some that are free and fantastic. But through the entire area the beat of the columnar structures is regulated to a common rhythm by the functional requirements of the masonry lintel. Even where vast vaults were employed, leaping across huge volumes of space, the columns with their structural discipline were inserted as free screens across the spaces, recalling the rhythmic beat of the rest of Rome.

The Greek cities were of such a scale that only a few buildings, superbly rhythmic within themselves but only modest in extent, could influence the extent of the entire city and, as symbols, dominate the less interesting sections. However, Roman ambition, and the concomitant scale of the city of Rome, demanded an entirely new principle of coherence and order. An individual building, or a series of individual buildings, without some binding element, would be swallowed up in the size of the great city.

So, as in law and government, the Roman genius produced the ordering device on a broad enough scale to meet the demands of the new dimension of communal activity. And today the remnants of the classical city of Rome stand as a monument to the success of this prodigious effort.

THE CITY

BAROQUE ROME

The map on the right, drawn fifteen hundred years later, is a fragment of the Giambattista Nolli map of Rome in 1748. Implanted upon the formerly disciplined plans of classical Rome are the confused forms of the medieval city, which have been reordered by the architectural discipline of the Baroque.

While this is a much tighter concept than that displayed in the map opposite (indeed the scale of the city was minuscule in relation to its former size), in the mind of Nolli and his contemporaries the exterior and interior public spaces were inextricably integrated into a singleness of thought and experience.

Here the rhythmic module is provided by the interior vaulted bay. The energy of the interior design, perfectly positioned and scaled in relation to the street and piazza on which it is placed, spills out into the void outside and animates the spaces of the city. The classical Pantheon is complemented by a Baroque fountain across the square: Vignola's Gesu Church debouches upon the square in front of it; Bernini's curve-fronted palazzo on Monte Citorio completes the ancient space movement and sets up tensions with the skillfully placed obelisk at the juncture of the broad and narrow squares. Most startling is the piazza in front of Sant' Ignazio, where the rhythmic forms of the nave and aisle vaults are extended across the square in the curved house walls which define the three interconnecting ovals in the plan. Here the inside spaces are an extension and completion of the experiences of the street, and at the same time extend their influence outward, molding the character, and in some cases the actual form, of the exterior spaces before them. (See page 126.)

Again we have the phenomenon of the development of a common and powerful discipline of design, and, in the extraordinary map, a mode of representation which is commensurate with it.

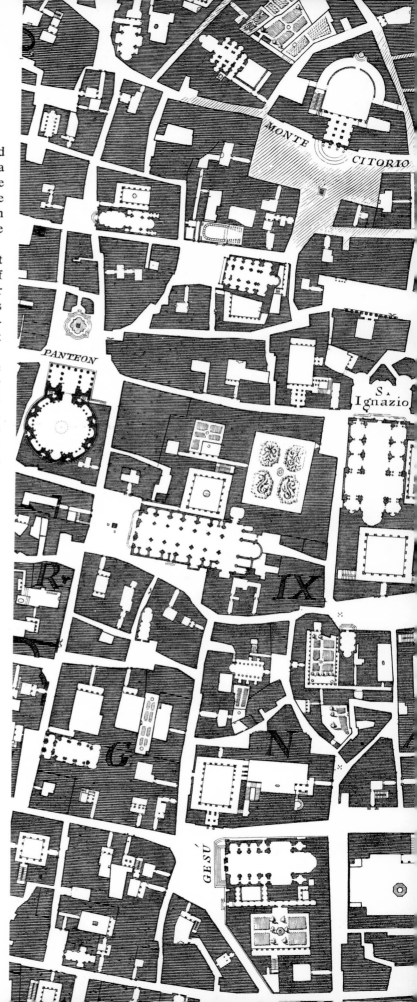

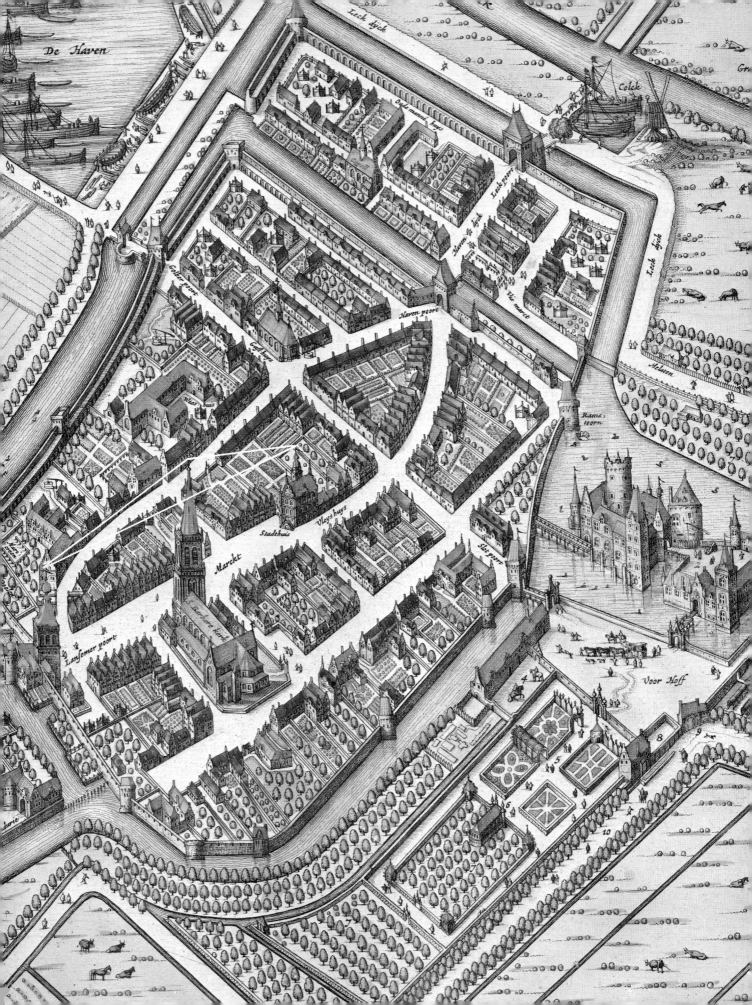

De Haven

Colck

Leck dijck

Onse vrouwe huys

Leck poort

Haven dijck

Leck poort

Leck dijck

Visch marct

Gasten poort

Slaven poort

Meulen

Rams
toorn

Gasthuys

Viesch huys

Vleys huys

Stadthuis

Marckt

Slot poort

Voor Hoff

Landsemer poort

Sint Jans kerck

4

5

6

10

7

7

8

9

DUTCH INTERLUDE

CULEMBORG

The Rome that we have been observing was the result of a vast undertaking in a city of strategic significance, produced with the help of the resources of the Roman Catholic Church. There is value in studying the parallel and concurrent activity in the small cities of Holland, where none of these conditions existed. All the energy and money for city-building was drawn from local sources, and the design was limited accordingly. Design was in a low key, expressing unselfconscious civic development of a scale and extent typical of a neighborhood renewal project in an American city today.

Culemborg, as shown in Joannes Blaeu's engraving of 1648, opposite, is a walled, moated city of medieval origin with a simple elongated rectangle as a market space. This central shaft of space provides the organizing element of Culemborg. The smaller spire over the gate, seen at the left, a powerful design feature at this end of the

market place, recalls the spire of the great church facing the square. This is further echoed by the modest turret of the town hall (the Stadhuis), which so splendidly corners the juncture of the street and the space of the market square. Again we see the will of the architect, in the first half of the sixteenth century, resolving the work of centuries by a single act. With no feeling for the necessity of the Baroque type of formal axial relationship with the foreground space, the designer has put his town hall building confidently astride this asymmetrical space and has given character to this end of the market square. By this third note of a point in space he has created a chord with the points of the spires of the medieval church and gate and so produced a design tension, a web of lines of force, passing above the simple polygon of space contained within the market square. This is a reaffirmation of design on a simple, almost humble basis.

ZALTBOMMEL

Zaltbommel is a somewhat larger and more complex city structure than Culemborg. Superbly the design articulates the anatomy of the city, and high above the flat Dutch plain the symbolic extension upward of its civic functions is etched against the sky.

The isometrical drawing on the opposite page shows the three principal spires. These serve as accents along the lines of movement afforded by the modified grid system of streets. As major focal points, these spires also relate to the spaces in the elongated market and its extension and to Nieuwstraat in front of the church.

In a country of vast extents of flat land devoid of great interest or remarkable natural features, the Dutch, with rare artistry, have set about remedying the defect by rearing city skylines that are total works of art. The engraving at the bottom of these two pages illustrates the success of this impulse in Zaltbommel. The perfectly scaled and complex tower of the church stands as the clearly dominating element, while the little spire

at the crossing is wonderfully recalled by the smaller, simpler, yet related tower and spire of the Gasthuys Chapel. The still smaller turret of the city hall provides the third important element in the chord.

With these architectural creations projecting into space in this wide-ranging system above the city and its streets, there is set into motion an ever-changing harmonic relationship between them as one moves about, both within the city and through the neighboring countryside. The familiar phenomenon is set into full play in which the nearest points seem to move most quickly across the objects in the middle distance, and those farthest away seem to accompany the traveler along his route. Thus a never-ceasing series of kinetic sensations is provided as one moves about Zaltbommel. In order for this phenomenon to be effective, the number of points must be few enough to be readily comprehended, and their position in relation to one another and to the city organism of which they are a part must be clear.

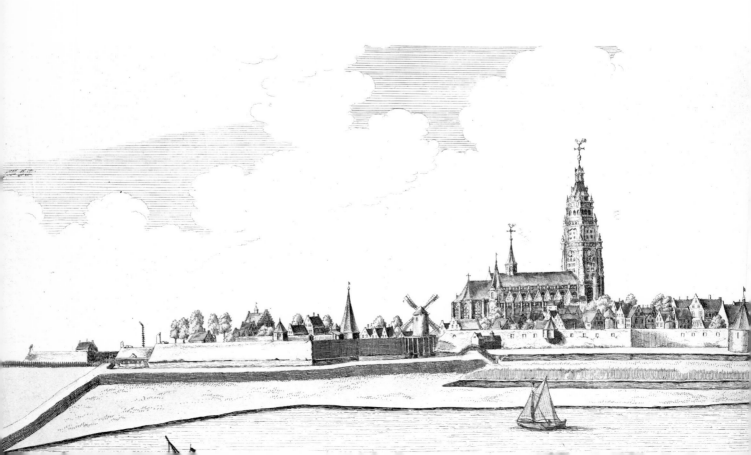

De Groote kerck
De Vogel
Bosch poort
Kruyttooren
De Nieu Straet
Nieuwe Straet
Nieuwe Straet
Gamerse Poort
Oenselse Poort
De Kat
De Nieuwe Haven
Gasthuys Straet
De Marckt
't Raedhuys
Gamerse Straet
Water poort
Steiger poort

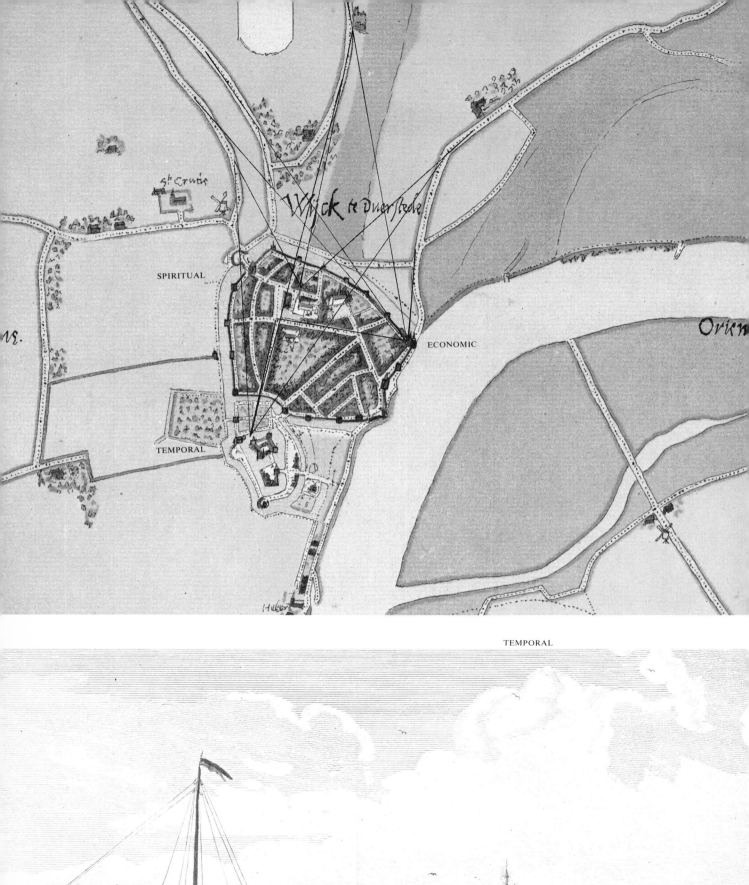

St Cruis

Wijck te DuerStede

SPIRITUAL

ECONOMIC

Orien

TEMPORAL

TEMPORAL

WIJK-BIJ-DUURSTEDE

In the little-known town of Wijk-bij-Duur-stede the principles of design exemplified in Culemborg and Zaltbommel are carried farther in a design structure of great simplicity. The three facets of town life: spiritual force, temporal power, and economic energy, are given symbolic expression in three buildings. Each one raises its characteristic outline against the sky and is so placed that it adds character to an area, and, by being interrelated to the regional movement system, provides a focal point of orientation. The first of these structures, the church with its blunted tower, is in the center of the town on the market square. The second, the turret of the local nobleman's palace, is on the edge of town. The third, about ninety degrees from the castle in

TEMPORAL   ECONOMIC   SPIRITUA

reference to the church, on the city wall by the river, is the windmill, seen in Jacob van Ruis-dael's painting in the Rijksmuseum (above).

The old map opposite, of Jacob of Deventer, made in the latter half of the sixteenth century, shows the town by the river in its regional setting, in all respects much as it exists today. The engraving below presents the city as seen from the river, the church in the center, the castle at the edge of the city on the left, and the windmill over the wall by the river to the extreme right. The map shows the continually changing vistas of the city that are provided by the subtly curving approach roads which alternately direct attention to one and then another of these three nodes. (Black lines overlaid.)

SPIRITUAL   ECONOMIC

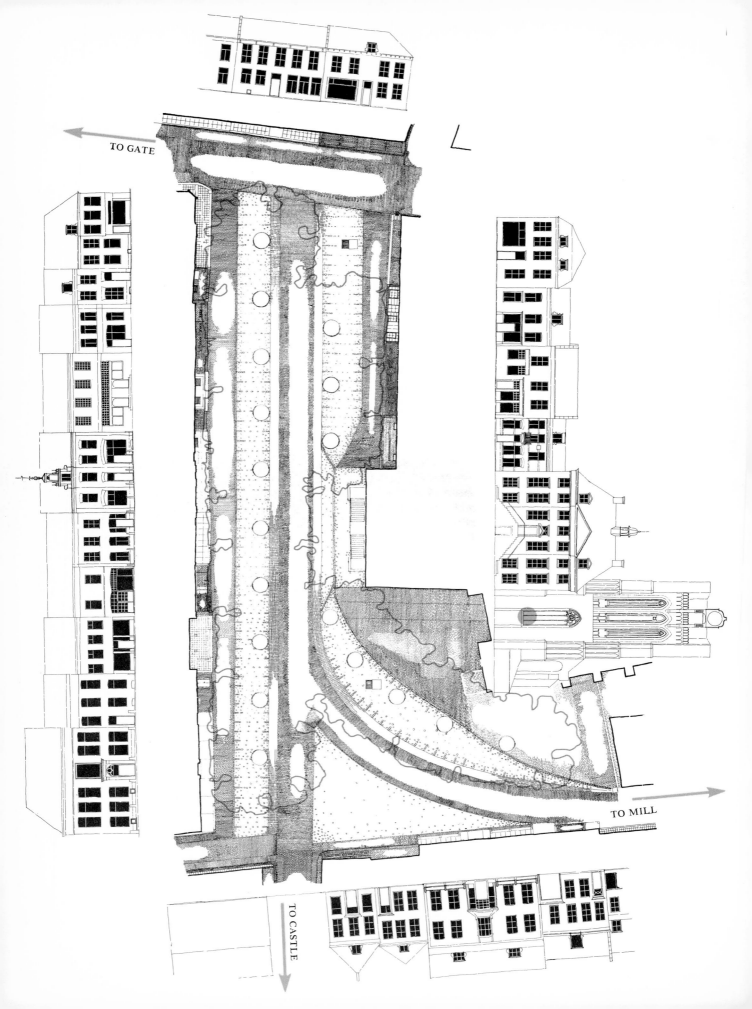

TO GATE

TO MILL

TO CASTLE

THREE SYMBOLIC NODES

As one approaches the central square of Wijk-bij-Duurstede from the countryside, the sense of orientation to the church tower, so strongly felt from a distance, is broken on arrival at the moat around the town, which one follows for a short distance to the bridge leading to the narrow gate in the town wall. From here one takes a street perpendicular to the long dimension of the market-place, so that the arrival at the town center is a sudden and exciting experience as the depth of the square and the church tower burst upon one's consciousness. At the far end of the little market-place is the juncture of two streets at right angles to each other; one of them leads directly to the castle, the turret of which provides the terminal feature of this vista, and the other to the windmill which dominates the skyline as seen down this street.

The organization of the little space of this square, presented in the drawing to the left, is very satisfying and handsome. The "new" seventeenth-century city hall is harmoniously placed and scaled with the medieval church tower, as shown in the 1745 water-color above. The trees (here outlined in green) are well located, the two wellheads effectively modulate the space, and the paving pattern expresses movement and rest, symbolizing the square's function in the total movement system.

In this square is one of the happiest examples of what is so admired in Piazza San Marco in Venice, the successful integration of structures of different periods into a total composition in which there is no compromise in the design of each part. The projection of the plane of the city hall well beyond that of the church gives the seventeenth-century influence a firm identity of its own in space, and the building of the two contemporary wellheads extends and reinforces this plane and, in design, unites this period with the earlier work.

The complete walling-in of the north end of the square by the structures on the north side of the perpendicular approach street contrasts splendidly with the point of juncture of the two right-angled streets at the southern end of the square, each expressive of another facet of the city's life.

169

170

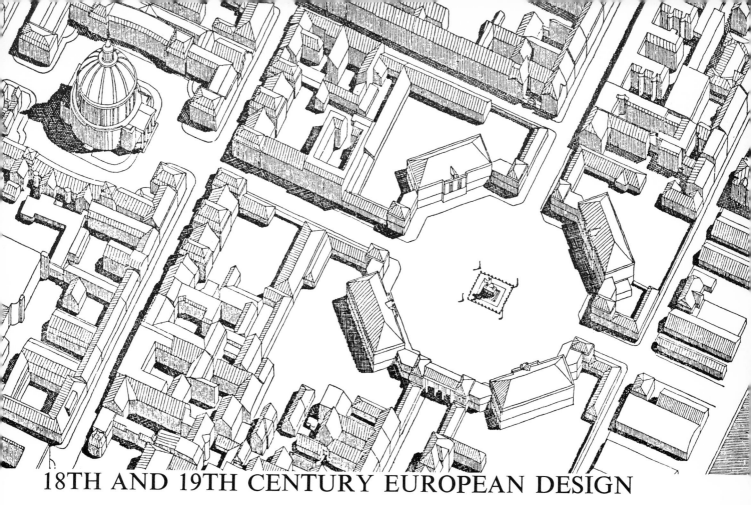

18TH AND 19TH CENTURY EUROPEAN DESIGN

The work we have seen in Holland and in Panza (pages 53–57) was the product of the intuitive medieval mind. Our attention is now drawn to modest small-city design after the effects of perspective and the rationalism of the Renaissance had disrupted the intuitive sensory reactions of the earlier designers.

King Frederik V of Denmark had Amalienborg designed by architect Eigtved in 1749, to stimulate development of some crown lands in Copenhagen. On these pages the drawings, from Steen Eiler Rasmussen's book *Towns and Buildings,* portray the original intent of the composition. The four palaces (now the residences of the King) placed on the angled corners of the octagon (Amalienborg Place) provide an ever-changing series of relationships with one another and also with the equestrian statue in the center of the place and the church dome that terminates the vista on the city side of the square.

The elevation drawing to the left shows in the foreground the original state of the construction of the palaces before the unfortunate second-story addition was built between the palaces and the end pavilions. The addition spoiled the function of the pavilions in setting points in space at the juncture of the square and street, and serving as a counterfoil to the mass of the palaces themselves. Behind are the outlines of twin houses at the end of Frederik's Street. In the background is the elevation of the Marble Church as originally designed by Eigtved, demonstrating the concept of the doubling of the scale of the church at each story as it rises from the ground floor, which is perfectly scaled to the residential design of the palaces. It is regrettable that the design actually adopted for the church had none of these characteristics.

The element that unifies this composition, that binds the city to the region as expressed by the port (the bulkhead is just visible in the extreme lower right corner of the perspective drawing) is the shaft of space defined by the street that runs from the river to the church.

It is this element of a shaft of space and its design thrust that provides the generating force of much of the finest eighteenth-century Northern European civic development.

171

THE SHAFT OF SPACE
GREENWICH

When the decision was made in England to build the great Royal Naval College, which later became the Naval Hospital, on the land between Inigo Jones's Queen's House and the River Thames, Sir Christopher Wren, after accepting the design commission, had to face the question of the relationship of the proposed great new structure to the old and relatively small building of Queen's House. His resolution, employing the principle of two transparent planes as the binding element, provides one of the most powerful inter-relationships of the structures of two periods.

Wren took the volume of Queen's House and projected it forward to the river to form the shaft of space which controlled his design. The photograph shows the plane determined by the mass of Wren's columns to the left, congruent with the plane established by the mass of Queen's House to the right. With the space shaft clearly established as a forward thrust of Queen's House, the question then arose of how to join the new composition to the space so created. The problem was solved by the building of two high-drummed domes at the center of gravity of the new group. This set into motion a counter-thrust of vertical forces which, in their impact with the ground, established pressures perpendicular to the forward movement of the central space. And so the whole was held in a state of dynamic equilibrium.

The widening of the space along the river, dictated by the position of Inigo Jones's earlier building block, connected the whole with the movement along the Thames and extended visually the vertical forces of the domes to the river space.

From engravings of the period, it looked as if Wren thought of tearing down Queen's House and substituting on the site a domed building of his own design, but apparently it was Queen Mary's idea to save the House. He therefore developed his whole plan with respect for the building he found there, and produced a clarity of relationship between the planes. Where they have this kind of relationship two planes must exactly coincide or be widely different. In contemporary practice, the influence of impinging planes established by neighboring buildings is scarcely ever considered in the planning of new structures.

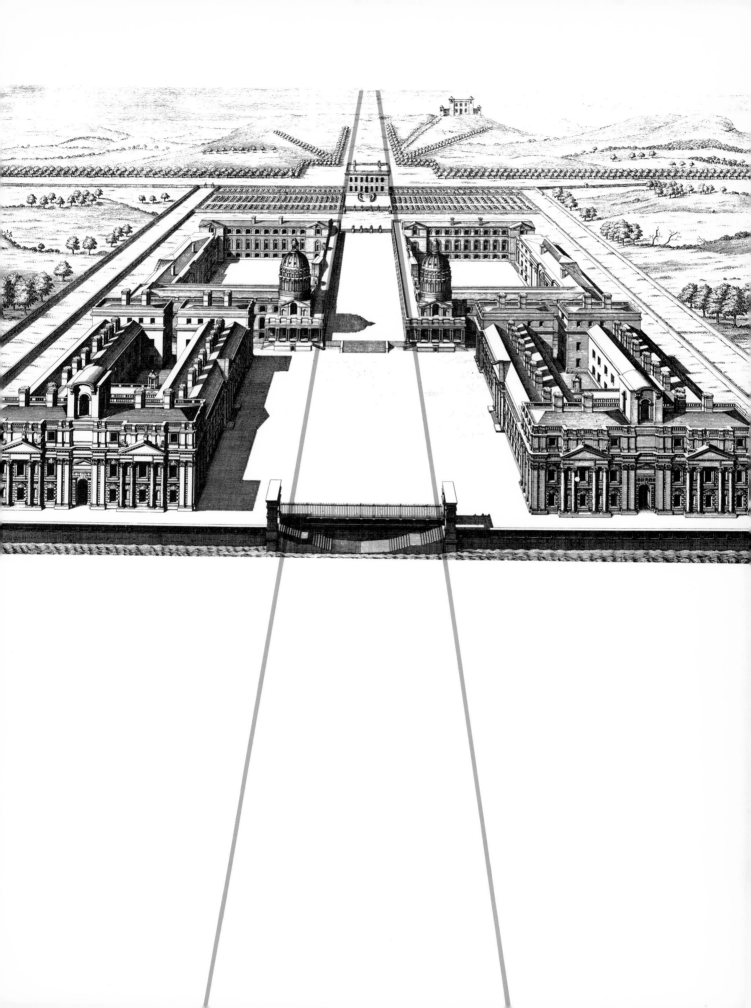

GENERATION OF ARCHITECTURE

In the town of Nancy in France the Place Royale (now called Place Stanislas) and the Place de la Carrière show the sensitive balance of forms, the harmony of dimensions and scale, the beautiful interrelationship of the minutest detail with the over-all design which might seem to be the work of a single genius. Nothing, however, could be further from the truth.

When Stanislas Leczinski, ex-King of Poland, then Duke of Lorraine, in 1752 set about to create in Nancy a Place Royale as a fitting setting for a statue of his son-in-law, Louis XV of France, he chose a site just to the west of the gateway leading from "Ville Vieille" to "Ville Newe" (see upper map, page 176), on land which was made available by the clearance of part of the old fortifications. His architect, Emmanuel Héré, had some latitude in determining the size and shape of the new square, but the greatness of his work is that its form is perfectly related to that of Place de la Carrière to the east, the dimensions of which were determined in the medieval period.

Curiously, the architectural details of the new square were almost exact copies of the design of the Hôtel de Beauvau-Craon, built in 1715 by Germain Boffrand, shown on the page opposite and indicated by the green arrow in the drawing on page 177. Héré enlarged the scale of the old façade, adding a crowning balustrade with urns and sculpture, and he varied the rhythm of the bays at the center and ends of the city hall, the terminal feature on Place Royale shown in the engraving from Patte's *Monumens érigés en France à la gloire de Louis XV* below. Yet the form of the typical bay is almost identical with that of the then almost forty-year-old palace shown opposite. Even the structures on the other side of the square, shown above, high enough to conceal the old ramparts yet sufficiently low to serve as a link with the medieval scale of Place de la Carrière, were essentially the lower story of Hôtel de Beauvau-Craon with the balustrade imposed directly on top. It may be that the old design was used on the insistence of client Stanislas, who took a lively personal interest in architectural matters. Whatever the reason, Place Royale proves that even when the architectural expression is limited to a predetermined formula, a great and beautiful work may be accomplished through the manipulation of the elements of mass and space and the skillful deployment of detail.

There are few examples in architecture in which the details serve as important a unifying role as do the gilded wrought-iron balconies, screens, gates, lanterns, and grilles made for Nancy by ironworker Jean Lamour. These animate the rather quiet architecture of Héré and establish transparent planes at the corners of Place Royal. Most important, they set up a tension between the various elements, binding mass and space together, and provide a rhythmically recurring sensation as one progresses down the main axis.

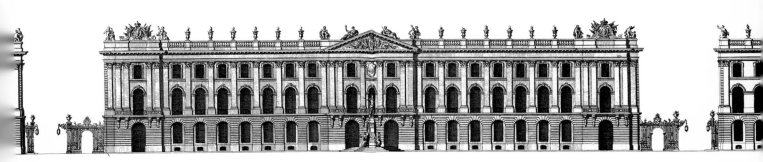

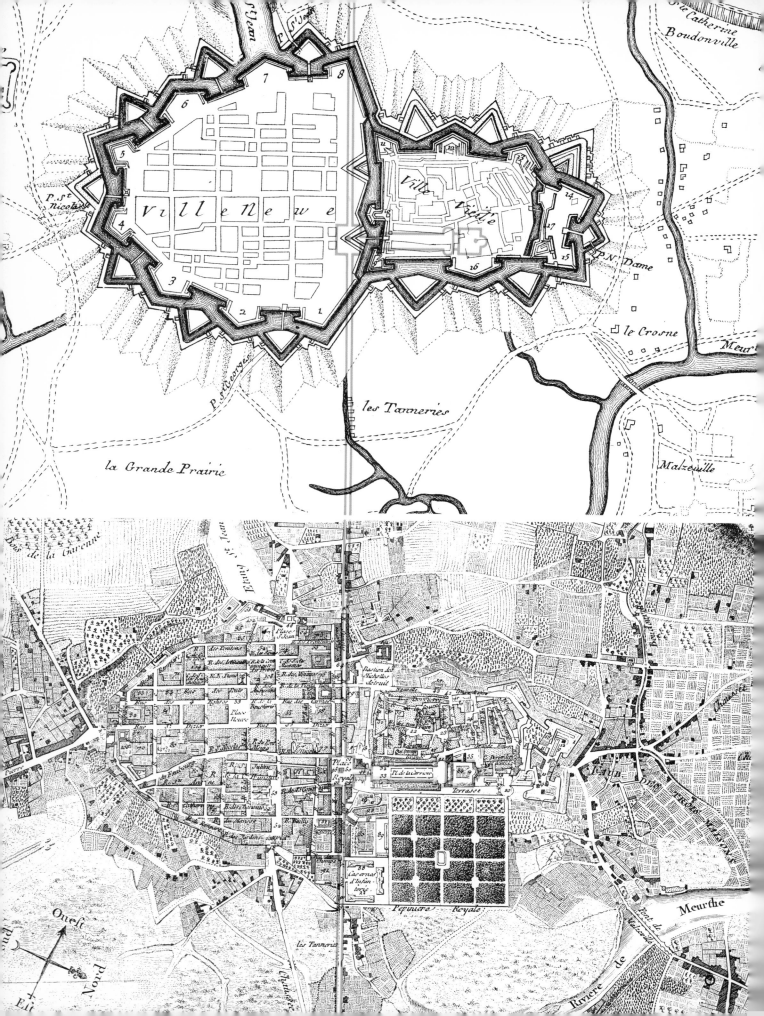

THE SHAFT AT NANCY

The two maps on the opposite page, that of the medieval, two-celled Nancy, above, and of the eighteenth-century Nancy, below, show vividly the impact of Renaissance ideas on medieval forms.

The new north-south highway with triumphal arches creating recession planes, which Stanislas superimposed on the self-completing, inward-looking medieval spaces, is shown in green extending across both maps, and is necessary for an understanding of the squares which he created (also shown in green).

This long street, passing through the "Ville Newe" brings to the old city the influence of the regional countryside and, conversely, extends the feeling of the city out into the surrounding land. The perpendicular extension of the design into the "Ville Vieille" from this artery of movement follows the form of the old medieval square shown on the upper map. The width of the square is the same as when it was used for jousting, and its termination is marked by the façade of the Palace of the Provincial Government, which stands on the site of the old medieval wall of the Ducal Palace garden. The entirely new scale of

design induced by the expansiveness of the Renaissance is shown by the large formal garden in the lower map. Tied in axially with the curved colonnades before the Government Palace, the garden today serves as a fine public park.

The drawing below shows in green the shaft of space set into motion by the central bay of Héré's city hall as it acts as a unifying force in the composition. Across Place Royale it is precisely contained by the walls of the low facing buildings in front of the Arch of Triumph. In Place de la Carrière it is defined by the inner planes of the carefully clipped rows of trees and finally it passes through the central bay of the Government Palace into the garden behind. Extending perpendicularly to it are green lines, suggesting the volume of the highway which intersects it.

Here again we find a regional movement system acting as the generating agent for a fine expression of urban design. Place Royale and Place de la Carrière can be fully understood only as they are conceived as playing their special roles in relation to it.

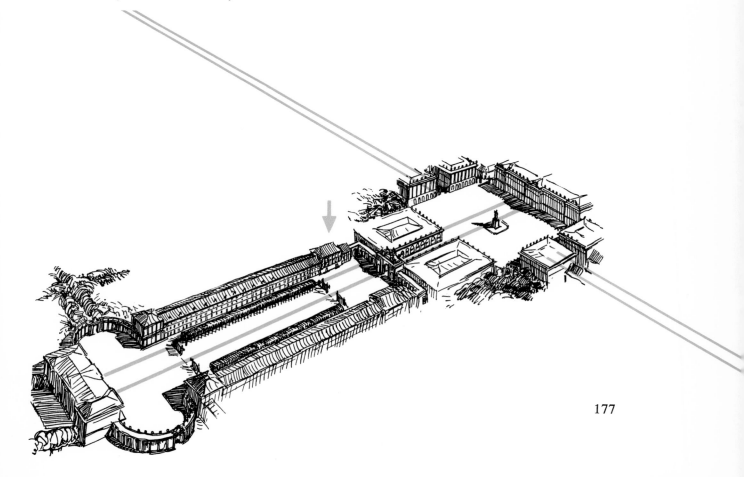

177

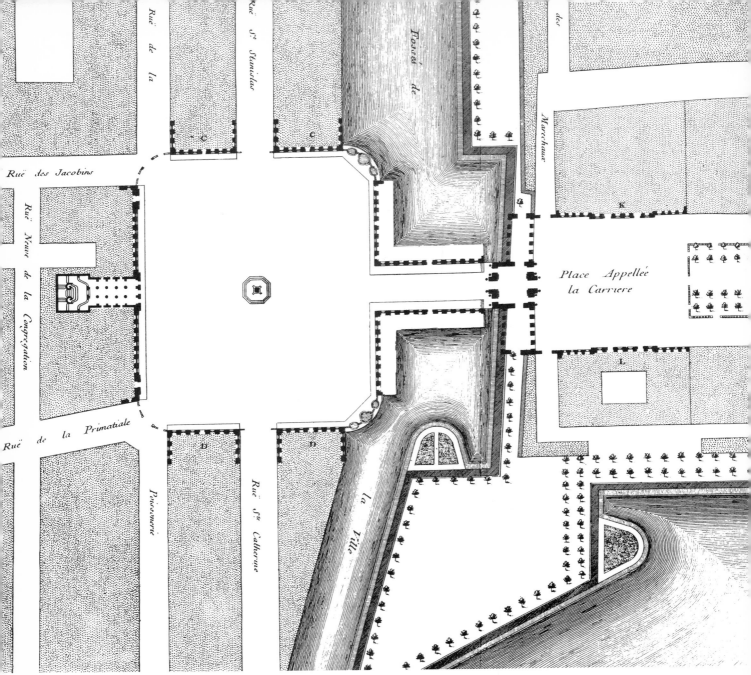

As we look at the perfection of this engraving from Patte (to which we have added the interior plan of the city hall lobby and stairway), it is difficult to believe that the shape of Place de la Carrière was established hundreds of years before Héré started work, and that the architectural form of the bays of Place Royale had been set by the pre-existing Hôtel de Beauvau-Craon, marked "L" on the plan. The façades of the old houses marked "M" were rebuilt by Stanislas at his own expense to accord with a regular rhythm.

That great work can be done without destroying what is already there has been illustrated earlier, but here a new element is added, that of sym-

bolically expressing in new structures the spirit of what has been associated with that particular space in previous history. Thus the Arch of Triumph, built by Stanislas, conveys the spirit of the fortified wall which divided the old medieval city from the new and recreates the feeling of the old bi-celled organic form. The terminal point, the Palace of the Provincial Government, is in what was once the garden of the Ducal Palace.

Place Royale is an expression of the broadening of Renaissance ideas. The long vistas and sense of connection with the regional countryside are afforded by the new central street which bisects it. Successfully placed against this is the

178

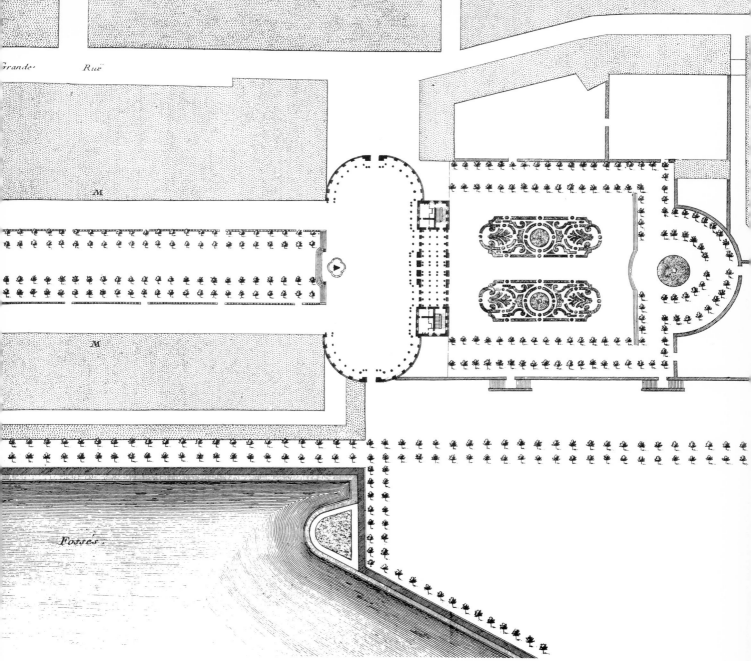

counter-movement of the perpendicular axis; the thrust of the space movement from the Place de la Carrière is received by the mass of City Hall. Here all is stone and iron. There is no interruption of the architecturally defined space except the statue in the center of the square. Unfortunately the original effect was ruined when the statue of Stanislas was substituted for the one of Louis XV, with consequent loss of scale.

The progress from this square to the area in front of the Provincial Government Palace is a remarkable example of a sequential architectural experience. First we encounter a narrowing down of space as we pass between the close-lying two-story shops. The experience is further intensified as we move between the tight confinement of the outer arches of the triumphal gateway. We are then ready for the change that greets us, a burst of space and the sudden intensity of green provided by the clipped trees in Place de la Carrière. Here green is used as a precious commodity, providing the main design quality for one of the spaces.

Reserved for the last, climactic experience is the great curvilinear space defined by the two exedra colonnades in front of the terminal Provincial Government Palace, which were faintly previsioned by the curved, transparent planes of Lamour's screens in the corners of Place Royale.

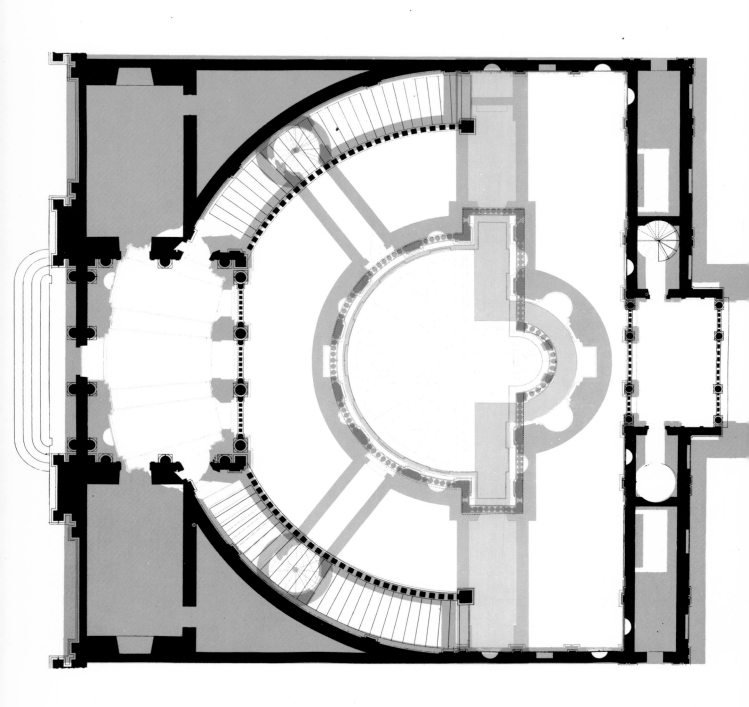

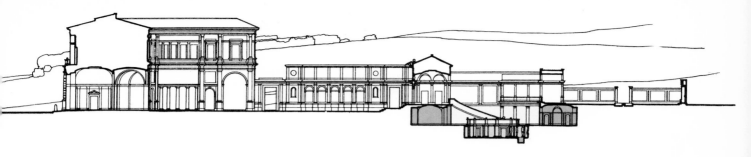

PRINCIPLE OF SCALE BY PLANE

The demands of the multiple scales of movement in cities have led to the increasing use of interrelated levels in design. Because so much contemporary work has been based on buildings resting on a simple earth plane, we have developed neither a firm philosophy nor vocabulary for the individual treatment of different planes. For guidance in this field we must look back beyond the last century.

One of the most masterful treatments of multiple planes ever achieved in architecture is the Villa Giulia in Rome, designed by Vignola in 1550, a section through which is shown above; the ground plan is below. Shown in yellow and blue is the remarkable three-level design which was hollowed out of the flat land for the sheer joy of creating vertical movement.

The illustration to the left, a detail of this part of the villa and a superimposition in color of three eighteenth-century engraved plans, demonstrates the interrelation of the forms and the complex system of circulation between them. The upper level is indicated in black, the intermediate level in lime-green, and the lower level in blue, the lighter blue being areas of water.

The value to the present day of this work is in the extreme difference of scale of the design, the quality of paving, and the character of form at each level. The form of the upper level is bold and almost austere, with its simple semi-cylindrical wall and curving staircase. The intermediate level is more complex and finer in scale, with its pilasters, niches, and curiously shaped opening into the lower level. The third level down is startlingly different from the two levels above. The scale of the paving, with its elaborate and complex shapes, is much finer, and the caryatids around the semi-circular canal in front of the grotto niches are in marked contrast to the character of the rest of the villa.

Once this principle is recognized and understood, there is today rich opportunity for articulation of overlapping planes by scale in the formulation of multi-level design.

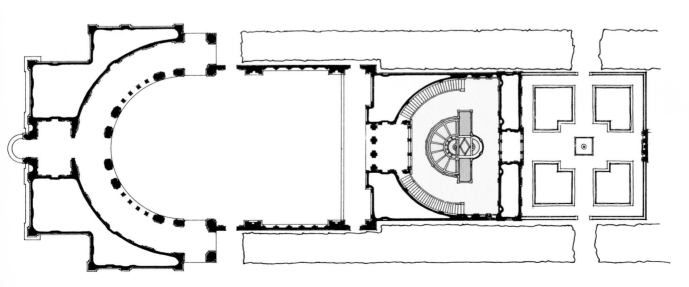

1:700

SINUOUS PROGRESSION THROUGH SPACE

There are those who will say, "Yes, but we are in a new age, our design should be based on new principles and not on the outworn composition of the Renaissance." While this is true, the interrelation between buildings, as for example in New York's Lincoln Center (insofar as interrelationship exists there at all), does not advance beyond Renaissance principles. In fact it fails to employ the full range of Renaissance ideas. Therefore it is appropriate to review such projects in relation to Renaissance design structure.

Indeed, except for Kenzo Tange's two magnificent Olympic Sports buildings in Tokyo (page 36), it is difficult to find two or more modern structures that are related to one another in anything except Renaissance design principles. Often no principles at all are employed.

However, there are examples of superb design under the Baroque influence which are free from the formal demands of axial symmetry. One of the most splendid is the English city of Bath in Somersetshire.

The aerial view on the opposite page shows the multi-curved structure of Lansdowne Crescent, the work of architect John Palmer. The photograph fails to convey the full three-dimensional complexity of the form because, in addition to the curves in the horizontal plane, the entire structure moves up a hill, down a valley, and up a hill again, thus creating a form in space comparable to Klee's "Sailing City," page 60.

The bottom photograph at the left presents the first impression of Lansdowne Crescent as it is approached from the east—a convex form of simple buildings stepped steeply up the hill, with the barest hint of a continuing space beyond. The middle photograph is taken from a point halfway up the hill. Here the convex mass recedes in importance in favor of the volume of space contained within the great curve of the houses on the hilltop, reaching a climax in the pedimented central pavilion. The top photograph portrays the replacement of mass by the dominance of space, and presents a major part of the sweep of the concave building wall, though even here it is incompletely revealed. The projecting curved bay of the house at the point of transition gives a sharp recall of the great curve of the mass which preceded the

concave sweep ahead. These pictures show only a fragment of the total experience that this work affords, for one continues around a new convex form moving downhill to a second curved pedimented concave group of houses on the second hill. This is design on a regional scale, containing no radical or unfamiliar architectural details or tricks, yet the whole is totally free of Baroque axial planning, a powerful statement of a space form.

This design was not born overnight. It was the product of a long and arduous search for form on the part of designer-builders over two generations, John Wood the Elder and John Wood the Young-

er, who planned and developed the extension of the medieval resort town of Bath from 1727 to 1781. The value of "feedback" is demonstrated here, a process in which design ideas are translated into action on a large scale, and each fragment of an idea which seems, upon realization, to be good, is seized upon and enlarged in scope in the next planning development. Indeed the concave curve of the houses built in 1754 around the circus of John Wood the Elder may well have provided the idea for the Royal Crescent, made in 1767, probably by John Wood the Younger, and this comparatively rigid design idea certainly was the point of departure for Lansdowne Crescent.

1692

1735

EVOLUTION OF BATH

The maps on the margins of these pages are largely self-explanatory as they present the story of the structure of Bath as it extends outward over the region. To the familiar inward-looking, self-completing form of the medieval city with the Abbey shown in black (upper left), has been added in the map below an area of speculation building in which John Wood in 1728 has introduced a new sense of order and scale in the form of the green rectangle of Queen's Square with his new houses around it, shown in black. Thus John Wood was, according to Nikolaus Pevsner, ". . . the first after Inigo Jones to impose Palladian uniformity on an English square as a whole." As shown in the upper map on the opposite page, this design element provided the springboard for the outward extension of the houses lining the new Gay Street to the three-arc circus, which acted as a point from which a further angled extension occurred, thus providing the seminal form which fathered all that followed.

1:14000

1765

The map at the lower right shows the fully developed structure which the speculation, planning, and building of the Woods achieved or influenced. The tense, closed forms of the Circus burst apart, in a sense, in the free-flowing, open curve of the Royal Crescent to the west, which was probably the work of John Wood the Younger. St. James's Square, with its diagonal corner streets, extends the design structure outward and serves as a link to the curvilinear Lansdowne Crescent.

In the other direction the Avon River is spanned by Robert Adam's Pulteney Street Bridge, which leads into the highly architectural, straight avenue of formal design terminating in a building at the edge of a park.

The photograph of Lansdowne Crescent (above) conveys the feeling of the interaction of town and countryside, of the richness that is obtained, not when two opposite forces blend together in a tasteless mixture, but when one emphasizes the integral characteristics of the other.

1810

1:14000

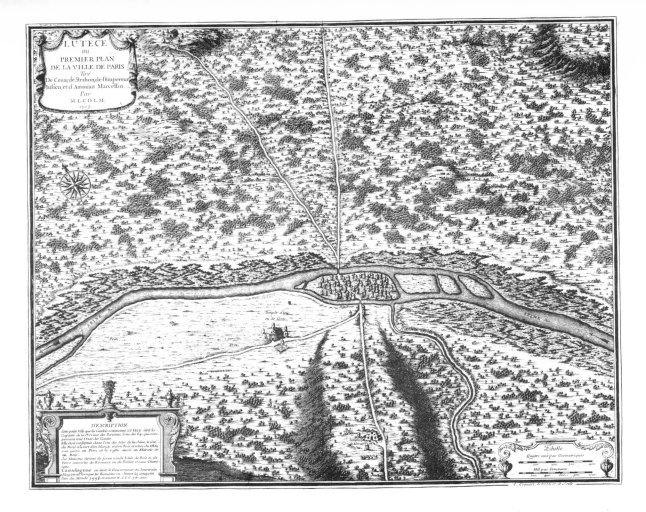

LUTECE
ou
PREMIER PLAN
DE LA VILLE DE PARIS
Tiré
De Cesar, de Strabon, de l'Empereur
Julien, et d'Ammian Marcellin.
Par
M.L.C.D.L.M.
1705.

DESCRIPTION
Cette petite Ville que les Gaulois nommoient LUTECE, étoit la
Capitale de la Province des Parisiens, l'une des 64. qui com-
posoient tout l'Estat des Gaules.
Elle étoit renfermée dans l'une des Isles de la Seine, la cein-
du Nord et vers l'Isles du Marais et des Bois, et celuy du Midy
vue partie en Prez, et le reste, aussi en Marais et
en Bois.
Ses Maisons étoient de forme ronde bâtie de Bois, et de
Terre couverte de Roseaux ou de Paille et sans Chemi-
nées.
Camulogene en étoit le Gouverneur au Souverain
de l'Autorité lorsque les Romains en firent la conquête
l'an du Monde 3998. et avant N.S.I.C. 56. ans.

Echelle
Quatre cent pas Geometriques

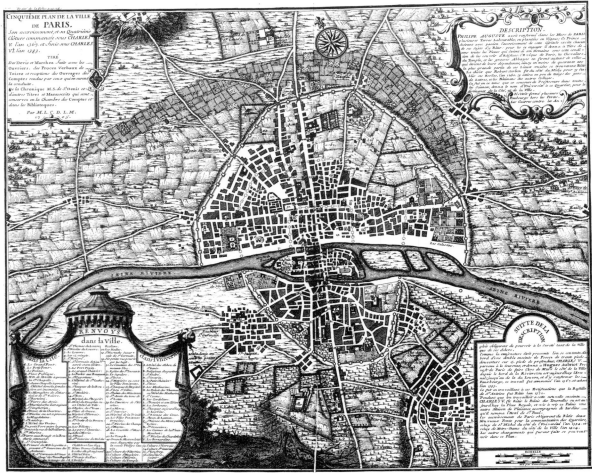

CINQUIÈME PLAN DE LA VILLE
DE PARIS.
Son accroissement, et sa Quatrième
Clôture commencée sous CHARLES
V. l'an 1367. et finie sous CHARLES
VI. l'an 1383.
TIRÉ
Des Devis et Marchés faits avec les
Ouvriers, des Procès Verbaux de
Toizes et receptions des Ouvrages des
Comptes rendus par ceux qui en avoient
la conduite.
De la Chronique M.S. de St Denis et de
d'autres Titres et Manuscrits qui sont
conservés en la Chambre des Comptes et
dans les Bibliotheques.
Par M.L.C.D.L.M.
1705.

DESCRIPTION
PHILIPE AUGUSTE avoit renfermé dans les Murs de PARIS

RENVOYS
dans la ville.

SUITTE DE LA
DESCRIPTION

ECHELLE

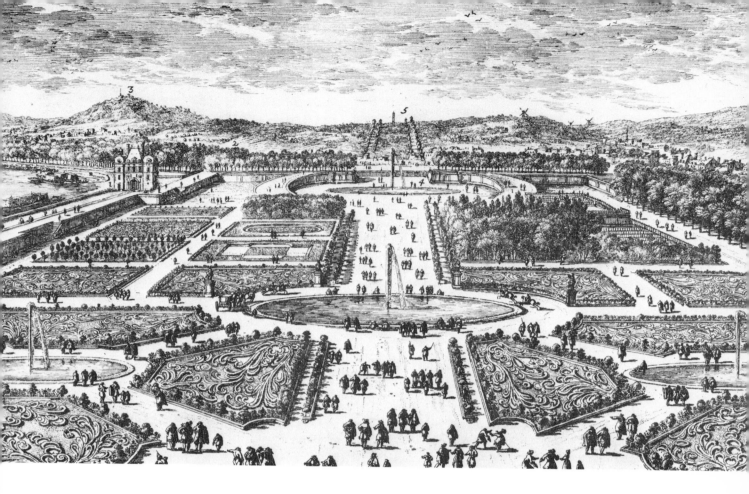

DEVELOPMENT OF PARIS

The records of the development of Paris enable us to see the full range of design forces at play from the Roman period to the present day. On the opposite page, the 1705 upper map shows the intersection of two movement systems on what is now Ile de la Cité, where the old Roman road crossed the River Seine. This established the design center and the lines of force leading to it, forming the frame of orientation for the classical Roman city.

The lower map, at the same scale, shows medieval Paris as it was from 1367 to 1383. Here the ancient crossing determines the center of the tightly developed town, the wall defining an area of intensity at the juncture of the movement systems. (This may be compared with the Klee drawing on page 129.)

The inner dotted line shows the position of the first walls built north of the river. These were moved outward by Philip Augustus in 1223 to the position shown by the outer dotted line. The pressure of city growth continued and the walls were further extended under Charles V and Charles VI to the position shown in this map.

For the next two centuries the development of Paris continued to be largely contained within the walls, and these were extended still farther by Louis XIII. In 1563 Catherine de Médicis introduced a new idea of Italian derivation, that of constructing pleasure gardens outside the city wall. This led to further extensions by Marie de Médicis, and finally to the breaching of the wall altogether and the brilliant axial extension of the old Medici gardens by the French landscape architect André Le Nôtre.

This set into motion a thrust of design which conveyed the energy, previously compressed within the city walls, across the countryside. The seventeenth-century Gabriel Perelle engraving of the Tuileries gardens and the embryonic Champs Elysées (above) depicts the hitherto unknown idea of a design element disappearing over the horizon.

187

PARIS — THE EXPLOSION

On these pages we see, in successive stages, the superimposition of Italian ideas on medieval-minded Paris, and the consequent unleashing of forces of a magnitude unknown in Italy.

The plan at the top, opposite, shows Paris as it was in 1300, a medieval walled city developed around the crossing of the River Seine. The Louvre Palace outside the walls, shown in black, is the point of origin of the design forces, the development of which is portrayed in these drawings.

The plan in the center is Paris in 1600, the white line indicating the position of the walls of 1300 north of the Seine, the gray showing the outward extension to the new walls responding to the pressures of city growth. To the east in black is shown the Bastille, and in green the row of trees planted along the wall, the first indication of the great tree-lined boulevard system to follow. The old Louvre, now completely surrounded by city development, is in process of rebuilding. Outside the new walls to the west is the Tuileries Palace, built by Catherine de Médicis, wife of Henry II, originally conceived as a self-contained, independent structure. To the west of this extends the Tuileries Gardens, still medieval in design with their directionless form of planting beds, yet heralding a new integration of city and countryside.

The lower map of 1740 (across both pages)

shows the maturing of Paris under Louis XV. Here the great concept of Le Nôtre, extending the axis of the Tuileries Gardens in the form of the green Champs Elysées, has become a dominant design element of Paris. The yellow lines show the later extension across the River Seine. The Tuileries Palace has been connected with the Louvre by the Grande Galerie built by Henry IV, providing a counterfoil for the axial thrust deeply embedded in the city. The old ramparts have been planted as continuous tree-lined boulevards, carrying forward the idea furthered by Marie de Médicis, wife of Henry IV, in her pleasure drive, Cours la Reine, developed along the Seine westward from the Tuileries Gardens.

A new breadth and freedom have been introduced in the art of civic design. The outward thrust of the movement systems, generated from firm building masses, penetrates farther and farther into the countryside. It stimulates similar axial thrusts originating in the châteaux and palaces about Paris, which also extend and intertwine, creating, in the late eighteenth and early nineteenth century, a form of regional development unique in the history of city-building.

Astride this ancient axis a new center for Paris is rising, La Défense, shown here with its buildings and its encircling expressways, helping to protect the old city from the onslaught of modern commercial development.

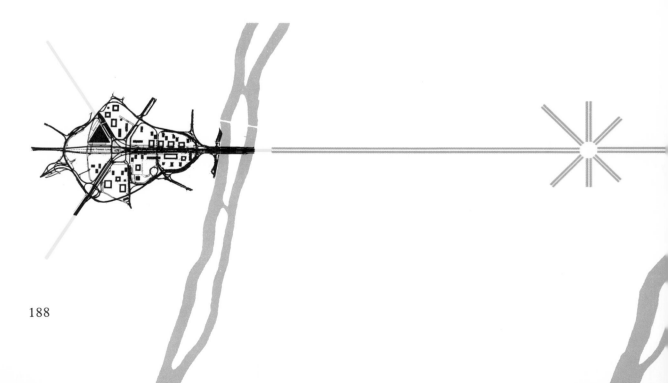

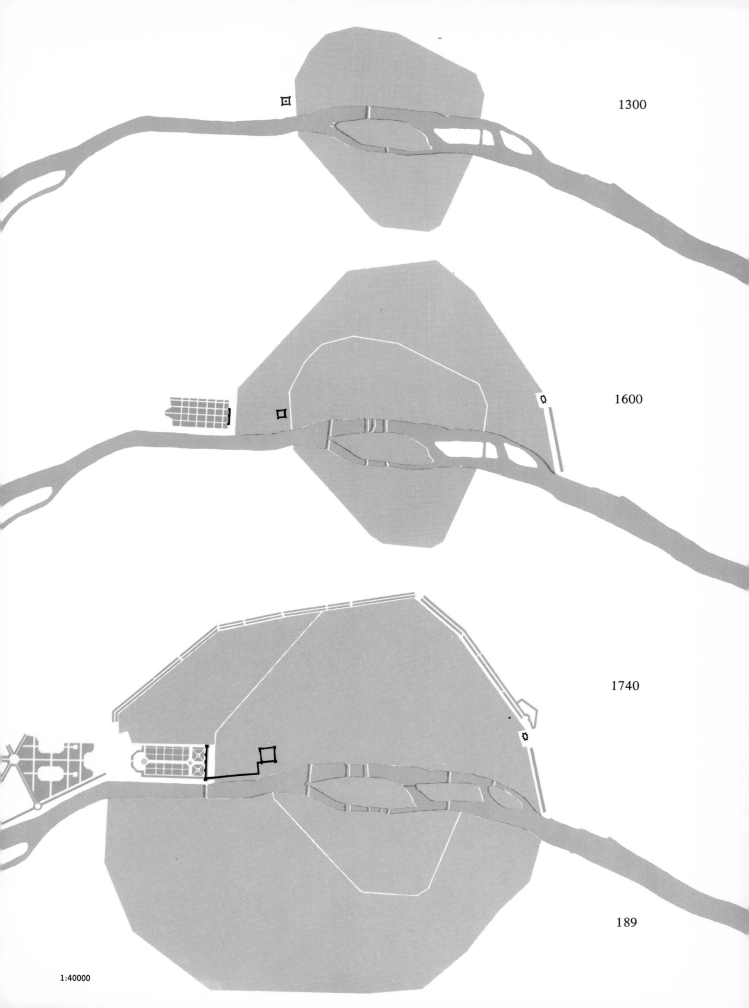

1300

1600

1740

189

1:40000

LE PONT NEUF R DAUPHINE

LA RIVIERE DE SE

ARCHITECTURE AND REGIONAL DESIGN

To the far left is a portion of the Legrand map of Paris as it was in 1380. Here the fortification walls, extended beyond the Louvre Palace (A), clearly define the beginning of the open land and contain the pressures of the city, except for some scattered development just outside the gate.

The near left engraving shows a portion of the Plan of Vassalieu, *dit* Nicolay, in 1609, of the Tuileries Palace, which Catherine de Médicis built outside the walls, and the gallery that was built along the Seine to connect it with the Louvre (here pictured in its medieval form). In front of the Tuileries extends the garden, an inward-looking self-completing design, devoid of axial emphasis and consisting of simple squares adjacent to one another. Nevertheless the wall had been breached and the idea of a relationship with the countryside established.

To the right is a section of the famous Michel Etienne Turgot map of 1734–1739, showing the complete transformation of the static Catherine de Médicis plan by André Le Nôtre. Graphically demonstrated in these three drawings is the expansion of the Renaissance idea as it was grafted onto French culture by the Medici Queens.

The whole nature of the Tuileries garden design is transformed from static to dynamic, and the thrust of the axis generated within the garden is extended outward by the Avenue des Tuileries, now the Champs Elysées. Not yet present is the Place de la Concorde, which was later to occupy the open ground between the Tuileries garden wall and the planted area of the Champs Elysées and would connect the central Tuileries axis with the area both to the east and across the river Seine.

These drawings show the beginning and development of a regional design idea, and they demonstrate, too, how a regional form can have its roots in so simple a matter as the shape of a garden plot.

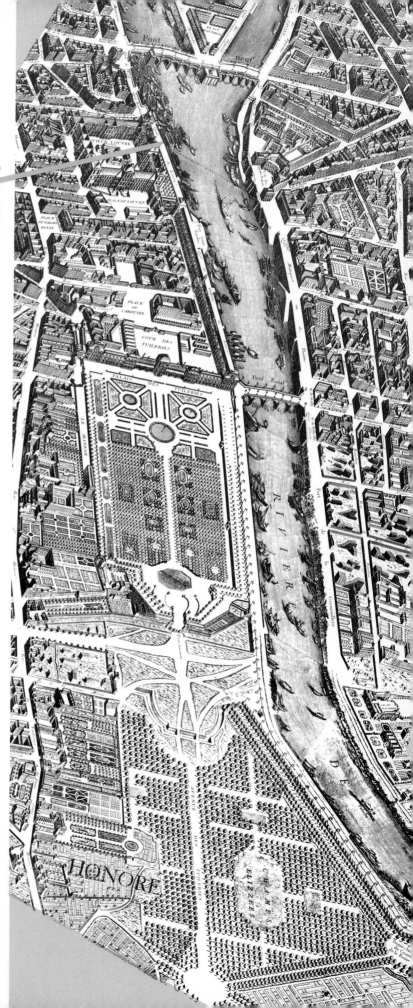

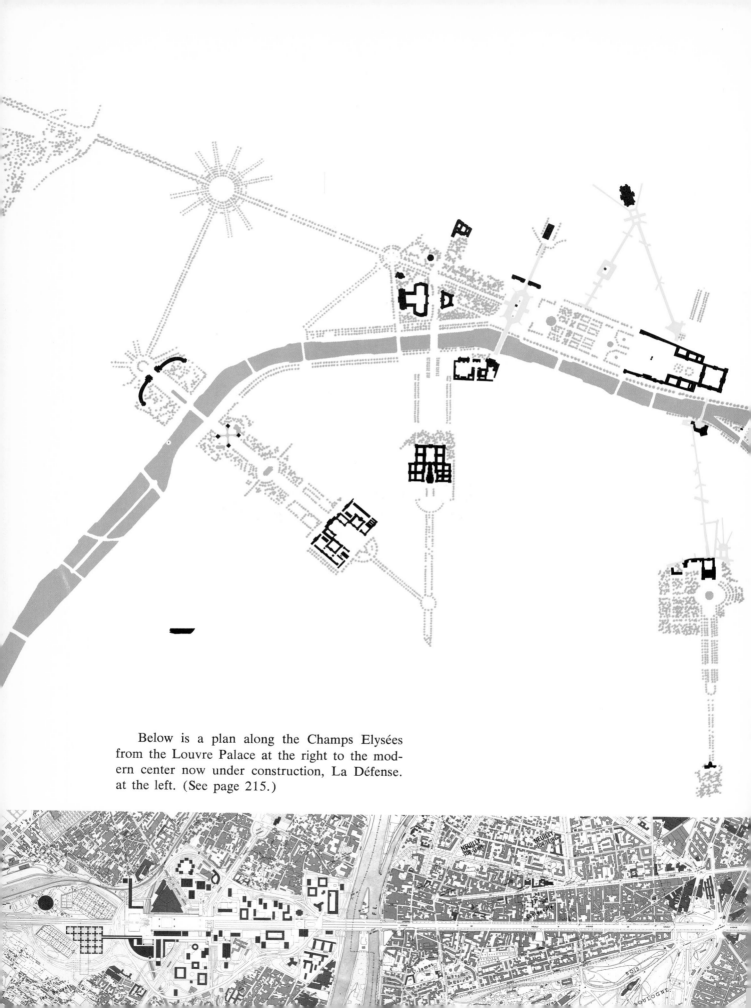

Below is a plan along the Champs Elysées
from the Louvre Palace at the right to the modern center now under construction, La Défense.
at the left. (See page 215.)

DESIGN STRUCTURE OF PARIS

Once the idea of the thrust of axial extension had been established by construction and planting on the ground, it became a dominant element in the later development of Paris and was applied with much skill by many designers over the years.

The river Seine provided the central spine for design growth. From it were extended perpendicularly a series of axial developments, notably the esplanade of the Invalides and the Champ de Mars with the Eiffel Tower. The pattern formed by them is strikingly similar to the designs by Paul Klee on pages 252 and 253. These developments were gradually interlaced and interconnected with the Champs Elysées and other boulevard extensions, forming the beginning of a regional network.

Napoleon I set about to clear out the old structures in the area that became the courtyard of the Louvre, and he ordered the realigning and completion of streets in neighboring sections. But it was Napoleon III and the achievements of Baron Georges Haussmann that led to the reintegration of the heart of Paris and a strengthening of its interior structure on a scale commensurate with the forces of regional expansion. This reversal of the direction of energy, from the outward explosion of the avenues and palaces of the Louis Kings to the implosion of the connecting and life-giving boulevards of Haussmann, is one of the most dramatic in any city. Each development was devised and inspired by social and economic forces far different from those prevailing today, but each has proved to be resilient, to be capable of providing a structure suited to modern needs.

The map on the following pages, engraved in 1740, gives a glimpse of the kind of quality the Paris region must have had when the entire area was dominated by a network of interlaced axes.

1:25000

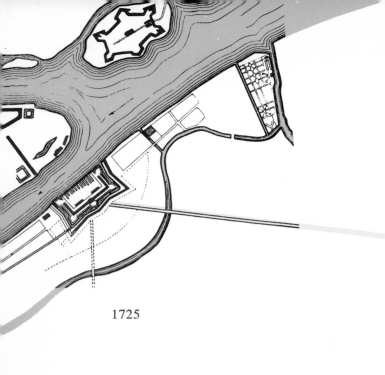

1725

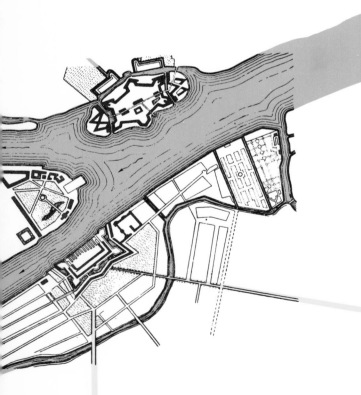

1750

1: 35000

EVOLUTION OF

Saint Petersburg (now Leningrad) in Russia is one of the few great cities built in its entirety after Renaissance design ideas had reached their full maturity. Its planners had available to them the experience of a broad range of completed civic works.

When Peter the Great decided he was tired of Moscow and wanted to create an entirely new capital for Russia, and in 1712 announced it would be on the banks of the Neva River, Paris had already achieved a dynamic scale.

In contrast to Paris, where the design forces burst outward from the old city, in Saint Petersburg the lines of force thrust inward from the regional countryside. Their convergence was at the one point of attraction which adequately symbolizes the underlying concept of the new city, the point of contact of man and the sea, the shipbuilding ways enclosed within the arms of the Admiralty. The convergence of these three lines of movement, the evolution of which is demonstrated on these pages, determined the form of the major elements of Saint Petersburg and provided a powerful framework for the subtle and highly refined design to be carried out later.

1725: Here is the early design of Saint Petersburg. The design tension has already been established between architectural elements on both sides of the river, appropriate for a maritime settlement. The pull from the hinterland is expressed in the yellow line, the first thrust of the single road from the east direct to the tower on the moated Admiralty. This building is the focal point in space, which, though completely rebuilt in subsequent years, retained its pre-eminence as the symbolic center of the city. The road from the southwest is foreseen as an idea, and the axial way does not exist.

1750: By now the plans have begun to take on the character of a city. Streets have been built, and the three converging ways are firmly established, although their thrust has not yet fully extended, in a design sense, to their objective, the Admiralty tower. The Winter Palace, later to be rebuilt, appears to the right. The multiple design interrelationships at this point have not yet been resolved.

SAINT PETERSBURG

1800: Here the three converging roads have been carried through to a definite junction with the still-moated Admiralty, but the spaces created are accidental and unintegrated as a total concept. The small church below the Admiralty later will be replaced by the Saint Isaac Cathedral, related in a design sense with the westernmost of the converging streets. On the banks of the Neva to the east, the Winter Palace has been rebuilt to its present form. Here, too, the residual open spaces are undefined, but contain within them the germ of the idea which was to be so powerfully expressed later. The crosshatch structure on the point which splits the river channel had been built to express architecturally the idea of the terrain. The next generation replaced it with a building perpendicular to the architectural mass behind it. As shown in the 1850 plan, this building asserted its design influence directly into the water by the curved bulkhead on its axis.

1850: This is the full realization of the whole series of design influences which had been building up over the previous hundred years into one of the most dynamic compositions ever made. Here we see the Admiralty rebuilt in a form reminiscent of the older building (see page 196) but on a much more powerful scale and in better relationship to the force of the axial thrusts. The original and the present elevations of the Admiralty are shown at the same scale, for comparison, on page 198. The Winter Palace axis has been extended southward by the great column which marks the focal center of the remarkable parabolic-shaped space defined by the Ministry of War, forged out of the old structures. The thrust of the space before the Admiralty is contained and turned back on itself by the enclosure of the area around the column. This provides a firm counterfoil for the elongated extension of the space west of the Admiralty, beyond the Cathedral of Saint Isaac, into the depths of the city.

The interaction of the cross-movements of this highly dynamic and extraordinarily shaped space with the extreme formality created by the symmetrical convergence of the three axes meeting at the Admiralty tower is one of the wonders of urban design.

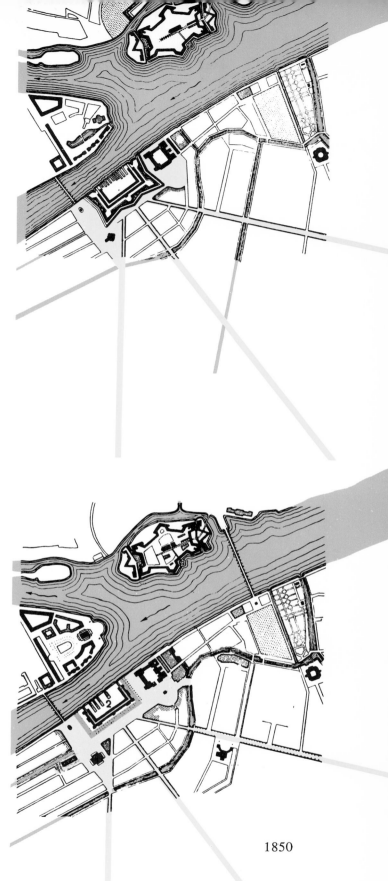

1850

1: 35000

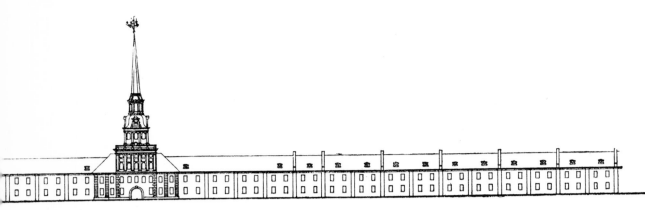

SAINT PETERSBURG TODAY — LENINGRAD

At the top of this page is the early façade of the Admiralty. This was replaced by the powerful design, almost a half-mile long, for the Admiralty on the left and the Winter Palace on the right, as seen in the drawing below. Here is the ordering of space on a vast scale. Far more important than the Baroque details is the complex interrelationship of the multiple-tiered rhythm set up by the bays and openings, a vivid expression of the kind of rhythmic effects on a movement system demonstrated in the Klee drawing at the top of page 252. The freshness of the colors — yellow, white, orange, and green-blue — infuses the spaces and modulates the movement.

The plan to the right shows the center of Saint Petersburg as it existed in the middle of the nineteenth century. Below this, to the left, is a plan showing the evolution of the form of the architecture at the point of separation of the small and great Neva rivers, and the way in which the idea had changed from the design of a single building to the design of an environment related to the scale of the region. To the right of this is shown the evolution of the exedra opposite the Winter Palace: the original shape of the place was determined by the two walls, one almost perpendicular to and one parallel with the former diagonal street leading to the Admiralty. The accidental and unrelated shape of the space proved to be an advantage when the urban renewal project removed that minimum of the city necessary to build up a form related to the palace axis. As much length as possible was used of the existing flat wall so that the necessity of extensive rebuilding was avoided. The construction of the curved connector to join the old wall provided a remarkable and far more exciting shape than a semicircle could give.

This is another example of great design produced by accepting an existing plan and turning its problems into assets, and today serves as the center for a great metropolis which has been renamed Leningrad.

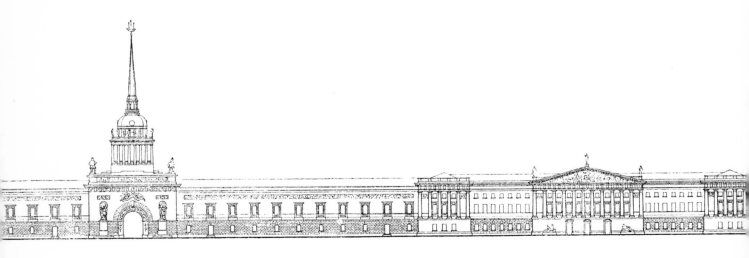

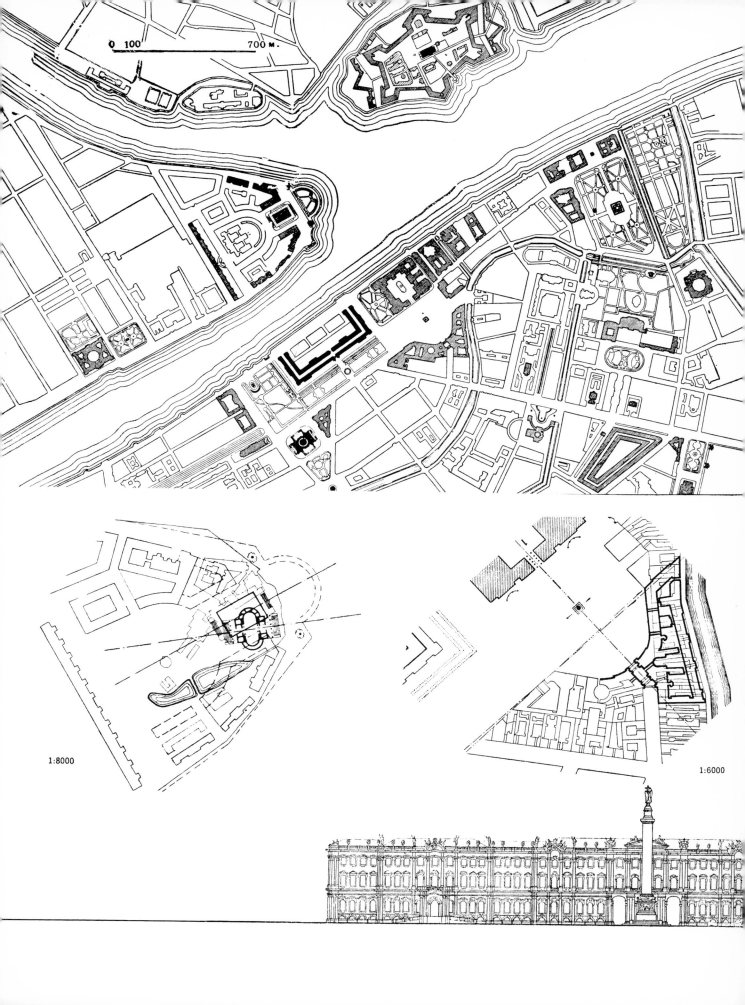

0 100   700 м.

1:8000

1:6000

JOHN NASH AND LONDON

We now come to a remarkable account of a man, a plan, and a city. The man is John Nash, the plan is Regent Street, and the city is London. As in the story of Bath, we are dealing with an architect-developer-promoter. But here the man started out as an architect, and the developer-promoter was the product of his desire to bring to fruition his vast architectural visions. In strong contrast to Bath with its open countryside, the heart of a completely developed section of London was the area in which Nash chose to realize his ideas.

The design structure of what he produced is demonstrated on the opposite page. Shown in green are the tree masses in the two great parks he planned: Regent's Park at the top and St. James's Park below. The yellow line represents the route of Regent Street, which connected the two parks, and in black are shown those locations which are now occupied, or were originally occupied, by structures of Nash's design or by those designed in close association with him and in accordance with the architectural requirements of his layout. In gray are shown important buildings relating to Nash's work.

Here is an example of the work of one man of inexhaustible energy, in which the vast design structure and the detailed buildings are inseparable, in which the buildings themselves carry forward the underlying design concept and make it work.

Around Regent's Park, like two hands clasping a precious substance, is the two-mile-long extent of terrace houses which give architectural definition to the park. The park, in turn, provides a fine setting for the terraces. Park Square and the semicircle of Park Crescent, shown in the recent painting above, serve as a powerful connector with the older Portland Place lined with Adam architecture.

The offset required by Foley House is made architecturally brilliant by the round portico of All Souls Church at the south end of Portland Place. The wide offset necessary to meet the axis of what was formerly Carlton House, now Carlton House Terrace, was accomplished by the great arc of the quadrant, which Nash had to finance himself in order to get it built. Finally, the sequence of movement was extended along the Mall (which lies to the north of St. James's Park) to Buckingham Palace, for which Nash made the original design. The Nash plan previsioned Trafalgar Square (in a form somewhat different from that built) and proposed a new street extending to the British Museum. If this street had been made, it would have further strengthened the organization of Central London.

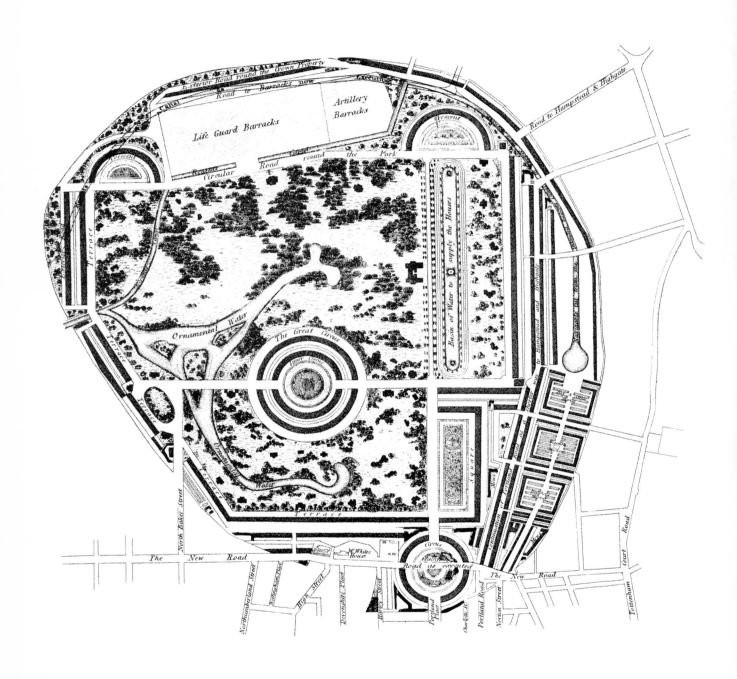

Map labels visible:

Exterior Road round the Crown Property
Road to Barracks now / Execution
Artillery / Barracks
Life Guard Barracks
Canal
Crescent
Road to Hampstead & Highgate
Crescent
Circular Road round the Park
Terrace
Basin of Water to supply the Houses
Terrace
Ornamental Water
Terrace
The Great Circus
Inner Circle
Communication of Portland Road to Hampstead and Highgate
Water
North Baker Street
Terrace
Square
Mews
Mews
Circus
The New Road
Northumberland Street
Nottingham Place
High Street
Devonshire Place
Harley Street
Duke of Hamilton
Mr White's House
Road as executed
Circus
The New Road
Portland Place
Charlotte St.
Portland Road
Norton Street
Tottenham Court Road

202

1:12000

EVERY MAN A KING

The first half of the nineteenth century (when Cumberland Terrace, shown above, was built) was a period of social upheaval in which rapidly expanding commercial and manufacturing enterprises had produced a great enlargement of the moneyed middle class. This led to a large-scale demand for residences, ample but not palatial in extent, which looked as much like palaces as possible. Nash's ideas fitted perfectly into this demand, and his architecture plus his organizing skill, applied in his vast concept of a new environment, produced the palace-like structure shown here in an engraving from a drawing by Thomas H. Shepherd.

Cumberland Terrace is a great sequence of theatrical effect, with projecting columnar bays, sculptured pediments, and triumphal arches leading to service yards. Yet it was so dear to the hearts of Londoners that, after the ravages of World War II, the deteriorated and partially damaged structures of this and the other Nash terraces around Regent's Park, property of the Crown, were rebuilt at great cost to look much as they did before.

Nash interwove his great terraces with the unbuilt spaces in a fresh and startling way. Shown opposite is his early design for the development of Regent's Park. This may be compared with the actual development, seen on the previous pages. The original idea connected the park to the city via Portland Place, with a complete circle of buildings, a "circus," marking the junction with the New Road, or east-west artery, originally designed to set the northern limit of London. The circular form was recalled in the two half-circle crescents to the north, and in the great double ring of terrace houses — the Inner Circus and the Great Circus — designed to give architectural form to the park. This plan stands as a milestone in the effort to produce an environment built on the economics of small-house ownership, while allowing at the same time the joys of relationship with nature previously associated with the country houses of the aristocracy.

DESIGNS AFFECTING EACH OTHER

A comparison of the intentions of Nash, as indicated in his plan of 1812 on page 202. with the actual execution on the ground shows an interesting change that occurred because of the construction of Saint Marylebone Church south of New Road at a point below the Great Circus. Originally Nash had planned to "turn his back" on the rest of the city by creating an unbroken row of houses extending west from the Circus at Portland Place to the juncture with North Baker Street, almost at the edge of the park. The decision in 1816 to build the new parish Church of Saint Marylebone enriched the design of the park and its setting because it prompted Nash to provide an interruption in York Terrace (shown below) and make another point of penetration into the old city, reinforcing that established at Portland Place.

The engraving to the right shows Saint Marylebone Church encased in the prism of space defined by the two ends of the buildings that make up York Terrace. Here, as at Greenwich, is an example of the interlock between two structures obtained by two masses at the opposite sides of the connecting plane. The church was begun in 1813 simply as a "Chapel-of-ease," but, as is shown in the drawing at right, it was extended, during construction, from its original narrow width by two projecting bays with two Corinthian columns, which have no function except to provide the volume necessary to receive the full thrust of the shaft of space defined by the ends of York Terrace. This alteration arose from a decision to designate the new chapel "the parish church of Saint Marylebone," but how much that decision was, in turn, influenced by Nash's offer of fine siting possibilities we can only guess. We do know, however, that the interaction of the series of forces at play produced a potent harmony between the work of two architects for two different clients, making a very important extension of a design structure.

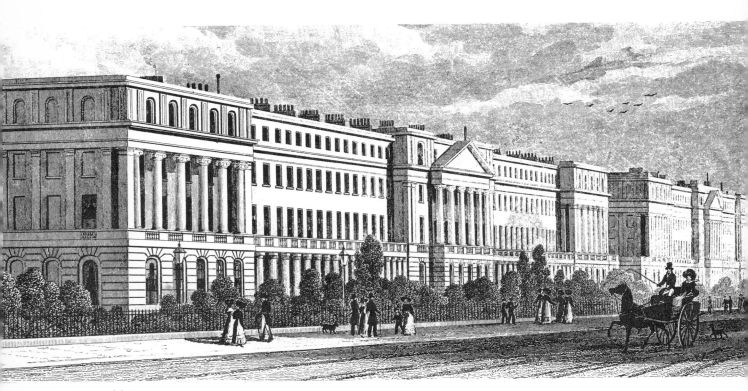

TURNING A CORNER

The early plan for Regent Street, shown on page 208, shows a continuous, smooth flowing curve from the end of Portland Place to a point north of the Oxford Street crossing. Later, Nash moved the position of Regent Street eastward at this location to avoid the disruption of the backs of the large houses on Cavendish Square. The offset as built was made by a much sharper bend because of a real-estate deal that Nash made with Sir James Langham, the purchaser of a portion of the Foley estate at the foot of Portland Place. This potentially awkward kink in the direction of Regent Street would have proved a disaster, had not Nash convinced the authorities to build All Souls Church on its present site and to designate him as its architect. It is a building which, by the adroit placing of its circular spired vestibule, does an astonishing job of turning chaos into order.

The engraving above shows a vista toward All Souls Church (on the extreme left), the terminal feature, from a point just below the change in direction of Regent Street south of the Oxford Street crossing. The dome here is the one shown on page 209. Below is a closer view from the north, showing the positioning of the circular colonnaded vestibule in the complex space of the elbow bend, and the successful transition which this design affords. Here is architecture fine in itself, yet architecture that is made to do its work in the larger scheme of things so well that it still conducts the movement around the difficult turn in Regent Street with power and grace, uncrushed by the intrusion of the ugly mass of the British Broadcasting Corporation Building, which has now been built beside it.

The 1851 balloon view of London on the right shows the skill with which Nash deployed his strong symbolic forms along his route to establish its entity within the old fabric.

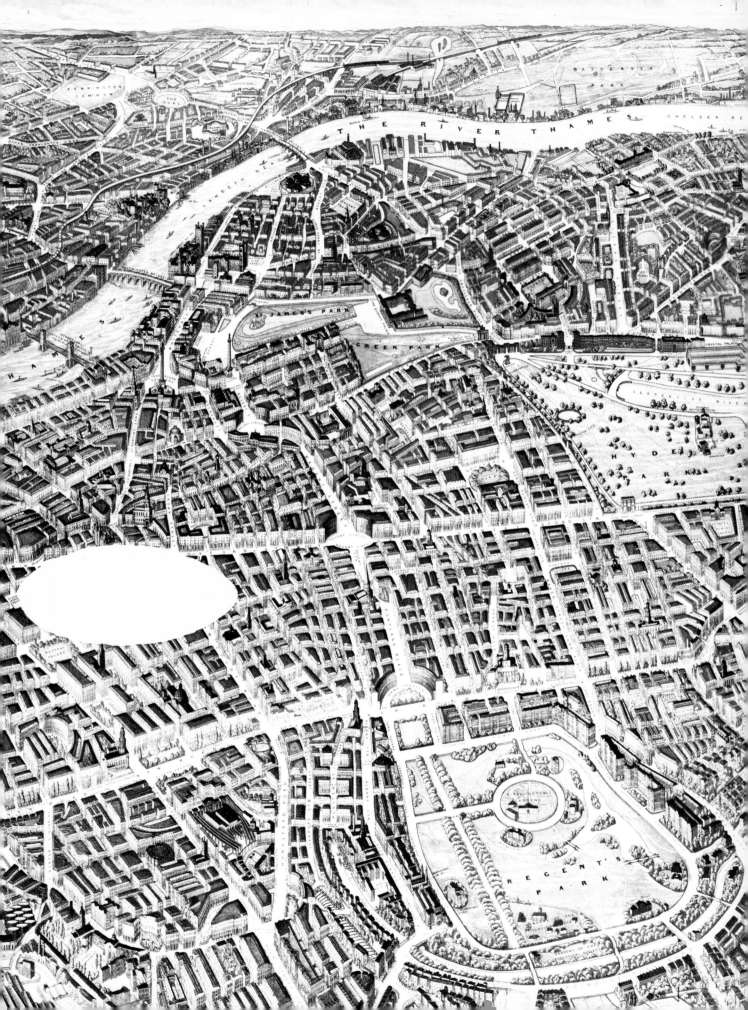

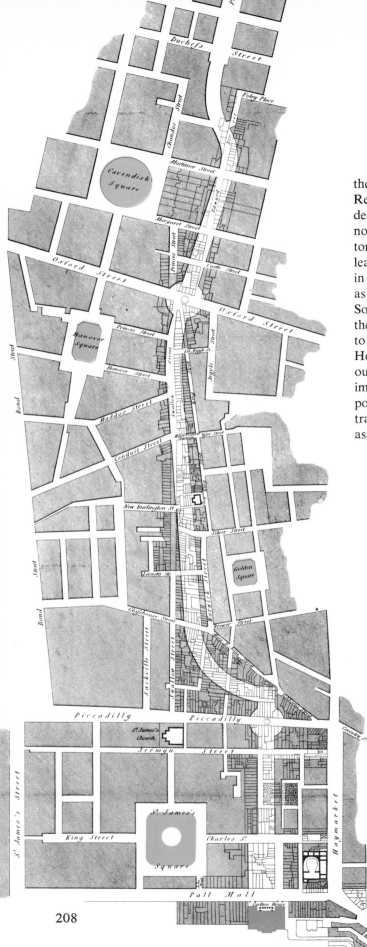

This map, made in 1814, forcefully portrays the courage of Nash's proposal for the location of Regent Street to connect Carlton House, the residence of the Regent, with the Crown lands to the north. Carlton House is shown in blue at the bottom of the map, with Portland Place at the north, leading to the Circus and Regent's Park, as shown in the plan on page 200. Nash envisioned the street as a connector between the jumbled pattern of the Soho area around Golden Square to the east, and the formal, organized, aristocratic section relating to Cavendish and Hanover Squares to the west. How well he did this is attested by the fact, pointed out by Sir John Summerson, that Regent Street immediately became (and remains today) an important center in the civic life of London, in contrast to other, more arbitrarily placed streets such as, for example, Kingsway.

1:6500

SINUOSITY OF REGENT STREET

Nash adapted the form of Regent Street to meet the functional requirements of the city, rather than imposing a preconceived architectural form on the fabric of the city. Where he met an obstacle he moved around it. Where necessary, he invented architectural forms to meet the requirements of his design structure.

The portion of Regent Street at the crossing of Oxford Street was determined by the depth requirements of the houses on the blocks butting onto Cavendish and Hanover squares. The circular non-directional form of the intersection with Oxford Street was conceived by Nash to avert the "fashionable objection" to residences north of that point. The superb handling of the changes in direction of the street by the cylindrical pavilions and flat domes of the bordering buildings under Nash's design, as well as the rich changes of rhythm and scale, is shown in the engraving above. The view is looking south at a point just south of the Oxford Street crossing.

Since one of the objectives of the street, in the first instance, was to connect the new park and its adjacent development with Carlton House (the residence of the Prince Regent), the architectural requirements of this building became a major consideration in the design. Nash extended the open space before Carlton House three blocks to the north and across Piccadilly to a terminal point now occupied by the County Fire Office. To take care of the offset between this axis and the line of Regent Street to the north, Nash originally planned a square with straight streets moving out of the opposite corners. This, however, proved to be too expensive, so the brilliant expedient of the arc-shaped street or Quadrant was conceived, designed, and even largely built by Nash.

By a curious irony, Carlton House, itself the inspirer of much of the design, was torn down shortly after the Regent became King, but Nash was able to turn the expediency to account in his design of the Carlton House Terraces, the Duke of York Column, and the great flight of steps that so splendidly connects the volume of his spaces in Regent Street via the Mall leading to Buckingham Palace.

THE GREAT QUADRANT

The great Quadrant is the consummate expression of the interaction of the design structure and architecture which Nash devised for taking care of the offset of Regent Street at this point. Although it is a satisfactory solution for the traffic flow, it certainly is not a design that would be produced if traffic were the only consideration. The County Fire Office (the terminal building at the right of the engraving on the opposite page) is the same building as the one shown on page 213 (in the center), terminating the extension of space from Carlton House. It serves to turn the corner architecturally and to deflect the movement into the Quadrant.

Not until his fifty-eighth year did Nash change from being a country-house architect to assume the multiple functions of city planner-designer-builder-promoter. This change, following his marriage, was due to his close association with the Prince Regent, later to become George IV. The association provided Nash with large resources and substantial influence, which he used with telling effect. In 1809 Nash was appointed architect to the Office of Woods and Forests. In this capacity he was asked to prepare proposals for the development of the Crown lands of Saint Mary-le-bone and their connection with Westminster. These led to the plan for Regent's Park and Regent Street. This sudden contact with the larger problem seemed to unlock great reserves of strength in Nash. It produced in him a drive of such propor-

tions that he was left unsatisfied simply with the creation of the government plan, and was led to invest his own money in the construction of those parts of the plan nobody else was willing to build.

The design and the idea behind Regent Street were such that most of its length could be divided into normal-sized building lots for separately financed units. There soon arose a number of projects for developments along the street. Many of these were designed by Nash, and others were by architects closely allied with him, so that considerable architectural coherence was attained along the route. But there was one section, the arc of the Great Quadrant, which could not be developed piecemeal, either architecturally or financially, yet the investors were reluctant to speculate the large sums necessary to build it as a unit in the early stages of the project. Undaunted, Nash stepped into the breach and realized this portion of his plan through the investment of his own funds.

All the buildings which Nash designed on Regent Street have been cleared away, and his smooth-faced façades have been replaced by the massive rusticated architecture of a later age. But the volume contained between them remains intact, and the spirit of the plan, the thrust of the movement, survives, proving that the skillful design of space can be more important than the design of buildings.

WATERLOO PLACE

The map opposite shows in yellow the space form imposed by Nash on the older mass of the building blocks (shown in gray) extending north from Carlton House, shown here in blue. In black are shown the principal buildings designed directly by John Nash in order to carry out the spatial design objectives. Above Piccadilly is the County Fire Office, connecting with the Great Quadrant, just described. To the right, across Haymarket, is the Haymarket Theatre, which provides a terminal for the vista from St. James's Square along Charles Street, which Nash extended to this point. This theater was originally in a slightly different location, but Nash persuaded the owner to move it to fit the plan, and also to engage him as the architect. The result is shown in the 1829 engraving below. The very satisfactory effect still persists, despite the replacement of all the buildings except the theater itself.

The engraving opposite, of the vista north from Carlton House, shows the flanking buildings, with the projecting four Ionic column bays, and the nearer buildings (also with Ionic columns in their central bays) successfully articulating Nash's space form and providing a proscenium kind of counter-foil for the deeply recessed façade of his County Fire Office. The four identically balanced buildings originally were all part of a single development. Although these buildings have been torn down long since, and replaced by buildings for separate, unrelated enterprises, the spirit of the interconnection of the building to the space has been retained, even within widely divergent building programs.

When the Prince Regent became King, he decided to move his residence from Carlton House to Buckingham Palace. Nash proposed that terraces of houses be built in the grounds of the old house, which was to be torn down and replaced by the York Column and a great flight of steps. The proposal was accepted, and thus Nash obtained income for the Crown from the old property and achieved a wonderful extension of his movement system. This ran from Regent Street and Waterloo Place, down to the Mall adjacent to St. James's Park (redesigned by him), and along the Mall to the terminal feature, Buckingham Palace. So it is that today one can travel in London from Buckingham Palace to Cumberland Terrace all along a way largely conceived, in both mass and space, by John Nash.

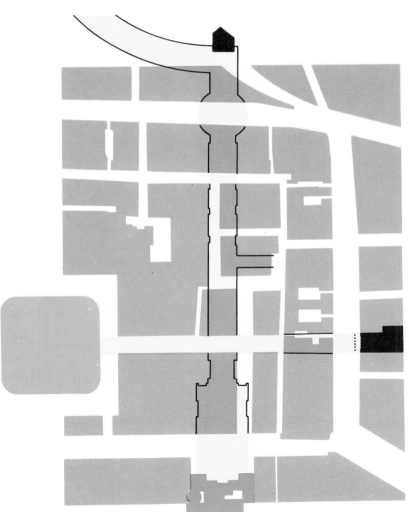

1:3500

THE TRAGEDY OF LONDON

In 1829, when the Shepherd engraving, above, was published, London, of all the European capitals, had the most delicate design structure. The product of hundreds of years of enlightened land subdivision by many landowners, this subtle intermixture of interconnecting squares and the marvelous skyline shown in the engraving above was particularly vulnerable and subject to attack.

The tragedy of London is that the people of that city neither understood this aspect of it nor took measures to protect it from the forces that were to come. The result is virtual ruination of large parts of London by high-rise structures that have been allowed to pop up at all sorts of miscellaneous places, ruining all sorts of formerly fine views, and the mindless proliferation of such structures continues. Most tragic is the fact that still there is no plan to meet this problem in the future.

This is not to say that London should have no tall buildings. It is to say that their location and design should be directed into intelligent channels. Stockholm, with its five Norrmalm Towers, has proved that an historic city can have high-rise structures without sacrificing its essential qualities, but here they have an organized and disciplined relationship with the regional transportation system which underlies them.

Happily, Paris has proved that the Stockholm idea can be successfully projected into the much larger and more difficult situation in that city. It is to be hoped that London will start on a plan of its own.

214

THE VISION OF PARIS

Except for one extremely objectionable high-rise structure, the seventeenth-century skyline of Paris north from the Louvre is undisturbed. Because Paris is providing, on a scale commensurate with modern demands, a new center to take the brunt of commercial expansion, there is a reasonable chance that the integrity of the historic city can be maintained.

The model below of this new center, La Défense, the product of a remarkable assemblage of managerial and design talent, shows the extent to which the old Champs Elysées axis is reinforced by the new movement systems. Clearly visible is the complex interweaving of streets, highways, and expressways which serve it. Not

visible is the new underground rail line from Place de l'Etoile which connects with the great pedestrian platform with its view down the Champs Elysées to the Arc de Triomphe.

The question of the effect of this development on the "Grande axe de France" was considered to be of such national importance that the selection of the design among those submitted by different architects was referred directly to the President, Georges Pompidou. It is a matter of international significance that the design selected preserved the integrity of the shaft of space projected by the Louvre and defined by the opening in the Arc de Triomphe. Here the decision that was made was right.

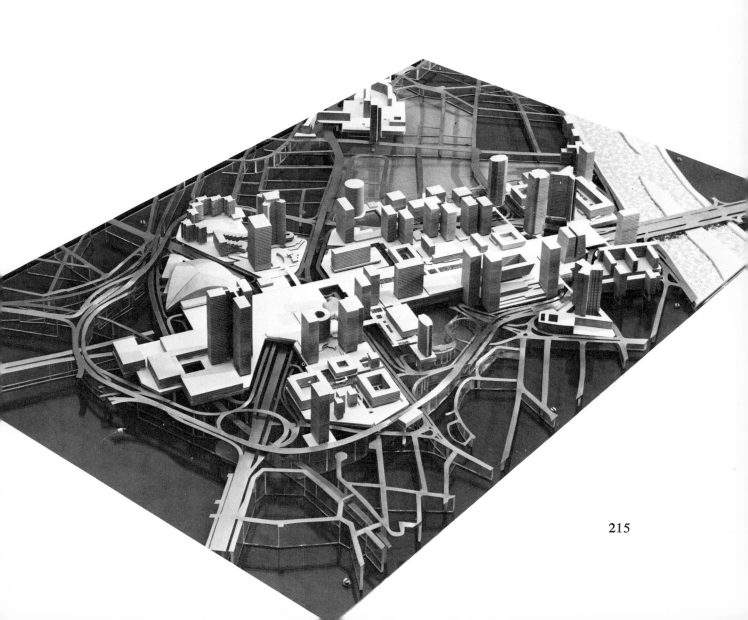

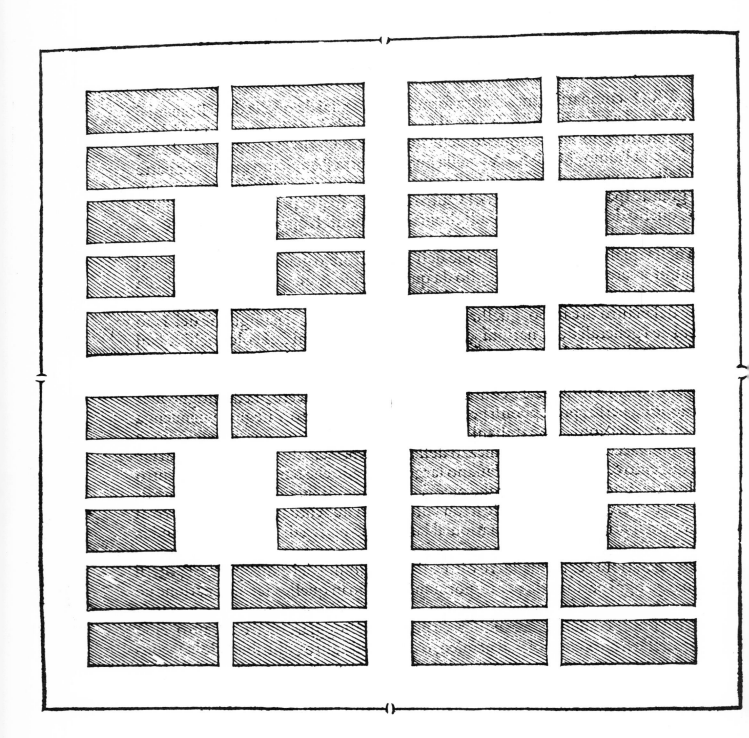

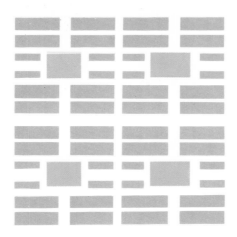

VITRUVIUS COMES TO THE NEW WORLD

The discovery of a remarkable document consisting of ten books on architecture, entitled *De Architectura,* by the Roman architect Marcus Pollio Vitruvius, who lived in the first century B.C., had a great impact on Renaissance work.

First translated in 1471 and widely distributed thereafter, this book contains much wisdom that is still applicable to the problems of architecture and of the architect today. However, one of its most important aspects is the stimulation it provided for creative thinking during the Renaissance period. The many editions that were published purporting to be based on Vitruvius are more valuable for what they add to Vitruvius than for the presentation of the original material.

The plan shown on the page opposite, from *L'Architettura* by Pietro di Giacomo Cataneo, first published in Venice in 1567, cannot be attributed directly to any suggestions of Vitruvius. Rather it should be viewed as a contemporary proposal for an ideal city developed under the stimulation of Vitruvius's Roman discussion of this subject.

Because there were very few completely new cities built in Europe following the widespread adoption of the Vitruvius cult, the full impact of the architect's ideas had to await expression on a city-wide scale until the founding of many new cities in the American Colonies.

The plan opposite contains the germ of the two most distinguished American city plans of the period, those of Savannah and Philadelphia. Whether there was direct knowledge of this design by Thomas Holme when he laid out the plan for Philadelphia for William Penn in 1683, shown below, or by James Oglethorpe when he designed the Savannah Plan in 1733, shown above, we do not know, but certainly all the major ideas of both plans are contained in Cataneo's book.

So the interaction of the classical rationalism of Vitruvius and the intellectual speculations of the Renaissance scholars finally received expression in the material fact of new cities in the New World.

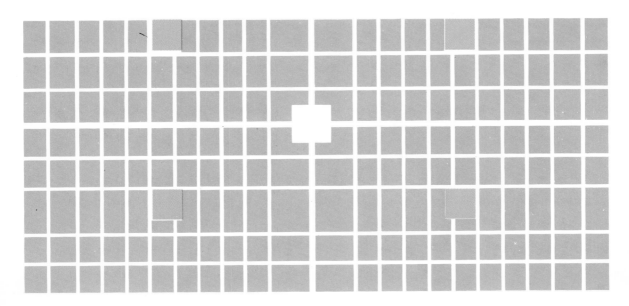

TODAY

MID-NINETEENTH CENTURY

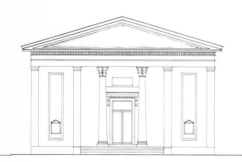

1850

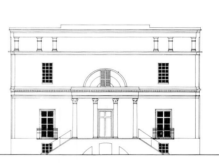

1819

1817

c. 1840 — ADDITIONS c. 1890

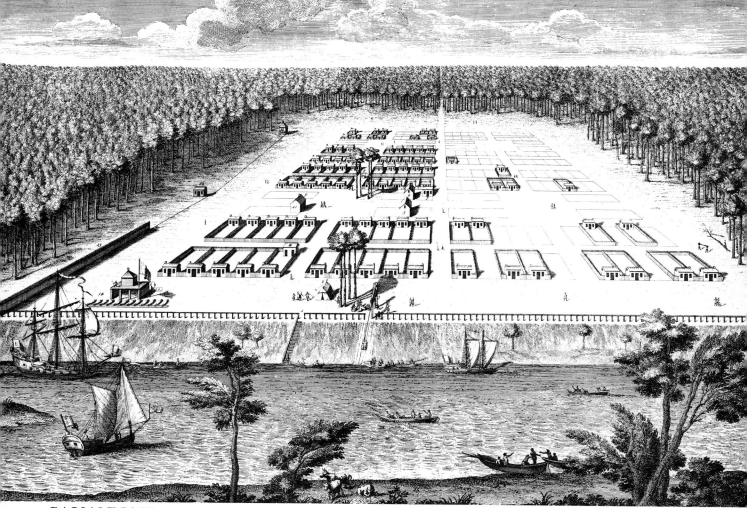

SAVANNAH

It is amazing that a colony, struggling against the most elemental problems of survival in a wilderness, should be able to produce a plan so exalted that it remains as one of the finest diagrams for city organization and growth in existence. The 1734 engraving of Savannah above, made one year after the city was founded, dramatizes the pioneer hardships and portrays the underlying ordering of the ground. The beginning of the city's three-dimensional expression is seen in the cellular units of the family houses which make up the larger cell of the square and the related blocks.

Extending from the river is the thrust of space of the highway between the four square-centered communities. This projects itself deep into the forest, providing the spine for the future extension of the city and a system of such order and clarity that it became the controlling element for the growth of Savannah for the next 120 years. Finally it burst forth in a major design structure, encompassing the city from one end to the other.

A plan of this degree of discipline focuses in icy sharpness the ability of the architect to give it architectural expression in the third dimension. The two narrow blocks on each side of the squares provide sites for buildings which inevitably are conspicuous, and quite evidently do or do not meet the demands imposed by the land layout. The series of elevation drawings on the page to the left show solutions by architects of many different periods as the ever-changing civic life of Savannah evolved over the constant of the planned land form. The most recent of these, the one of our own day (in the upper left-hand corner) undoubtedly was thought of as traditional in its design. In reality it accords with the firmly established tradition in all except its two most important aspects, scale and proportion. The lesson of meeting the responsibility of the site, beautifully demonstrated in all the work from the Colonial through the Victorian period, was available on the ground, but the designer of today failed to see it.

219

1733

1735

1790

1:19000

SAVANNAH DESIGN STRUCTURE

The extraordinary cellular unit consisting of the central green square and the twelve blocks associated with it, as John W. Reps has pointed out in *The Making of Urban America*, "provided not only an unusually attractive, convenient and intimate environment but also served as a practical device for allowing urban expansion without formless sprawl."

The diagrams on this and the opposite page show that the cellular unit, the square and its twelve blocks, not only served as a fine module for growth by accretion, but also had within it the elements of growth by extension, because of the outward thrust of the linear connections between the central squares. The total effect is an interaction between two patterns, the gridiron web of streets dividing the basic units, and the web of green spaces and their green links which overlies the geometry of the streets.

The design growth of Savannah was a simple accumulation of related cellular units, bound together by their own internal characteristics, until a period following 1856, when the total mass of the city had reached such proportions that a design restructuring of the city was needed. This restructuring occurred with remarkable force in the latter half of the nineteenth century, as the last diagram on the opposite page shows. The central spine of the third cellular unit from the left was made the dominant spine of a design structure embracing the entire city of that time. It became the foreground of the domed city hall on the waterfront, from which extended on both sides a formal park and the great Factors' Walk and warehouses along the river shown in black on the plan. During a later period a large new park was added at the southern end. It was on an entirely different scale from the old squares and extended the influence of the central design element into the hinterland.

This is one of the clearest examples of city growth by design, and of a restructuring following a period of growth by accretion, a design extension

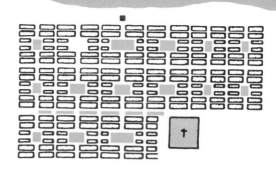

1815

consisting integrally of land planning and architecture. In our time cities must go through a new phase of restructuring to meet the new dimensions of regional scale, much of which will be provided by the design of expressways. The challenge is to relate the new design structure to the existing operative principles of organic growth as successfully as the planners did in Savannah in the latter part of the nineteenth century.

The actual impact of the Savannah system of land organization is both practical and delightful. There are efficient streets on the normal gridiron pattern which bypass the square-centered community, and which, by the very fact of their large scale, are more efficient traffic carriers than through streets at every block would be. The Savannah planners have been wise enough to use wide tree-lined boulevards in place of the ordinary streets at intervals, marking stages of growth parallel with the river. This gives a sense of large-scale orientation to the street network, and an added rhythm to progression away from the river.

The visual effect of looking down lines of squares is exciting and constantly different, each square having its own special character and those in the central axis being strongly marked by monuments. Yet the total impact is just the opposite from the single pull of a great axial plan such as that of Paris or Washington, which is based on a single movement system. Because there are squares in all directions, a sense of being within a complete organism is created, a kind of simultaneity that is most satisfying. When one is within any of these squares one feels entirely removed from the rushing traffic of the surrounding streets, which crosses but does not parallel the lines of sight. It is enormously to the credit of the city fathers of Savannah that the traffic has not been allowed to cut through the green squares, despite their vulnerability under this plan. The cars have been allowed to park only on the square which was originally the market (shown in white on these plans).

1856

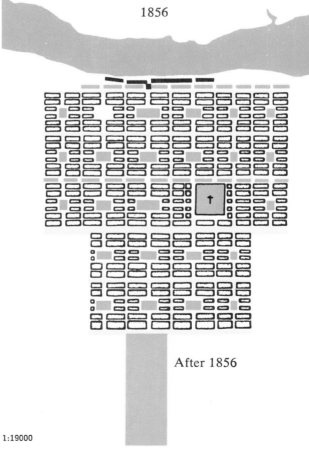

After 1856

1:19000

221

FEDERAL DIGNITY

The design plan for Washington, unlike that of Savannah, has received world acclaim, but for reasons quite different from that of the original intentions of its creator, Major Pierre L'Enfant. The 1792 plan, opposite, which was Andrew Ellicott's version, and the great regional plan, shown below, show that it was L'Enfant's idea that the seminal source of the design for Washington would be the meeting of the city and the river, and that the design of the city would join the force of the region, the Potomac River, thus placing it in common with other great cities, such as Venice, Florence, and Saint Petersburg. So from the White House (marked President's House on the maps) there would have been a great sweeping view down a long stretch of the Potomac, and from the Capitol a vista across an expanse of the water of the river as a foreground for the Virginia hills. Indeed, the geometry of the mall design at the point of junction of the two axes and the river is angular, and would appear incomplete except as seen as a design of both land and water.

The thinking of the designers of the present century was not in harmony with a concept of such breadth. In 1902 the members of the Mc-Millan Commission desired a contained, self-completing, and comfortably inward-looking idea, rather than a dynamic interrelationship with the region. In its proposals it blocked off the view from the Capitol by the Lincoln Memorial, and the White House vista by what later became the memorial to Jefferson, which shut out the river.

The Washington that was built as a consequence of the McMillan plan is a beautiful city and a joy to be in. However, this does not dim the freshness of L'Enfant's original concept, nor does it prevent one from thinking of Washington as it is and Washington as it might have been.

The Ellicott version of L'Enfant's plan, opposite, in common with the Nolli map of Rome on page 161, expresses graphically an integration of exterior space planning and architectural design. This is especially evident in the Capitol building and in the White House. We are thus reminded that this interrelation, so obscured during recent years, was contained in the original plan for the capital city and that it would be patriotic to revive it today.

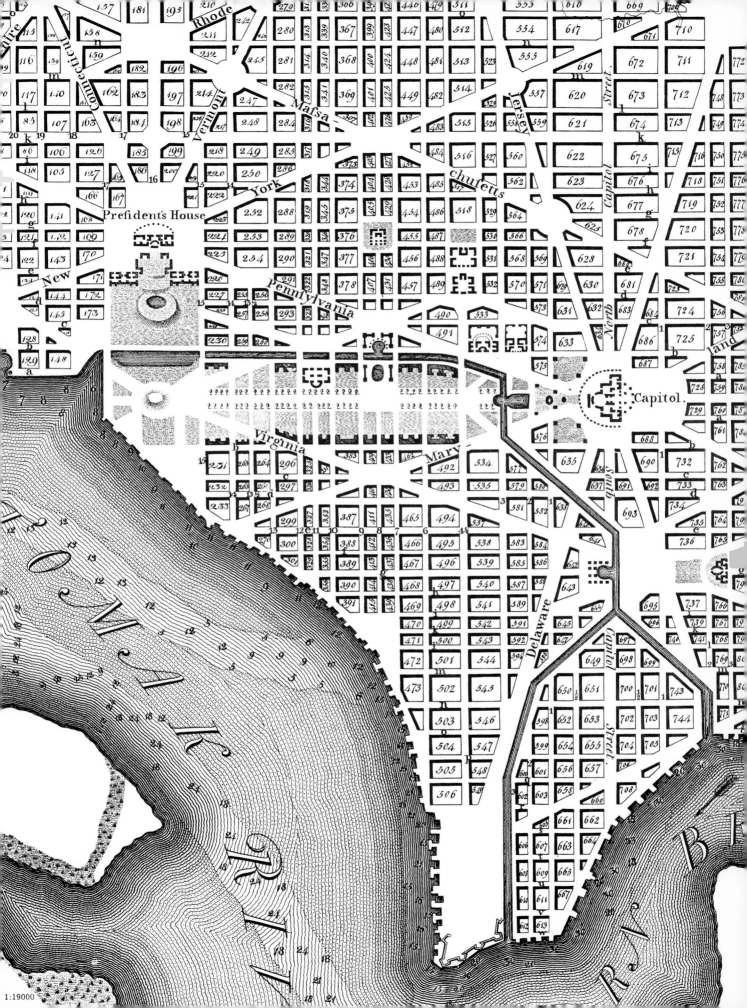

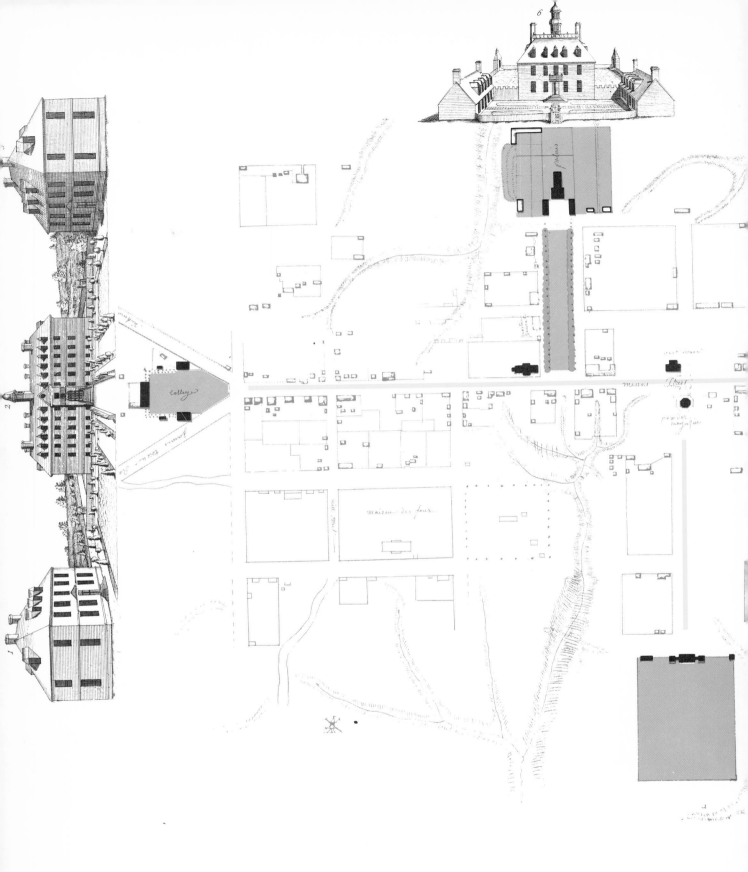

COLONIAL PROGRESSION

The color diagram overlaid on the Frenchman's map of Williamsburg of 1782 here emphasizes the greatness of the design composition of this city, and reminds us that the principles it embodies are at the root of the American tradition.

Starting at the left, at the gate of the group of buildings of William and Mary College (shown in black), the Colonial politician attending a meeting of the State Assembly would have proceeded easterly toward the H-shaped State House (three-quarters of a mile away), which was the other visual terminus of Duke of Gloucester Street, the main street of the city. Leaving the college, he would pass along two blocks bordered by houses, to the churchyard on the left, and the church building with its spire which provides the pivot to the cross thrust of the tree-lined mall, extending the space of the street north to the focal Governor's Palace with its symmetrical outbuildings, also in black.

A small block separates this linear cross-space from the square with its central court house on the north and octagonal powder magazine on the south side of the main street. South of this is an open space which formerly led to Tazewell Hall, with its outbuildings, once the architectural terminus to this vista. The rhythmic progression proceeds along the contained space between the next two blocks with their dense development of buildings, to the State House, which dominates the space that opens up around it.

In this simple, unselfconscious composition, the architecture and the space-planning are one, although done by many different people at different periods. The great act of reconstruction of Williamsburg by the Rockefeller family has brought about a revival of interest in the details of American Colonial life. Not to be forgotten is the lesson of the design of the city as a whole.

GLORY OF EXUBERANCE

The restrained dignity of the Colonial period in North America, not uninfluenced by the relative scarcity of resources in the new land, gave way to the great burgeoning of energy and activity during the Victorian period of industrial expansion. In various places the exuberance coming from the new-found strength of the young countries received expression in building on a fresh and daring scale. None was more totally glorious, or more expressive of a vast regional concept, than the group of government buildings in Ottawa, the capital of the Dominion of Canada.

These old photographs, borrowed from the historical archives, show the skyline of Ottawa before the disastrous fire of 1916, and before the replacement of the rather complex original Parliament building tower by the taller, starker Peace Tower. The photograph above shows the superb way in which the design of the pyramidal library dominates the full sweep of the Ottawa River around the hill on which it is built, establishing a pivotal point in space, and asserting the functions of man within the great landscape. Originally all the other architectural features were gauged to reinforce this basic design element, such as the Parliament building tower as shown above, just to the left of the library spire.

Although the handsome Peace Tower is too self-assertive to play a fully harmonious role in the total ensemble, the basic forms of this vast group of buildings and the terrain on which they stand are so strong that, under the rebuilding, little harm was done.

Ottawa now is laboring with the question of how to adapt the city to the demands of modern commerce, without destroying the delicate interaction of the river and the sky as modulated by these buildings. The city has shown its deep concern that nothing be done to detract from the government buildings, which is a good thing because this group in its setting is one of the finest expressions of Victorian exuberance in the world.

LE CORBUSIER AND THE NEW VISION

The kind of tumultuous richness which Ottawa represents obviously heralds the end of a period, and indeed it was only a short time later that advanced architects "lowered the boom," swept away all the richness and the accumulated debris of Victorian architecture, and in its place inserted a vision of austerity and order such as that contained in the Le Corbusier drawing above. In the short time since this great revolution, the counter-

revolution has already established itself, and richness and even capriciousness of form are now subjects for accolade. Once again, axial symmetry is fashionable and the twisting of function to fit an arbitrary form is carried on to a degree beyond that tolerated under the Ecole des Beaux Arts design principles. To be sure, classical columns and pointed arches are no longer used, but these were never as important as mass and land design. So it

228

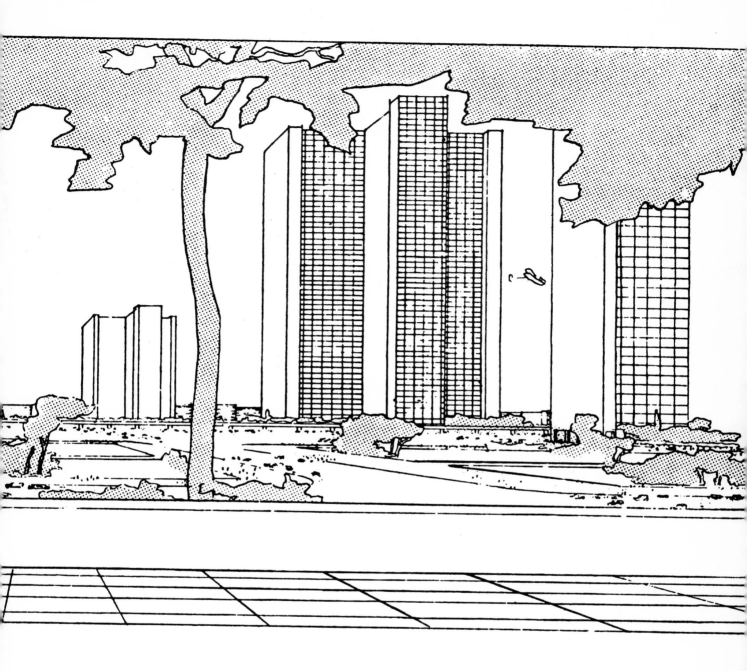

may be asked what happened to design in a deeper sense, or did anything important happen at all?

As Brunelleschi was the great figure connected with the origin of the Renaissance, and yet never participated in its broader application (indeed it may be debated whether he even previsioned it), so Le Corbusier is the great figure of modern architecture. Like Brunelleschi he planted the seeds for the larger application of the principles of the modern movement, and certainly he previsioned it, as this 1922 drawing indicates.

Le Corbusier's life and work force us to consider our position today in relation to an evolutionary development of which he represents the source, and they pose the question of how the principles he helped to formulate can be applied, not to the design of an individual building or two or three, but to the design of the total environment.

229

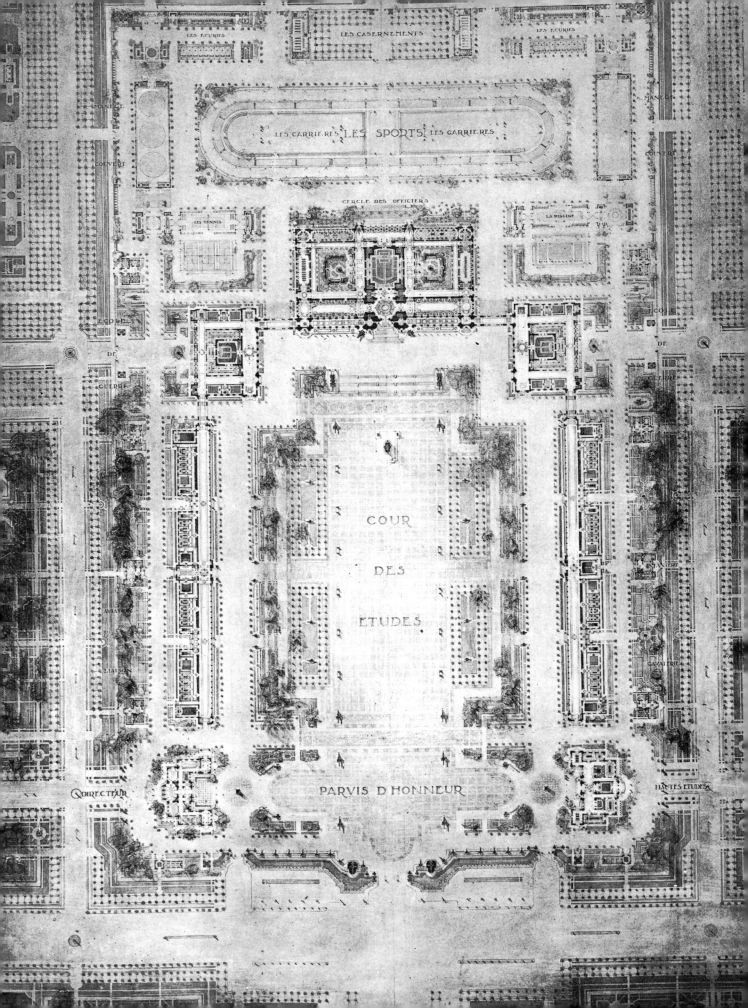

THE GREAT AMPUTATION

The Rome Prize drawing of Monsieur Giroud, shown opposite, was made in 1922, about the same time that Le Corbusier produced the drawing reproduced below. Here we see the overlapping of the two phases of development, the Beaux Arts plan marking the close of one phase, the Le Corbusier drawing heralding the new.

Whatever else one may say for it, the Rome Prize drawing is an attempt at a vast and coordinated design for land development. The building forms are derived from the land design. The very representation of the buildings by their structural points of contact with the land rather than by their mass as blocks, shows clearly that the designer was thinking of the flow of space through them. His design presents space as one totality, interior and exterior; indeed there is not too much distinction between the two. The exterior form of the buildings is determined by the shapes of the rooms serving the various functions. Every part is coordinated with every other part in the design sense. There is complete mastery of scale from the most minute to the broadest forms. However, this type of exercise had become separated from reality. It represented academic caprice, and was swept away.

The drawing of Le Corbusier below clearly shows one of the most decisive consequences of the architectural revolution, the cutting off of the building from the land. The mass of the structure is suspended above the land, and the design of each is independent of the other. In this drawing the buildings are extended in a formal, rigid geometrical pattern over the countryside, and the paths on the land wander in their own curvilinear system. This concept, in the hands of a master, can produce great work. However, the effect on the architectural profession was a disaster. No longer was the designer subject to the discipline of land design. Since the design of the building and the design of the land could now be treated separately, and since most architects were interested in buildings and not in land, the result has been concentration on building design independent of its environment, and the thoughtless, arbitrary placing of it on the land, without regard to total design principles. By the great liberation of Le Corbusier, the great surgical amputation of the building from the land, we have a new liberty of design for which we have paid a great price because, in the process, the total environment has suffered.

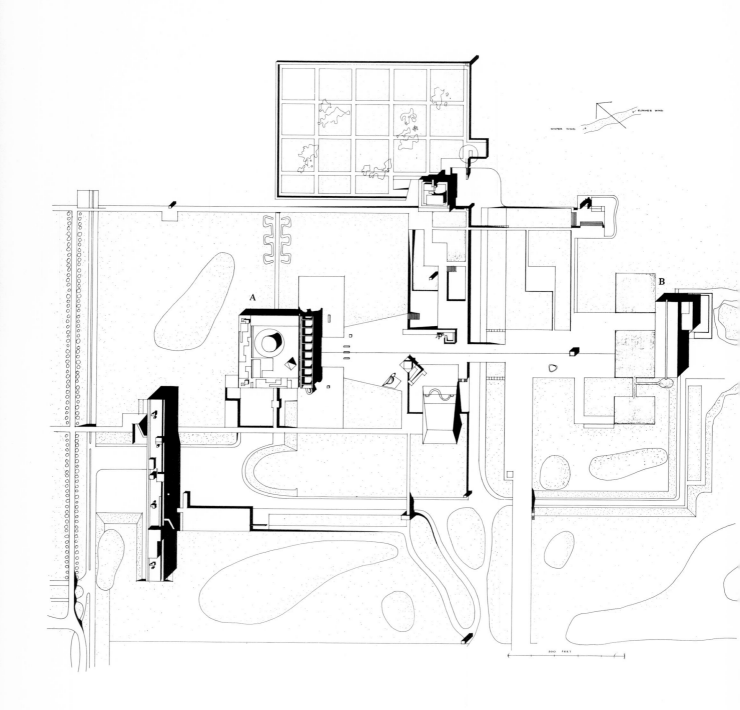

A

B

SUMMER WIND

WINTER WIND

500 FEET

1:5000

PAINTING ON A CLEAN CANVAS — CHANDIGARH

When Jawaharlal Nehru wanted to express the burgeoning vitality of the New India by building a new city, Chandigarh, he turned to the greatest architect Western culture had produced, Le Corbusier. He gave Le Corbusier carte blanche to express the highest aspirations of modern design. What Le Corbusier did with that assignment stands as a measure of our grasp of large-scale design at the present day.

The photograph above, one of three views of Chandigarh, presents a vision through the controlled eye of the camera. In reality the human eye at this point would take in a larger horizon and would be confronted by the adjacent wastelands. While Le Corbusier planned a formal paved connection between his buildings in the governmental group, and also planned an additional structure that has not been built, his buildings are so far apart that they fail to master the space they are in, and will continue to fail to do so, no matter how much paving is built.

Even the architecture of the piers of the Assembly building, marked A on the map opposite,

so dramatic in perspective, reduces to matchstick proportion when seen edge-on along the central spine of movement from the Supreme Court building (B on the map). Le Corbusier's antipathy to the city of Chandigarh was so great that he created artificial mounds, seen in the photograph above, to screen off an awareness of its existence from his architecture. Despite the amazingly brilliant examples before him of the works of the Moguls, and then of Sir Edwin Luytens in New Dehli, in which the public architecture stood proudly overlooking the city, illuminating its parts and the life of the people within it, Le Corbusier was blind to the design requirements of relating his buildings to the city, and, indeed, of relating his buildings to one another.

Le Corbusier was a great master, and his place in history is invulnerable. From him we have learned many of the principles of modern design which we use today. But from his completed work we cannot learn directly about the application of these principles to the larger problem of the city. For this we must look elsewhere.

233

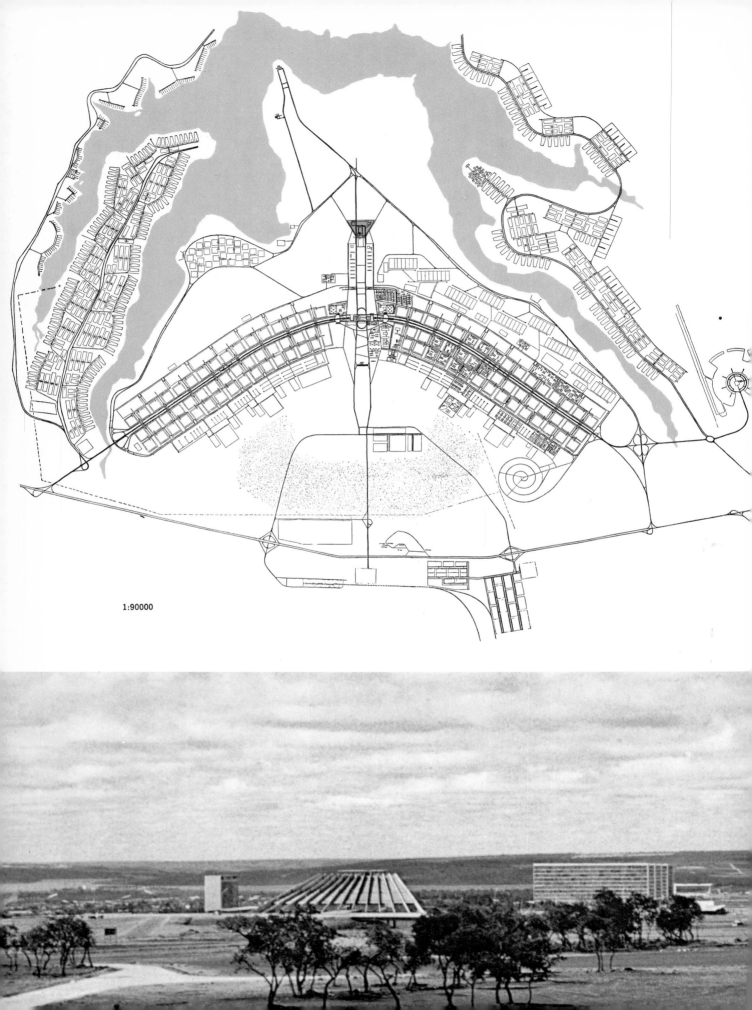

1:90000

THE GREAT EFFORT—BRASILIA

Much maligned by critics, too many of whom have never seen it, Brasilia stands in contemporary architecture as the most significant example of a city designed as a whole. And it would be foolish indeed for architects not to take advantage of the lesson it offers.

Unfortunately, Brasilia cannot be understood except as experienced on the ground in the city itself. One reason for this was pointed out by Lucio Costa, designer of the basic scheme for Brasilia. Before I visited the city, he said that Brasilia could be apprehended only in relation to the clouds which, continually passing overhead, throw changing pools of light and shadow over the architectural forms. While the contrast between unchanging architecture and ever-changing elements and details such as the splashing of water in fountains, or the flapping of flags in the wind, has long been a principle of urban design, in Brasilia the element of change is provided by the formations of clouds which constantly encompass the entire city and become part of its dynamic design.

Without seeing it except in illustrations, I myself had condemned Brasilia, and in the appendix to this book I have included the statement I would have used here if I had not visited the city. I had judged the shaft of space between the identical ministry buildings (seen below) as inadequately terminated by the slender mass of the twin administration towers behind the dome of the Senate and the saucer of the House of Representatives. Only after viewing the site at first hand did I realize that the space is the whole stretch contained within the bowl-shaped hills surrounding the city. All the building mass is sculptural form, and this articulates the total space design on a breadth of scale hitherto unknown. As seen in the photograph below, the warm tones of the pyramidal-shaped opera house at the left and the curved cathedral to the right contrast with the white exterior of the government buildings.

Costa made it clear that Brasilia was never intended to be a model for a typical city. It was meant to be a unique capital for a great nation. The plan at left shows the character of his design. There is a central shaft of space forming a monumental axis from the television tower (tiny green triangle) on the top of a hill to the triangular Plaza (in green) of the Three Powers, overlooking the lake, where the major functions of government are concentrated. Perpendicular to this axis stretch the two curved, winglike residential areas, down the center of which runs an expressway. At the point of juncture of the expressway and the central space is an extraordinary bus terminal and the "Highway Platform" shown on page 239. Parallel with the expressway, and two blocks removed from it, is a pedestrian shopping strip tying the residential areas together.

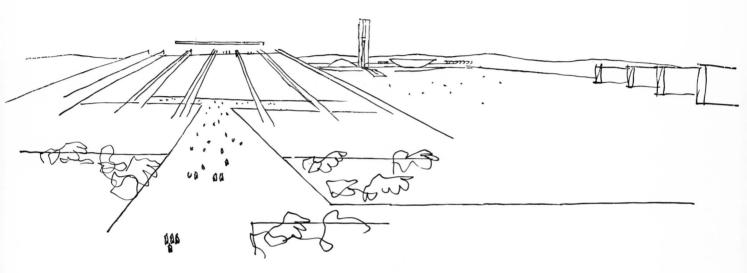

AUTOMOBILE-PEDESTRIAN RELATIONSHIPS

In Brasilia the principle of interrelated opposites has received exceptional architectural recognition through the contrasting demands of the automobile and the pedestrian.

Brasilia is probably the only city that employs an expressway as the central feature of its residential areas. This represents an unabashed expression of the importance of the automobile in contemporary life. At the same time the city offers for the pedestrian a number of areas that are totally removed from vehicular traffic. The most remarkable of these is illustrated opposite. The entire roof of the Congress Building is paved with marble, and access to this balusterless pedestrian area is provided by the ramp leading up from the ground below. The space is powerfully modulated by the great saucer-like form of the House

of Representatives which rises from it, and by the dome of the Senate which is just visible to the left of the photograph, next to the twin shafts of the Administration Building. Unlike the mass-enclosed pedestrian spaces we have observed, this one is a plane suspended in space. It is totally devoid of mass definition and provides a superb vantage point from which to experience the rhythmic outflow of the structures of Brasilia as they penetrate the space volumes defined by the natural features of the region.

The drawing above, by Oscar Niemeyer, the architect of Brasilia who designed all the major buildings and many of the minor ones, further emphasizes the concept of buildings which of themselves do not attempt to confine spaces, but rather play their role in continuous space.

237

HIGHWAYS AS ARCHITECTURE

Because buildings are traditional and expressways are not, facilities for the movement of the automobile, for its stopping and for the disembarking of its occupants, have until now been thought of as comparable to plumbing facilities — the subject of design for somebody other than an architect. But in Brasilia the highway has come into its own as an architectural work and is an integral element in civic design.

The photographs above and below give some sense of the form of the highway structure in relation to the mass-space form of the monumental government buildings. The photograph opposite, showing the interior of the bus terminal (the exterior is seen to the right of the upper photograph on this page), conveys something of the feeling of orientation that greets one on arrival at this central point. The building is an extension of the expressway structure and is indivisible from it, every part of it relating to the design of the city as a whole.

The fact that the volume of space of the esplanade between the Congress Building and the television tower is penetrated by the vertebrate structure of the expressway becomes the occasion for a monumental architectural expression in this remarkable work which Lucio Costa calls the "Highway Platform."

ARTICULATION OF SPACE

The distance between the Administration Building and the Supreme Court in Brasilia, 1000 feet, is 500 feet shorter than the distance between the Assembly and the Supreme Court in Chandigarh, but this alone does not seem to explain fully why the tension in Brasilia is sustained, and the buildings and their setting make a total composition of powerful impact.

The reasons for the marked contrast between these two major works of our own day present a fruitful subject for analysis, out of which a deeper understanding of contemporary design could grow.

Among the more obvious differences are the bulk of the capitol building in Brasilia, which has no counterpart in Chandigarh, and the design of the structural members, which in Brasilia present substantial mass to the frontal view. Also to be found in Brasilia is the subtle articulation of the intervening space by sculpture, benches, and beautifully modulated paving, as seen below.

This great plaza responds well to the assembly of masses of people, yet it does not depend on crowds to produce an experience that is deeply satisfying.

ARCHITECTURE WHICH INTERLOCKS

It seems appropriate to repeat the title used on page 72, which led into the discussion of the agora in Athens. I have done this because in Brasilia there is a re-emergence of the principles of interrelation of buildings displayed in the earlier work. The forms of the Supreme Court building, in the left foreground, the saucer of the House of Representatives, and the twin towers of the Administration Building are so powerful in their own right and so powerfully interrelated that they sustain tension across a space very much larger than that of most traditional compositions. The photograph makes clear the correlation between the curved concavity of the base of the roof supports of the Supreme Court building and the curved convexity of the House of Representatives saucer. It also shows the harmony of the curved line of the left edge of the central column in relation to the saucer

and the sharply vertical line of the right edge adjacent to the clean vertical form of the towers.

This harmonic reverberation between buildings does not depend on one carefully posed photograph; it is ever present and intensifies as one moves around the buildings.

The solution of the problems of design of our contemporary cities does not stem from forms or from relationships that are as symmetrical or rigidly geometric as those of Brasilia. Kenzo Tange in his Olympic buildings in Tokyo (page 36) has shown us a new geometry of relationships in the design of two buildings, and this could be extended to a larger composition.

The gift of Brasilia is not primarily the form of its structures or the formal symmetry of its composition, but rather the reformulation of the vision of the city as a totality.

PROGRESS THROUGH COLOR

In the planning of Panza in Ischia (as we have seen on pages 53-57) and in the planning of Peking in China (to be seen on pages 244-251) the experience of progression through space was powerfully modulated by the dimension of color. In both these cases the experience of colored space was transmitted directly by the architecture.

In our contemporary Western culture we have not accepted strong color as a major dimension of architecture. In Rotterdam, however, and in a number of other places, especially in Europe, this desire for color is met by the use of flowers.

In the United States, in pursuit of "variety," flowers of many colors are used together. The result is that there is no progression or change if the flowers relate to movement over an extended distance. Indeed, the same could be said of building types in some contemporary subdivisions. Types A, B, C, and D, each one different from its neighbor, when strung out along the street become monotonous in their repetition.

In Rotterdam, as these photographs of the great Lijnbaan project show, the color is massed into large zones where the progression of movement is articulated, and a counterfoil is provided for the interest of the people as they pass through the spaces.

This full completion of the plans of the city not only provides raw space but invests it with the qualities of life and change.

This does not involve only sculpture and flowers. As Larry Smith and Victor Gruen have pointed out in their book, *Shopping Towns USA,* the physical environment must be enriched by various kinds of events, which good management must provide, and, to compete with suburban shopping centers, central city spaces must have management which is comparably good. The space by its very dimension must be a proper vessel for the activities it is to contain, not too large and not too small, and so formed as to foster the accidental encounter.

PEKING

Possibly the greatest single work of man on the face the earth is Peking. This Chinese city, designed as the domicile of the Emperor, was intended to mark the center of the universe. The city is deeply enmeshed in ritualistic formulae and religious concepts which do not concern us now. Nevertheless, it is so brilliant in design that it provides a rich storehouse of ideas for the city of today.

PROGRESS THROUGH COLOR AND FORM

The old Chinese drawing, and the photograph of the Altar of Heaven, at left, and the curved canal in the Forbidden City, on the opposite page, give some indication of the experience of progressing along a Chinese movement axis. In full play are all the elements of space design that we have been discussing, from the analysis of the Guardi drawing on pages 24 to 27, to this point. If we study this progression in terms of the impact on the sensibilities of the participator as he moves through these spaces, the true nature of the design can be felt. Here are the joy of ascent and descent, the recession planes and the penetration in depth. In the roofs and the columns are concavity and convexity. This is architecture that connects with the ground by multiple platforms and that cuts the sky in a never-ending series of undulating lines and curving shapes as the points in space move across one another in the view of the participator progressing up the central way.

More clearly than elsewhere, the design is the sequence of progression. The buildings are all of a uniform modular system, the proportion and dimensions of structures increasing with the number of bays, according to definite rules of progression. With such rules the designer is forced to depend on means other than aggrandizement of architectural mass for effect.

The picture of the Altar of Heaven, opposite, shows in pure form the use of architecture to modulate the experience of progression through space. The central axial movement is contained and directed not by architectural mass but by the design of the paving in a simple earth plane. The act of progressing into a more intensely sacred space is achieved, not by a wall which encloses a space, but by a free-standing gateway astride the paved articulated line of movement, its only function being to demarcate a point in movement or a moment in time in a chain of movement-experience.

The Altar of Heaven itself, the most sacred place in China, where twice annually the Emperor made sacrifice, is the purest possible space experience. The three cylinders, each defined by one of the three tiers of ascending balustrades, set into motion vertical shafts of space articulation. The climax of the experience is the point of meeting of the stairway and the sky.

The full-bodied "baroque" form of the curving canal in the outer court of the Forbidden City, the "River of Golden Water," right, punctuated by the bulbous tops of the marble balustrades which line it, shows that within the rigid discipline of a traditional system of architecture, such as the Chinese imposed upon themselves, there was adequate room for rich expression, here, appropriately, in the realm of land design.

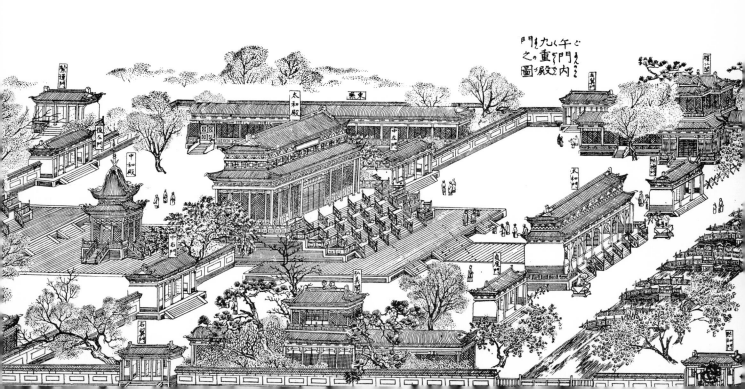

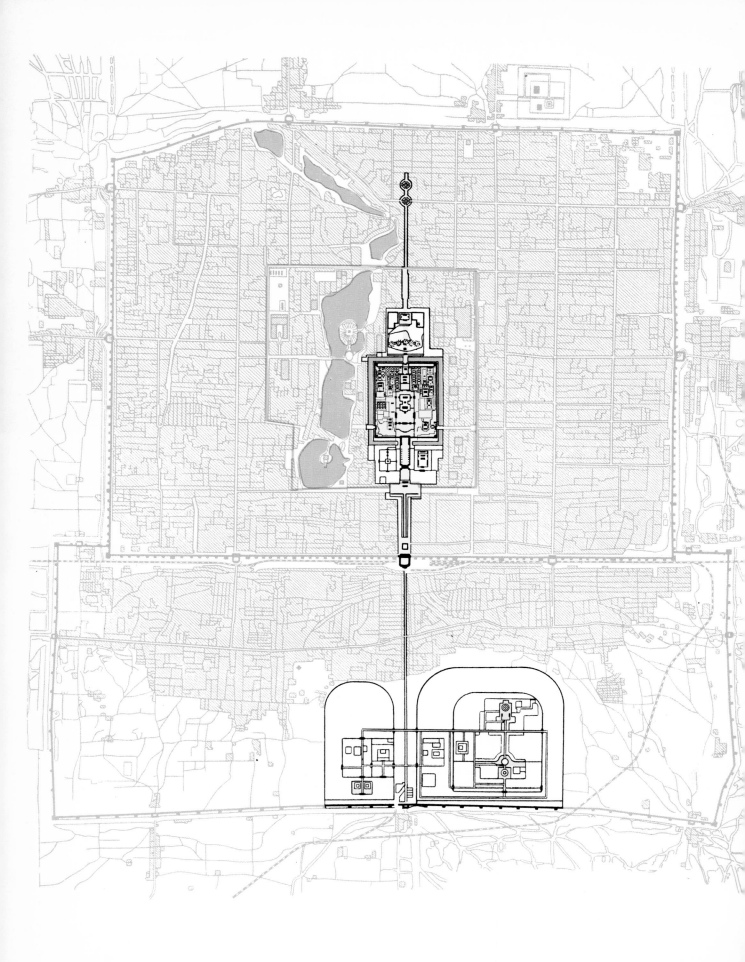

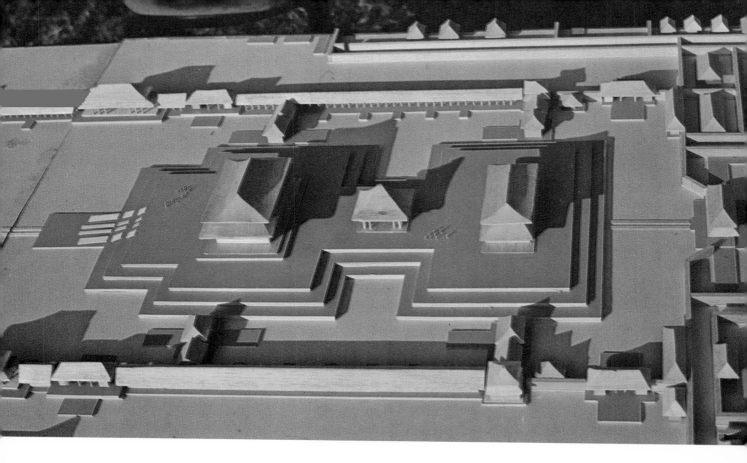

SCALE AND DESIGN

The central design structure of Peking, emphasized in the total plan of the city, is shown opposite. The approach from the south across the plain leads to the central gateway in the great wall, which opens upon the paved way between the Temple of Agriculture to the left and the Temple of Heaven to the right. The design of these spaces, in turn, is excellently related to the central movement system, providing a series of perpendicular and parallel modulations in reference to it.

The fundamental character of Peking is expressed by the central movement through four areas, each of which has its own particular color. The southern rectangle, with its enclosing walls, the Outer City, has buildings with black roofs. These prepare the eye for the fresh experience, after penetrating the wall surrounding the hollow square, the Inner City, of the brilliant blue-purple tile roofs and red doors with gold ornaments. Next comes the gate to the Imperial City, outlined in green. The rhythm of space contraction and expansion intensifies until the space is reached before the Wu Mên or Meridian Gate (shown on pages 244 and 245), heralding the Forbidden City, the home of the Emperor of China.

From this point the experience of entering into the outer court with its curved canal, and finally the central court with the Throne Halls, is one of unbelievable color intensity. The yellow and gold roofs surrounding the blue sky create a sensation of architectural power which has no parallel. The progression moves across the northern leg of the moat enclosing the Forbidden City and up Coal Hill and down again, and on to the Drum Tower and the Bell Tower, where it expires before the northern city wall is reached.

In actual fact, the size and mass of the Hall of Supreme Harmony, shown in the color photo on page 244, is no greater than that of many of the buildings encountered on the three-mile progression up the main axis from the outer gate. The principle of dominant mass, central to most Western monumental civic designs, is totally absent. Indeed, the Hall of Supreme Harmony is invisible except when seen from the central courtyard.

The power of the experience lies in the utilization of anticipation and fulfillment, in the setting up of a rhythm of experiences in time, a sequence of sensation that keeps mounting in intensity. Space and color are the major modulators, and the climax is indeed an adequate one for the center of the kingdom.

249

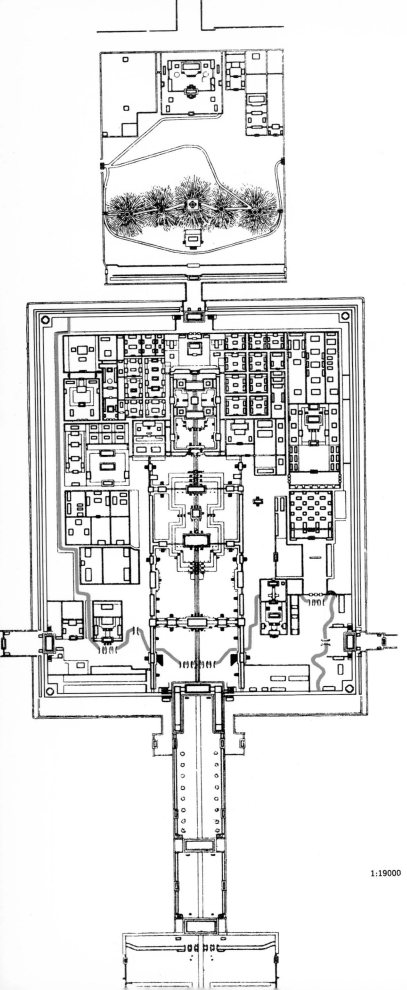

FLOW FROM SCALE TO SCALE

The plan of Peking is probably the only plan of any city that can be enlarged from scale to scale, and yet at each scale, whatever its extent, can hold together as a total design. At each level the city asserts its own design coherence but contains within itself the seeds of a different design order that will emerge as dominant if the scale is enlarged or reduced.

The drawing at left is an enlargement of the central axial element shown in the plan on the previous page. This extends from the gate at the entrance to the Imperial City to Coal Hill, which lies north of the Imperial Palace. As one moves through archways into walled courts and back into archways again, there is a clear rhythmic modulation of the northern axial movement based on openings and closings of space, with a systematic intensification of the rhythm as the throne is approached.

There are cross axes and side units which counterfoil the central design. Although there is heavy axial balance, there is not a rigid axial symmetry; the balancing buildings may be quite different in design, and, beyond their formality in the central spaces, the water courses are allowed to meander freely within the formal areas.

The rectangular moat enclosing the Forbidden City decisively cuts it off from the remainder of the urban complex, and provides a rich color element in its reflection of the red walls and yellow-roofed pavilions along it.

1:19000

The enlargement, shown here at right, of the central palace space from the plan opposite provides a rich and superbly modulated design which has its own coherent qualities. The visitor to this area would have passed through the Meridian Gate, across the "River of Golden Water" on one of the five bridges, and arrived at the Gate of Supreme Harmony shown at the bottom of this plan.

The central system of design consists of three principal pavilions, the Hall of Supreme Harmony to the south, the Hall of Protecting Harmony to the north, and the square hall between, set on an H-shaped mound which is built in three tiers, each with its rich balustrade of white marble, punctuated by great gold-plated urns. The space in which the mound is located is divided into three zones by walls which cut across the mound. The earth forms, which are basic to the whole design, and the space modulation determined by the planes of the walls, each have their own independent but interrelated existence.

Peking emphasizes the dominance of land-form design in great and extensive work. The levels of the land, the cutting of the land by channels of water, and the creation of land mounds at the climax, determine the architecture of the city. While the planes of the walls define space areas, the buildings, minor in mass, create points of repose and accomplishment.

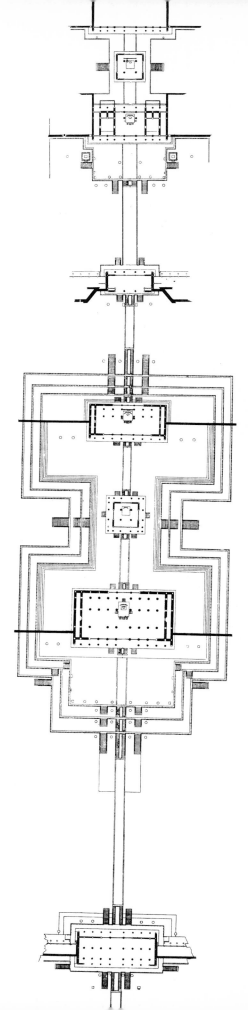

1:2250

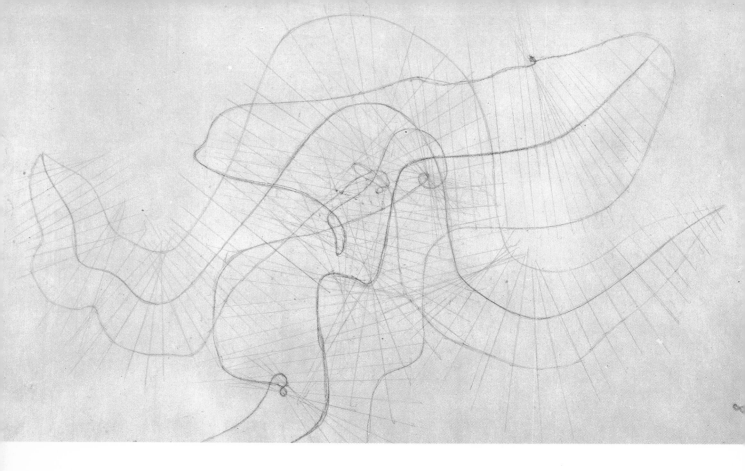

SIMULTANEOUS MOVEMENT SYSTEMS

A great difference between the cities we have studied so far and the city of today is the application of mechanical power to the movement of man through space. This relatively recent development sets up an entirely different kind of time-space perception. Up to this point the rate of speed of movement through space was much the same whether a person walked, rode on horseback, or drove a carriage. Thus the urban designer dealt with one basic system of perception.

The enormous increase in the size of the metropolitan region today requires an entirely new scale of image if the region is to hold together as an entity. Thus, for instance, Manhattan Island as a single mass furnishes the image of the center of the New York region. The immense horizontal expansion of the region has demanded drastic increase in the speed of getting about, and so the region has become overlaid with a complex series of transportation methods, each with its own rate of movement and its own system of perception attached. Up to the present, each of these

systems has been thought of separately, just as, at the beginning of each new period of architecture, the building is conceived of as separate from the ground. Yet the image of the region is derived from the series of impressions produced by all these systems interacting with one another and with the impressions gained while moving about the ground on foot. All these movement systems must be thought of simultaneously if the region is to produce the impression of a coherent whole.

Even our very administrative organization is pitched against this. A great bureaucracy and a wide range of vested interests are built up separately behind each type of transportation, and there is scarcely a beginning of understanding of what simultaneity would mean.

The responsibility for dealing with these complex systems as a coordinated unit is not normally assigned to anyone, yet it is here that lie the wellsprings for the design of the city of the future. Out of an understanding of this will come a discipline that could produce order on a metropolitan scale.

252

We must now confront directly the question of the nature of the discipline that will produce unity in the complexities of the evolving urban region.

"In necessariis unitas; in non necessariis libertas; in utrisque charitas [sic]." These words, an American variation of an ancient aphorism inscribed around an eighteenth-century portrait of the Reverend John Lowell and other Massachusetts dignitaries, meaning, "In essentials unity, in nonessentials liberty; in both charity," help to give us the clue. It now becomes our task to separate the essential from the nonessential.

The Klee diagram to the left consists of two central lines of movement, and the remainder of the design is the effect of these two movements simultaneously on the field. From them radiate perpendicular lines of influence, the energy of which, derived from the central spine, expires in the field. The outer lines define the extent of the fields that are influenced by the two central systems. The extreme complexity at certain points is still entirely within this simple three-part discipline. The parallelism between this diagram and the plans of the Acropolis of Pergamon and of Paris is shown on pages 62 and 192. Doubtless many other parallels will come to mind.

Within the concept of the Latin aphorism, the two central lines of movement are the essentials, the public aspect, or the basic design structure. The outer rays and the forms produced by their interactions are the nonessentials, the individual works, and therefore suitable subjects for freedom. The two Klee drawings to the right are an enjoyable statement of the range which this freedom may take. In the diagram above there is variety in each of the individual works which move off the central spine of movement, but all are related by a keenly felt common discipline of rhythm and form. In the lower drawing each artist is a prima donna, expressing himself in a form as different from his neighbor's as he can make it; yet the whole has a kind of unity only because of the powerful cohesive effect of the central line of movement, which binds them all together and from which they derive their strength.

It is by an understanding of this distinction between the essential and the nonessential that the architect will be free from unnecessary controls and the designer will produce great civic design.

Discipline

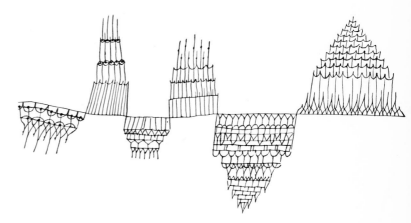

Freedom

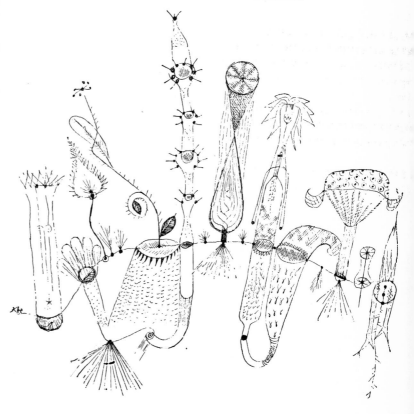

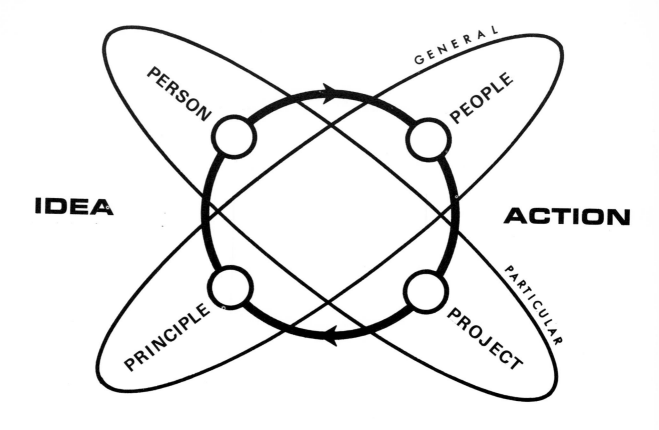

DECISION MAKING

The way in which decisions are made becomes a key element if one thinks of architectural form in terms of growth. On the following two pages are portrayed the growth of the pedestrian systems in central Montreal, developed under the guidance of Vincent Ponte, and in central Philadelphia. On the opposite page the growth of the Philadelphia system is portrayed as it existed simultaneously as an idea in the minds of the public, the idea insofar as it had been resolved into engineering plans, the idea as it existed in the mind of the most imaginative and forward-looking designer, and the idea insofar as it had manifested itself in terms of construction on the ground. Each of these four tracks has its own morphology, rate of change and history of evolution; each interacts with the others in varying degrees. The diagram to the right attempts to symbolize this process, showing horizontally the different states of the design idea in the interest of simplicity here including only two of the four simultaneous tracks.

The diagram above attempts to identify the focal elements in the interplay between idea and action just discussed. These are divided into the general and the particular. Thus the distinction is made between the project and the principle from which it was derived, and which its use will influence, and between the general prevailing opinions and attitudes of the people as against the points of view and proposals of those persons who make up, at any one time, the most active and articulate leadership. Here, again, there is continuous cyclical interaction, not just a one-way street. The leaders may influence the people and the people influence the leaders, or change them. The nature, competence, relevance and, hopefully, inspiring qualities of the design hypothesis that is fed into this process has a great influence over the direction that it takes, and on the relative position of the four focal elements. In the diagram to the right the circular movement illustrated above is stretched out to produce the spiral, the vertical dimension being time.

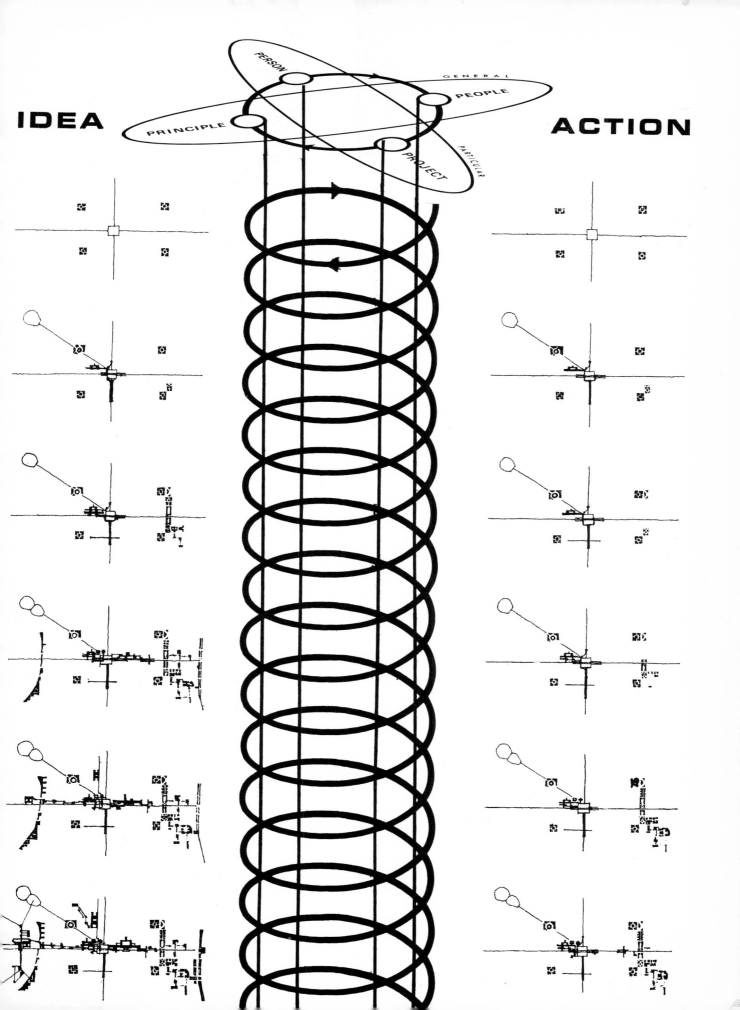

IDEA

ACTION

PERSON

GENERAL

PEOPLE

PRINCIPLE

PARTICULAR

PROJECT

GROWTH OF FORM

PEDESTRIAN SPACES

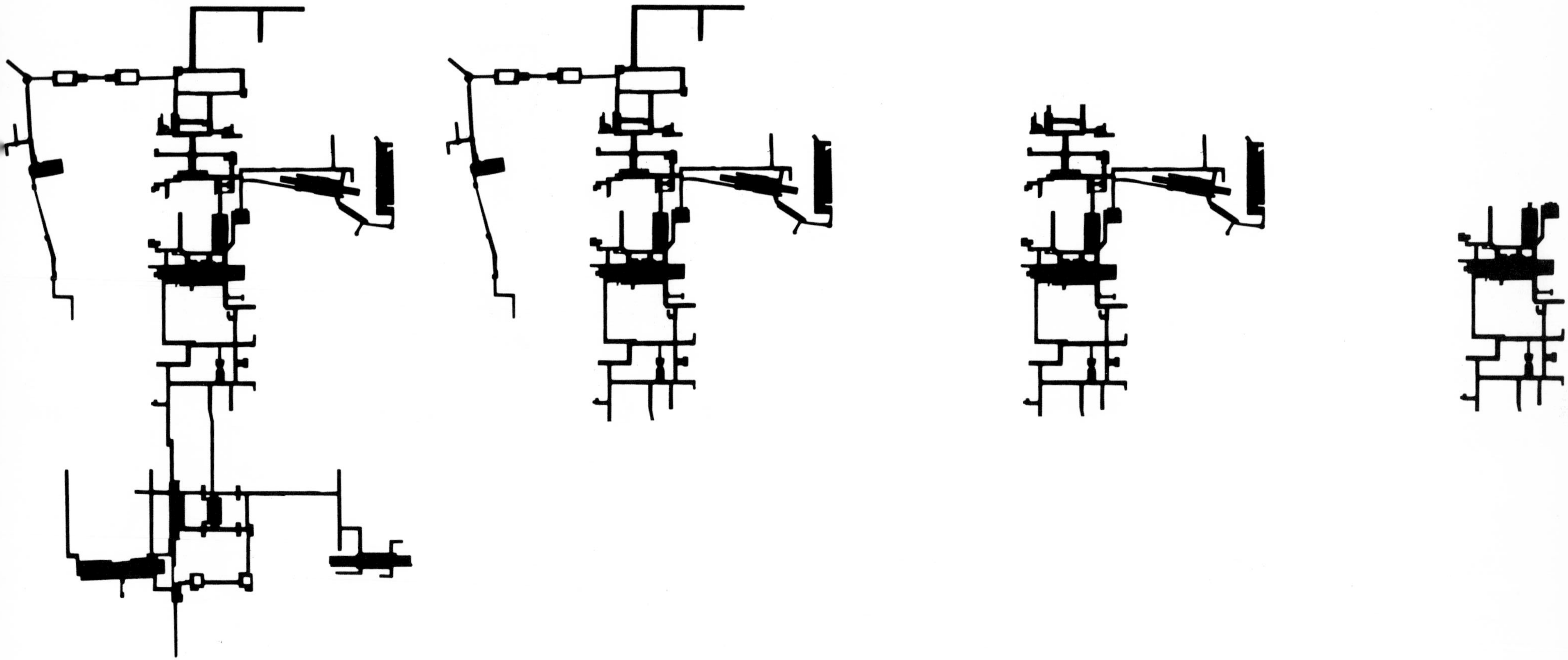

MONTREAL

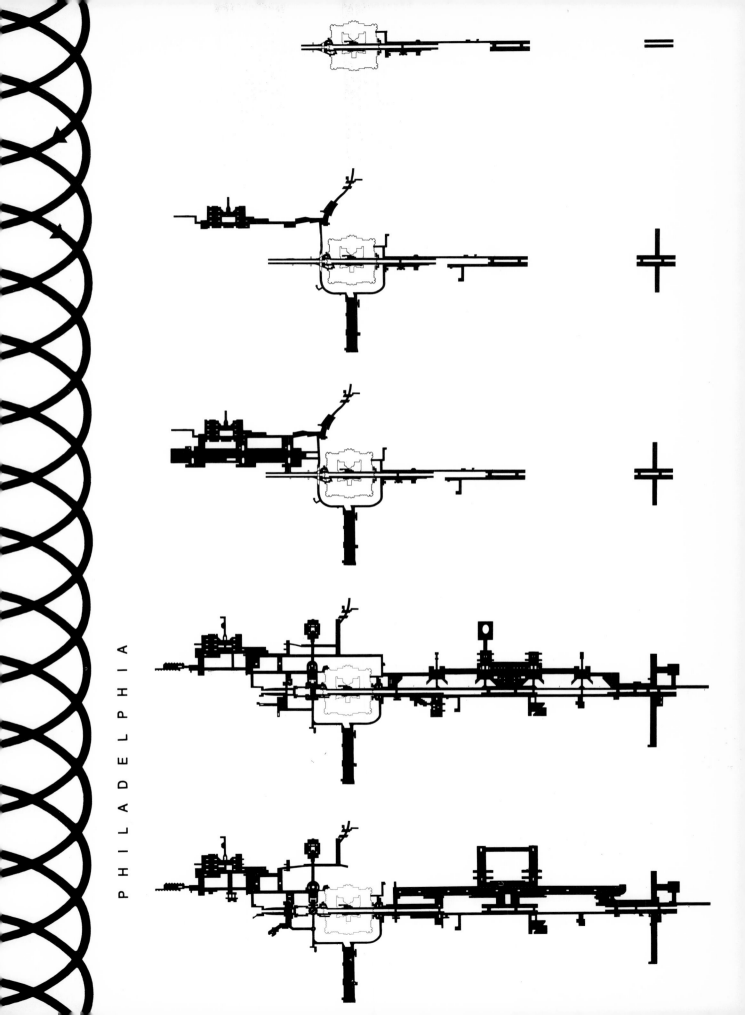

PHILADELPHIA

CYCLICAL FEEDBACK

In 1968 on the Aegean Sea, at the Sixth Delos Symposion conducted under the guidance of C. A. Doxiades, noted Greek city planner, a discussion took place on the parallel between biological processes and human institutions. British biologist C. H. Waddington asserted that technology must permit people to be involved in the evolution of their own environment. Robert A. Aldrich, United States pediatrician, developed the model of the DNA molecule containing the code for man, so arranging and organizing cellular growth in the body that an individual man is produced. Each man contains the code for an environment, and the DNA is selected to remain active in the future according to the quality of the environment which man has produced, in a never-ending cycle. He compared the process with a guided missile, the guidance system consisting of the interaction of internal and external controls. Jonas E. Salk, inventor of the Salk Vaccine, noted that the DNA molecule is getting longer and longer. He pointed out that man was implicit in the earliest DNA, but that to anticipate man at that time would have been impossible. Waddington presented the view that we should organize the process for shaping the future rather than deciding what the future ought to be.

The diagram on the opposite page and those on the following two pages present a model for such a process related to city building. The DNA function, so clearly present in the processes of nature, offers a useful parallel in considering the planning function in human institutions. Rather than imposing a rigid plan for the future, or, indeed, a series of rigid alternatives to choose from, it may be seen as a continuing process of hypothesis formation and reformation in response to feedback. On this basis it is seen as a continually changing system of order which is capable of influencing a multiplicity of individual actions to interrelate to such a degree that some sort of coherent organism is produced. In this sense it contains the code CITY in the same sense that, biologically, DNA contains the code MAN, and, in the same sense, it must reconstruct itself as it receives the impact of the ever-changing environment.

After extended communications some portion of the physical proposals that are contained in the initial hypothesis will be accepted and, through constructive technology, will be realized on the ground, and so become part of the living processes of people. By the very fact of their existence they will have a direct impact on some portion, large or small, of the lives of a varying number of people.

The tragedy of urban design today is that this effect on the quality of life of people of what is actually built is not given the emphasis it deserves, yet it is here that the vital element of feedback is generated. If the designer cuts himself off from the impact of feedback, or if he imposes a filter under which he exposes himself only to that portion of feedback he wants to receive, the entire cyclical process is maimed or halted.

Just how the reality of the impact of concepts, ideas, institutions, processes, proposals, and built environment on people's lives can best be communicated to the persons and institutions responsible for formulating new proposals for city building is very much undetermined. The social sciences and particularly the behavioral sciences should be engaged. Unfortunately these sciences have, in the past, visualized their role as that of observers of social phenomena, and therefore of studying the social acts of the past. To be effective in terms of city building, the social sciences will have to recast their thinking to recognize the general speeding up of the pace of development, the phenomenon of simultaneity, and develop methods of measurement of social change in terms of people's states of mind, of the fundamentals of the quality of life, through social indicators which are sufficiently sensitive to respond to change quickly. These should be designed to provide the administrator with a continuous flow of insights so he may reformulate the hypothesis in the light of the reality of the impact of the program on people's lives. This may well be the major thrust of the innovative effort of the social sciences over the next several decades.

On the following two pages I have attempted to indicate diagrammatically the actual process of hypothesis formation and reformation within this system.

IDEA

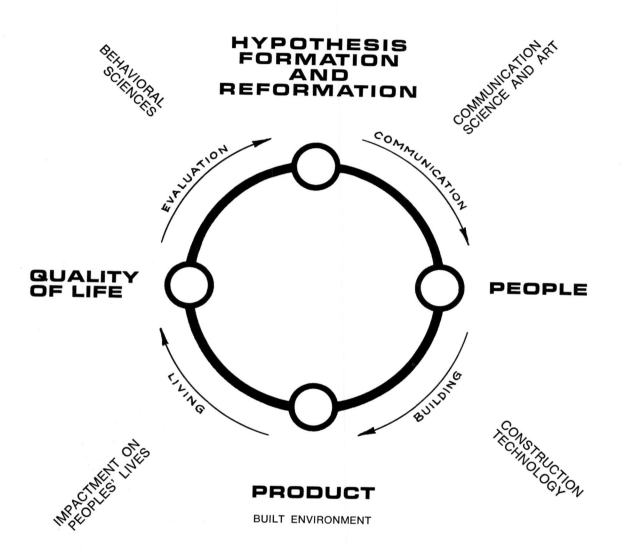

HYPOTHESIS FORMATION AND REFORMATION

BEHAVIORAL SCIENCES

COMMUNICATION SCIENCE AND ART

EVALUATION

COMMUNICATION

QUALITY OF LIFE

PEOPLE

LIVING

BUILDING

IMPACTMENT ON PEOPLES' LIVES

CONSTRUCTION TECHNOLOGY

PRODUCT

BUILT ENVIRONMENT

ACTION

IDEA

HYPOTHESIS FORMATION AND REFORMATION

#1 An hypothesis consists of some model for a system of order, for an interrelationship between several separate elements so as to create a new entity. If it is structured clearly and is communicated to the people involved, they will view its several parts, and, in accord with the binary system of the computer, accept some elements and reject others. The column on the immediate right presents four hypotheses developed in sequence. The column on the far right shows those parts of these hypotheses which are rejected by the community; the center column indicates the parts which are acceptable to the community.

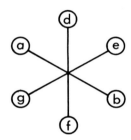

#2 The result of the first go-round of the feedback cycle is the destruction of hypothesis number 1 by the community. The product which survived community review is not a system of order but rather several disconnected elements and relationships (top center column). It is (or should be) now the function of the planner to use these elements as the basis upon which to structure a new hypothesis. Additional elements and new connections must be added to reformulate a whole.

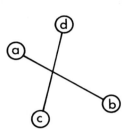

#3 Hypothesis number 2 is acted upon by the community (which may be a neighborhood group, the members of a school board, the citizens of an entire city, or, indeed, the United States Congress), which rejects most of the new elements and relationships (middle diagram, per right column) but which accepts elements "e," and thereby establishes the new direction of thrust which becomes the crucial force in the further hypothesis formation. This, as seen on the right, grows more complex.

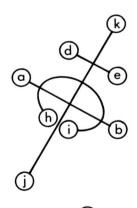

#4 The community rejects the central line of authority in hypothesis number 3 but otherwise finds it acceptable. The hypothesis reformulator restructures it into the form shown to the right. Three new elements are added, the central line of authority is replaced by an open vector or direction of thrust, and this hypothesis is found acceptable by the community and so is built. Thus it becomes the subject of evaluation to determine whether, in life use, it actually fulfills its objective.

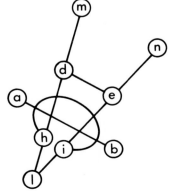

ACTION

COMMUNITY
+
ACCEPT

COMMUNITY
—
REJECT

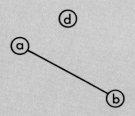

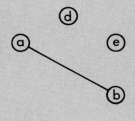

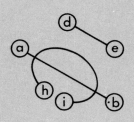

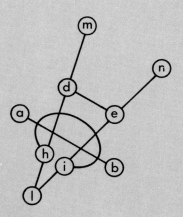

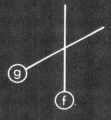

Note that several hypotheses in the left-hand column form no coherent sequence, nor do the elements of community rejection above. The portions of the disparate hypotheses acceptable to the community (center column) make a pattern of coherent growth. The form of the final system is implicit in each step of community acceptance, almost as though the community previewed the final product.

SYNTHESIS

The most noteworthy aspect of the process portrayed on the previous two pages is that the final hypothesis is the creation of neither the community nor the designer, but is the product of the interaction of each.

For such interaction to be productive, two conditions must be present:

1. An understanding on the part of both the designer and the community of the nature of the process and how it works.

2. A willingness on the part of each to plunge into it fully, to give of themselves, to submit to the discipline it entails, and to bring to it, fully, the creative input it demands.

Continued exposure to participation in this process will have a profound effect both on the individuals and on the institutions which surround them.

For the purposes of architecture it will require a rethinking of the fundamental relationship between the professional and the client, as well as who the client really is. Traditional habits of architectural arrogance will have to give way to an honest commitment to the principle that the client has a role. Traditional commitment to the interests of the individual client will have to give way to a more inclusive definition of client, under which concern for the immediate employer is extended to take into account the people and the community which surround him. For this to be fully incorporated into the rules, procedures, philosophy, and practice of architecture, landscape architecture, and urban and regional planning, a basic reshaping of the professions and their educational institutions is required.

For the individual designer, architect, or planner, nothing less than a revolution of his own self-image is necessary. However, if he proves to be capable of embarking on the process, if he is able and willing to expose himself fully to feedback, including the pain this implies, and in a valid sense, employ the feedback in hypothesis reformation, he will find that he himself is greatly changed by the interaction; that he is tempered by the heat of the confrontation, and that, after some time, he will not be able to tell in hypothesis formation how much is the product of his own internal drives and how much comes from his immersion in community values.

For the community this process means a new articulation of leadership and a new development of procedures, of delegated responsibility for negotiation, of quick review and decision making. It involves acceptance of the value of professional input (not necessarily from outside the community), and it involves abandonment of the simplistic notions that have grown up around the words "advocacy planning" under which it is assumed that those persons who, at any one time, purport to represent the community, actually do, and that they, of themselves, can do the whole job with no outside help.

For the individual in the community the fully effective operation of this feedback cycle involves some degree of self-restraint and self-discipline because it implies listening on both sides. However, when the individual in the community finds by doing that the process is really working, his view of himself and the society in which he is functioning will so radically alter that the changes will come about quite naturally.

Finally, it is important to stress again that hypothesis formation and reformation may occur anywhere, within the profession, within government, within the community, but without it the process will be meaningless.

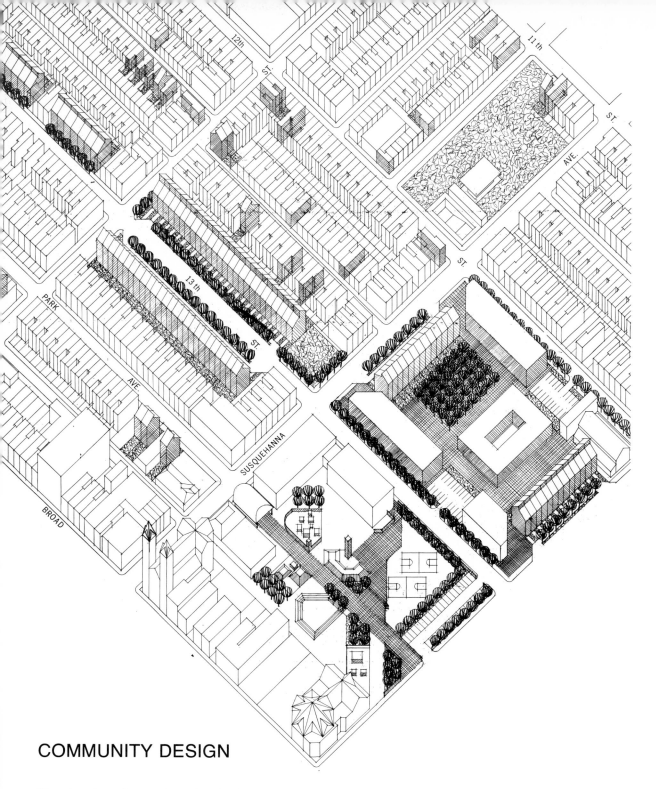

COMMUNITY DESIGN

The drawing above, done by Patric B. Dawe for the Philadelphia City Planning Commission, shows how a plan for an old neighborhood can give a new sense of orientation by articulation of movement systems and by injection of new structures and open spaces which respect and enhance the structures already there. Instead of tearing down the whole area, new houses are inserted into the old fabric lot by lot as gaps occur, thus giving an or-ganic revitalization which strengthens rather than destroys community institutions and psychological and human associations, Erikson's radii of signif-icant relations. (See pages 46–47.)

This plan shows that very strong design articula-tion is entirely consistent with a process that involves residents in playing a vital role, and a program that preserves most of the existing community.

PUTTING IDEAS TO WORK—PHILADELPHIA

The essential nature of the "design idea" or "design structure" can now be examined, with the help of Paul Klee and with the actual example of the three towers in Society Hill, Philadelphia, by architect Ieoh Ming Pei.

The left diagram, by Klee, below, consists of nothing but lines and suggests, in its entirety, channels of movement through space. The right drawing below, by Pei, a part of his design for Society Hill submitted to the Redevelopment Authority on behalf of his client, Mr. Zeckendorf, bears a curious resemblance to the Klee pattern and shows that he was thinking of the placement of his three towers in relation to the thrusts of movement in the pedestrian system around them. Here we have a design structure consisting of two elements: the paths of movement, shown in hatching; and the mass of the five towers, three in Society Hill and two by Washington Square to the left. It is the combination of the mass of the towers and the space of the movement that constitutes the essential design structure. When this is once established, the architect, working within the remaining area, is freed of rigid controls except as they are demanded to maintain the integrity of the design structure. Thus the architecture may not penetrate the upper air, which must be reserved for the five points to retain the essential order. The entrance into the area of his design must be related to the form of the movement system, but beyond this he may have latitude of design.

A basic design structure is the binding together of perception sequences shared by large numbers of people, thereby developing a group image from shared experiences and so giving a sense of underlying order to which individual freedom and variety are related.

It may be asked how this differs from all the pedestrian-oriented designs in history, and why the point of simultaneous systems at different speeds, discussed on page 252, is emphasized. Here Pei has given a brilliant answer because he has so placed and designed his towers that they relate with sensitivity to the delicate and fragile eighteenth- and nineteenth-century structures that form their foreground on the west and south, yet at the same time they serve as a powerful articulation point in relation to the fast movement on the Delaware Expressway, dominating the sweep of the regional flow of the Delaware River. (See pages 296 and 297.)

On pages 266 and 267 is shown the evolution of the design structure in Society Hill, from the idea in the 1947 Better Philadelphia Exhibition to the fully matured design of today. On page 266 are two of the five squares of the original 1683 Penn Plan for Philadelphia, Franklin Square to the north and Washington Square to the south. Connecting these two is the monumental Independence Mall extending northward from Independence Hall, the most important historic shrine in the United States. This, with the 1944 proposal for the eastward extension of the historic park to bind together three additional historic structures, is the work of architect Roy Larson. The proposal for the network of garden footpaths is mine. These paths, separated from the streets, pass through the middle of the blocks and extend the pedestrian system, linking together a number of old churches and houses in the Greenway System.

The plan on page 267 shows the extension of the design structure to the Delaware River, and, in the other direction, its link with Washington Square. Also seen (in red) are several contemporary buildings, including the five Pei towers. The circuit of movement was extended and completed on the north by a pedestrian system connecting the waterfront with Christ Church and the Friends Meeting House, and a synagogue designed by Louis Kahn. The new structures are integrated with the movement system, which in turn was derived from the natural features and regional topography, the total providing the design structure preordering the area.

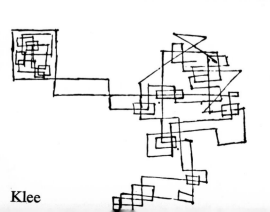

Klee

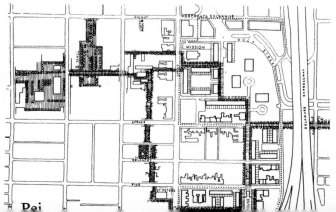

Pei

PAINFUL SEARCH FOR FORM

1947

While the form of the Pei towers in Philadelphia may seem obvious now, it is the result of a long and painful search. The design I made (right) for the 1947 Exhibition had a series of slabs arbitrarily placed on an inward-looking system and failed to provide any elegance or order to the area around. The plan was so timid that it provided for a strip of light industry between the apartments and the river, and recreation on the river was confined to a small marina between commercial piers.

1957

After a ten-year lapse during which the historic areas continued to decline, architects Vincent Kling, Roy Larson, and Oskar Stonorov were engaged to reconsider the 1947 plan, and they produced the proposal shown here. The sweep was enlarged as a continuous design from Washington Square to the river, but the wide scattering of the complex forms of the tall towers and slabs raised difficult questions about the relationship with the eighteenth-century buildings in Society Hill.

1958

The Redevelopment Authority retained architect Preston Andrade, working with Willo von Moltke of the Planning Commission staff, to refine further the proposals for the area, prior to advertising the project for bids. The great advance was made to simplify the mass of the apartments into six towers (three at the waterfront and three at Washington Square), but even here there was a six-story apartment slab opposite the most precious eighteenth-century landmarks on Third Street.

1960

The competition was won by Mr. Zeckendorf, undoubtedly primarily because of the brilliant design of his architect Ieoh Ming Pei, lower right. It may be asked what latitude is left for the architect if there is a directive for the competition as specific as the one shown above. Pei answered this question by incorporating the good qualities of the earlier design and carying it on to a much higher level. The apartment slabs are replaced by three-story town houses which provide a splendid transition from the Colonial houses across the street to the three towers. (See page 297.)

INDEPENDENCE HALL IS CIRCLED.

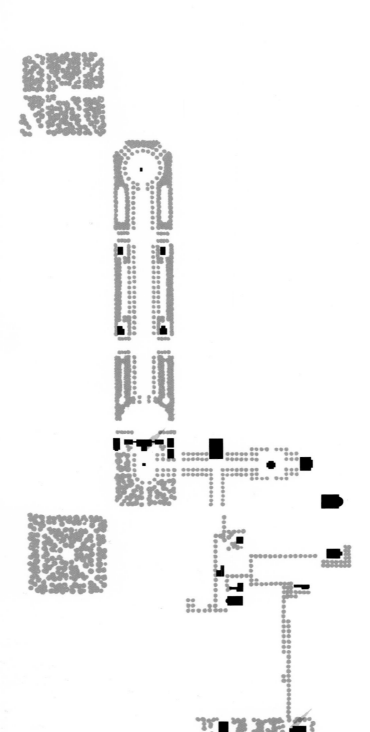

1947

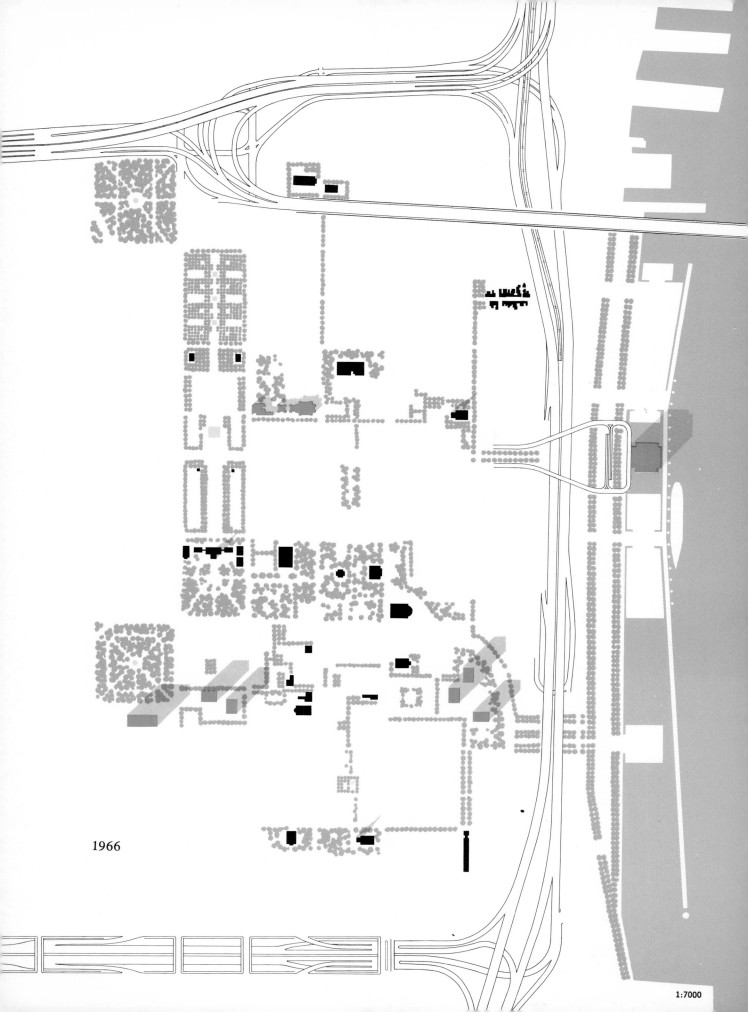

1966

1:7000

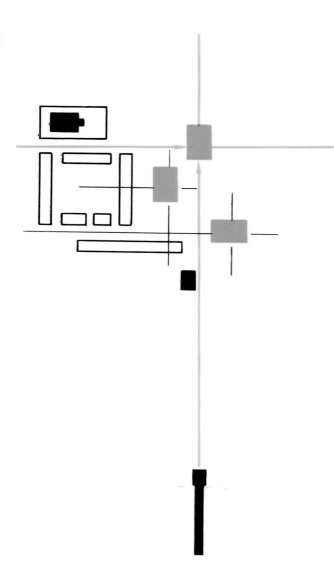

FORM DETERMINED BY
DESIGN STRUCTURE

The diagram at left shows that the position of the three Pei towers was precisely determined by design forces impinging on the site from the outside, rather than being arbitrary placement related only to the site itself. As built, these three towers resolve the design structure and serve as visual linkages between the pedestrian and automobile systems.

The northern tower is on the north-extending axis created by the eighteenth-century market in the bed of Second Street, and in the other direction by the line of the Greenway extension past historic Saint Paul's Church, shown in black. The southernmost tower is on an axis with a movement determined by the depth of the historic houses on Spruce Street, and the intermediate tower is the logical resolution of the positions of the other two. None of these can move in any direction without destroying the unity of the design and the larger system. Indeed, a test of almost any design is whether the buildings can be shifted without damage to the plan. Here, the answer would be no.

On pages 270 and 271 is shown the evolution of the entire design structure of Center City in which the elements described in this section are woven together into a total three dimensional system of space organization. In black are shown Independence Hall, the Art Museum at the end of the Parkway, and City Hall at the Intersection of the two 1683 William Penn axes. The central core of most intense activity is shown in gray, threaded through by the ever-growing pedestrian system one level beneath the street, shown in yellow, and the footway one level above the street connecting with the department stores shown in white.

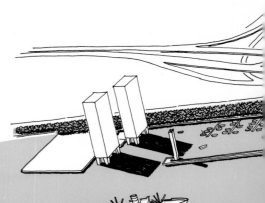

FROM FORM TO ARCHITECTURAL EXPRESSION

We have seen how form grows out of design structure, these two representing two essential phases of the design process. There is a third and interrelated element, namely architectural expression. Louis Kahn has made the distinction between form that "belongs to everybody" and design that "is the architect's own." I would add the design structure as a necessary first element, and replace Kahn's "design" by "architectural expression."

In the case of the Pei towers the function of relating the nineteenth- to the twentieth-century city would have failed if Pei had not detailed his towers with supreme sensitivity to this requirement. The actual architecture, in which the wall supports the structure, evokes the muntined windows of the eighteenth-century buildings, and is based on the same structural principle, but also is powerfully effective seen from the expressway and the river.

The restraints or freedoms of architectural expression are determined by the role that the building plays in the larger design structure. The drawing below, of Robert Geddes' design for the development of the Delaware waterfront, presents the case.

With respect to the five Pei towers in Society Hill, shown with red tops, the land area consists of

a confusion of eighteenth- and nineteenth-century structures, with garden footpaths threaded between them. Therefore, if there is to be order, it will be order in the sky. The perfectly positioned shafts of the identical Pei towers provide this discipline, encompassing the space like calipers, and by the tension between them give order to the entire space.

The Geddes plan is quite the opposite. In it there is order on the ground. The long disciplined rows of trees and the uniform base line of the embarcadero give a unified platform from which may spring buildings of most startling variety at carefully modulated points. Here the architect of each may be a virtuoso and indulge in self-expression in the way suggested in the lower drawing on page 253. Because the buildings have clear individual positions in the larger design structure, and because there is order on the ground, the architectural expression may be most individualistic and still an over-all order will be achieved.

There is a striking architectural parallel in the design of two buildings, the Château de Chambord which has order on the ground and tumult in the sky, and the new Boston City Hall which has opposite characteristics.

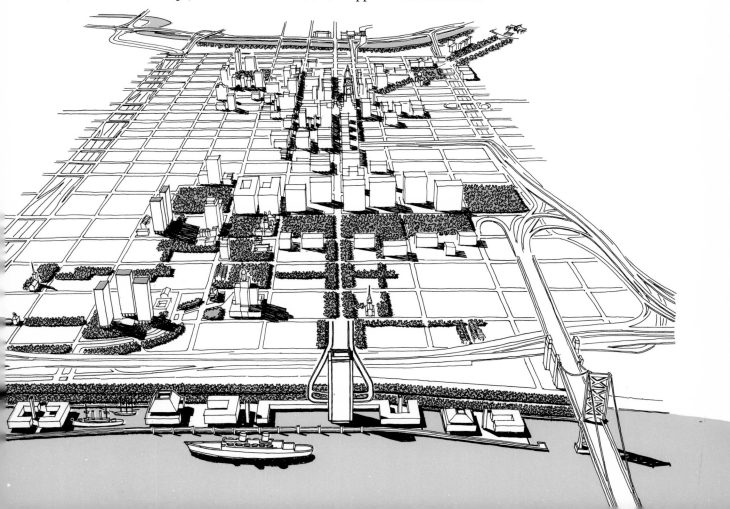

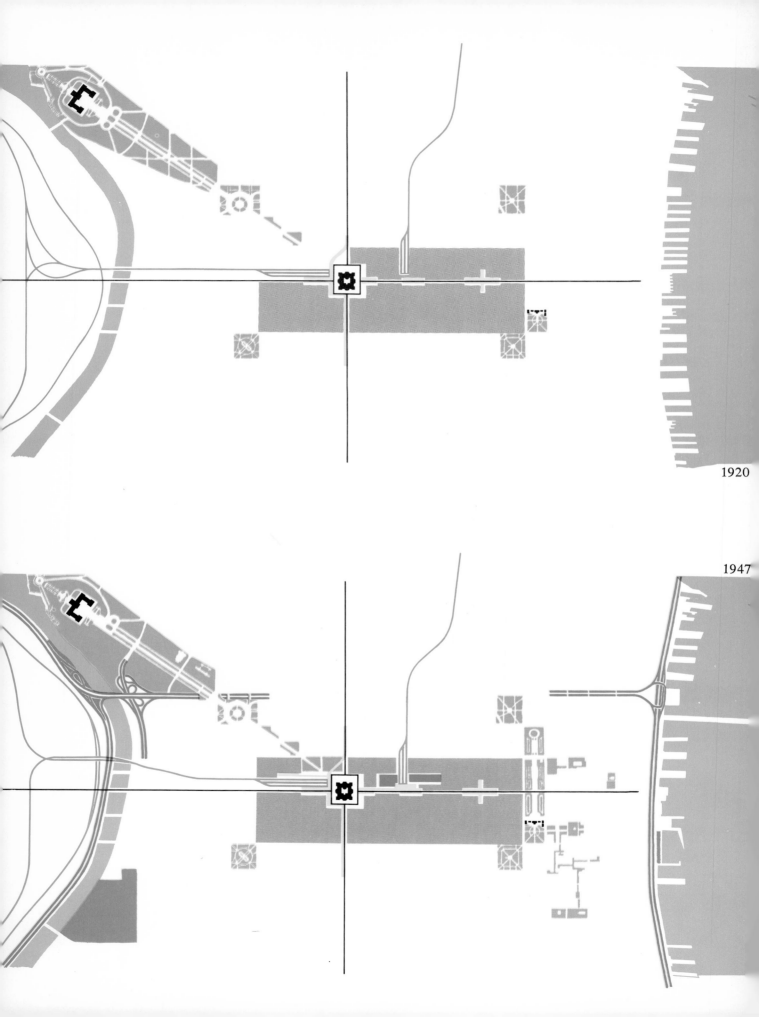

1920

1947

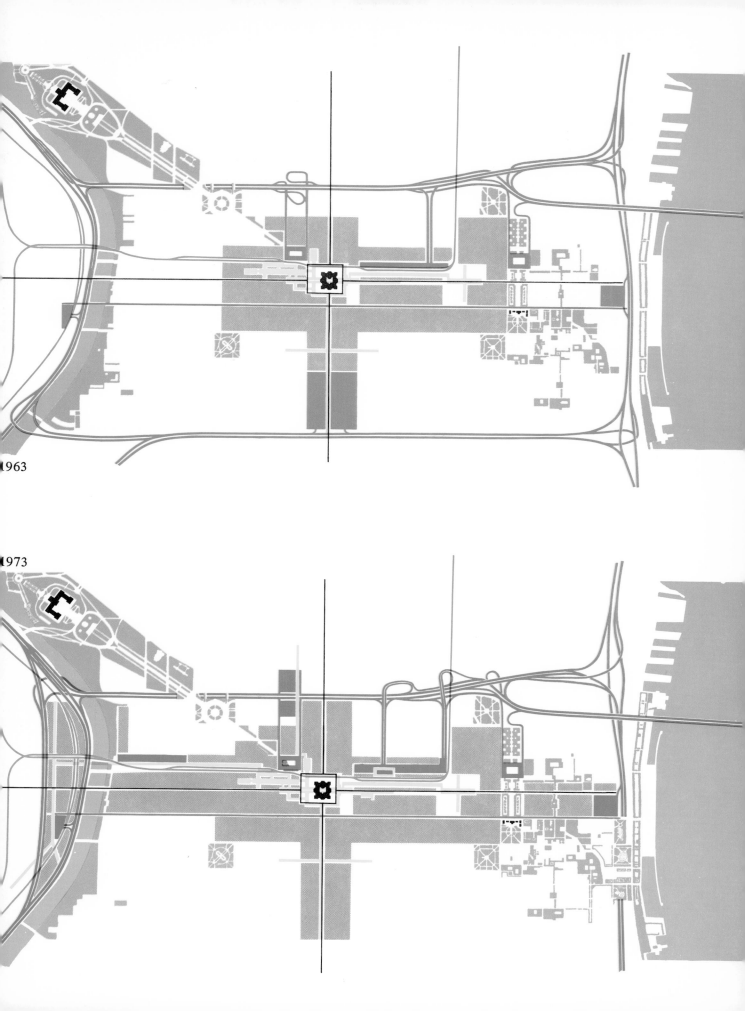

1963

1973

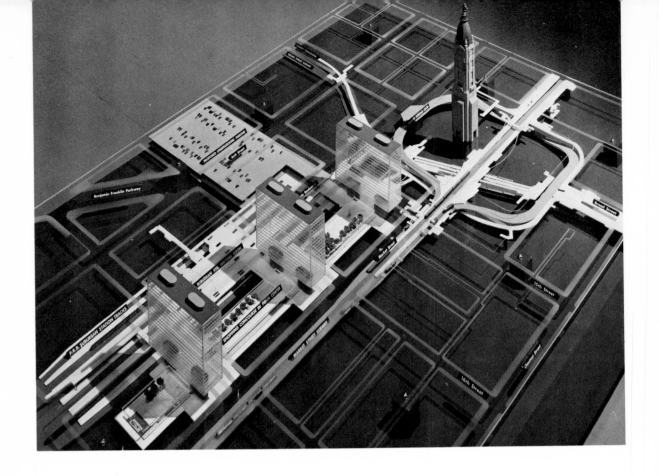

GENESIS OF THE IMAGE

Because Society Hill is peripheral to the most intense civic core, the separation of the pedestrian and the vehicular movement system can be achieved on the same ground plane. As the designer moves into the core itself, the separation can be achieved only in the third dimension, by the establishment of multiple overlapping planes of movement at different levels. This is seen in the Penn Center Project developed by the Pennsylvania Railroad on the site of an abandoned elevated track.

In the original 1952 City Planning Commission proposal for this area the dominant pedestrian movement occurred one level below the street on the plane labeled "Shopping Concourse in Penn Center" in the model above. This plane, with its gardens open to the sky, and extending beneath the streets the whole length of the project, was relegated to a subdominant position by the modification of this original plan which provided

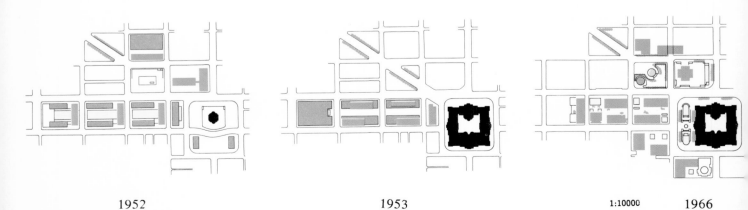

1952   1953   1:10000   1966

for roofing over most of the space. Ever since, the lower-level plane has been seeking to emerge into the sunlight and has succeeded in doing so to a remarkable degree. Three steps in the evolution of the plan are shown in the diagram opposite, in which the lower-level plane, as it is exposed to the sky, is indicated in yellow. City Hall is shown in black.

The first step after the rejection of the City Planning Commission's 1952 plan was the preparation of a new one by Robert Dowling in 1953. This accepted the continuity of the lower-level pedestrian plane and its connection with the subway, underground commuter railroad, bus terminal, and parking garage, but it roofed over the space in its entirety. The Planning Commission suggested that the roof be pierced at three carefully distributed points to bring some light and air to the lower level. The suggestion was incorporated into the official plan and has been carried out. The IBM Company not only gratuitously added another garden space, but, in accordance with the plans of Vincent Kling, consultant to the Planning Commission on the original proposal for Penn Center, built a series of levels within the building as steps down from the street to the pedestrian plane. The Central Penn Bank Building, also designed by Kling, added another opening. The decision of the Philadelphia City Government to purchase the narrow block just to the west of City Hall eliminated the proposed building which would have cut off the view of City Hall Tower from the Penn Center esplanade. This block allows room for another garden in the plaza, linking the understreet movements to the Municipal Services Building to the north. (See pages 278–279.) In this building, also designed by architect Kling, there is a remarkable expression (shown in the Arnold Newman photograph below) of the emerging importance of the lower-level pedestrian plane in the two-story glass-enclosed lobbies within the volume of the building. This is a re-expression of the original idea.

THE IMAGE MATURES

The photograph opposite is approximately the view out of his car window which the traveler experiences upon his arrival downtown. This lower-level garden, also visible in the left side of the model below, embellished with a fountain by Gerd Utescher paid for by schoolchildren's pennies, serves as an attractive entrance to center city and is, so far as I know, the first garden ever built in a subway.

Construction of this garden set into motion the process described under "The Nature of Design" on page 33. As thousands of people — businessmen, professionals, politicians, shoppers and workers, as well as people just out for enjoyment — encountered, experienced, and moved through this space, the principle of lowering the earth to the subway level, of visually connecting the lower and street levels, of punctuating the continuity of sensation of going downtown by a stimulating and orienting experience immediately upon arrival, moved from an abstraction into an experience shared by large numbers of people. Because this experience was found to be pleasurable by these people, and because it was evidently not an isolated thing but

a link in a chain of experiences, the consensus that developed naturally extended itself into further continuities, links, and connections.

The model below, developed by the Philadelphia Department of Public Property, is the outgrowth of this shared experience. Here are shown, by means of transparent planes, the complex interactions and cross connections of the multi-level intersecting subway and subway-surface systems (blue), and the network of pedestrian units (brown), linking all the parts together.

The physical form represented here is the product of an unusual process of design. The Department of Public Property involved architect Vincent Kling not as a consultant to McCormick Taylor Associates, the subway engineers, but as co-partner with equal status. Thus the subway became not an engineering form decorated by an architect but an extension of architecture underground.

The illustration on pages 278 and 279, a cross section perpendicular to the main axis of Penn Center intersecting the two circles in the model below, shows how the original idea for Penn Center has grown.

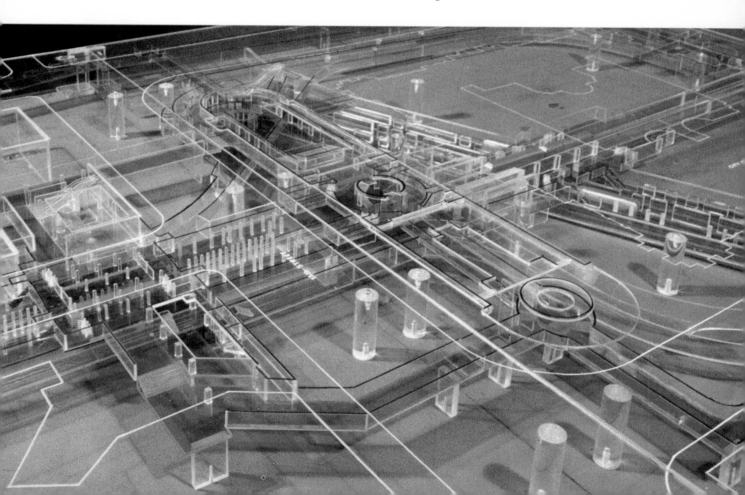

MOVEMENT SYSTEMS IN ACTION

The basic idea we had been struggling for since 1947 received its most lucid expression in the two models shown on the opposite page, prepared by the architectural firm of Skidmore, Owings and Merrill for the Market East project. The upper model shows the interaction of the movement systems in their pure form, subway and railroad, blue; pedestrian concourse, red; street level, orange; bus and parking, yellow; elevator cores, white. These are presented as the generators of architectural form, and below is the model of the form so generated.

On this page, below, is a drawing by Thomas Todd, of Wallace, McHarg, Roberts and Todd, architects, of the proposed design structure for downtown Buffalo, showing the application of this principle to an entire center city. The elevator cores rise out of a land area richly modulated by separated vehicular and pedestrian movements on different levels, and again there is an interweaving of the old and the new.

The drawings on the next two pages show how, east of Penn Center, branches from a central pedestrian movement system were extended into three separate building projects where they became the core of the building design, each designer working out his own resolution of the interconnection of the various levels with each other and with the outside, this resolution forming the central focus of each plan.

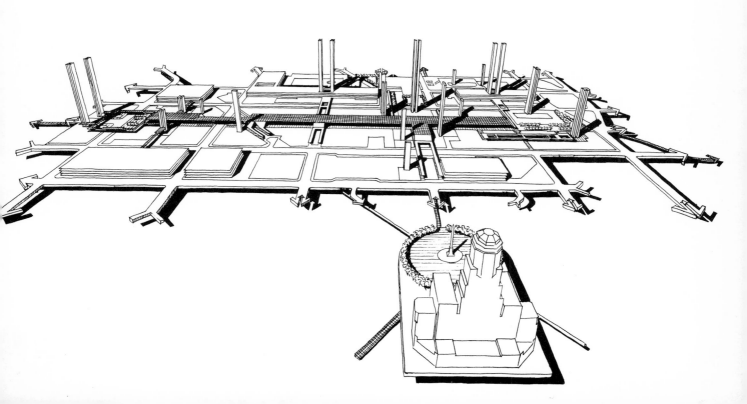

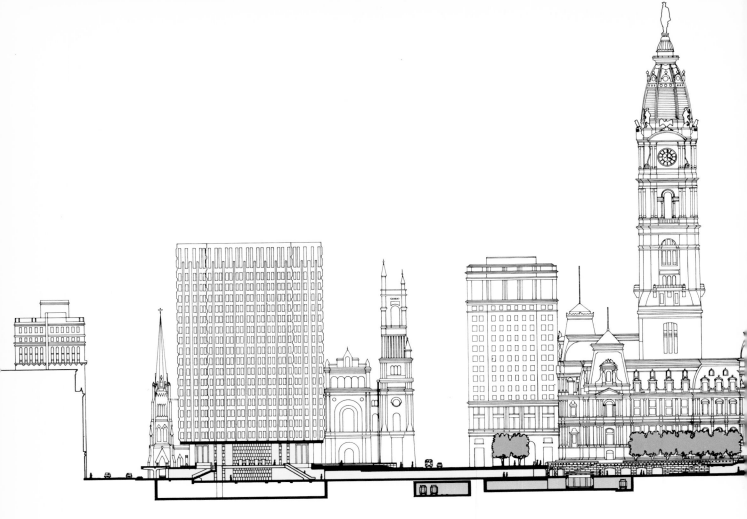

Above is the Municipal Services Building with its two-story glass-walled lobby, illustrated below, which functionally and visually integrates the below-street and street levels and brings the street picture into the building.

Above is West Plaza, a sunken court adjacent to City Hall, which provides an open-air experience in the continuity of pedestrian movement below the street (yellow) and brings light into the subway (blue) two levels down.

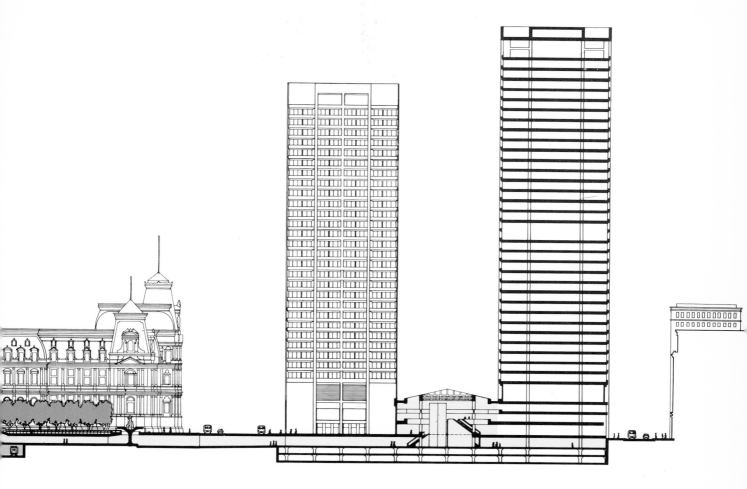

The drawing below and the one to its left show the sunken court, its cascade and stairways, and the splendid views it provides of the ever-orienting City Hall and adjacent buildings, two of which have a direct axial relation with it.

Above is a section and below a drawing of the 1500 Market Street development with its central glass-roofed galleria extending up from the pedestrian plane, a still different architectural expression of the connection between levels.

279

BEGINNING OF
ARCHITECTURAL EXPRESSION

The building of the pedestrian movement system in Society Hill to the east and Penn Center to the west emphasized the need for a connecting link through the rather rundown retail area of East Market Street. This would reinforce the shopping area and establish a link between the three department stores at Eighth and Market Streets and the business activity clustering around City Hall. The answer to the need was Market East.

Here the basic concept was a pedestrian area punctuated by gardens one level below the street, accessible to the subway, and an extension of the underground commuter railroad system. The shops at street level were set back behind covered walkways, and above the street a continuous shopping promenade connected with the bus terminal and parking garages with their own ramps to the expressway. The four department stores were joined to the promenade by glass-enclosed bridges above the street. The architectural expression of enrichment of points of entry at the three levels is depicted in these 1960 perspective drawings by Willo von Moltke. Below at right is shown the view into the open garden from the windows of the subway cars, at center right is the view from the street, and above that the shopping promenade as it overlooks Market Street and the subway train beside the garden below.

As in Penn Center, when the work was started there was no program. Many architects and planners felt that nothing should be done until a program had been formulated. But by that time it would have been too late. The spatial organization of the regional movement systems itself produced a hypothesis for a program, and, once this was clearly expressed (as illustrated here), it set into motion the process of democratic review, controversy, and feedback, so setting up a force which brings about design.

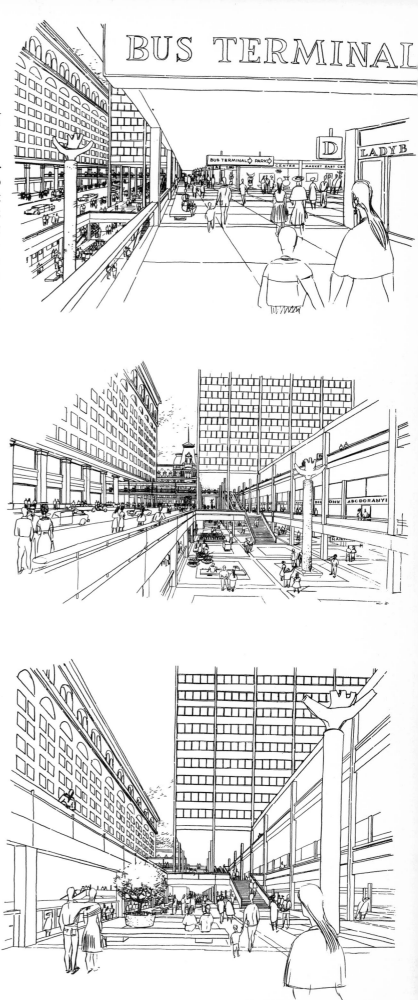

DEMOCRATIC FEEDBACK

The planners of the system shown on page 281 thought they had done a good job, but the economic analysts took a different view. The division of retail activity into three levels created more linear foot frontage of shops than it was felt at that time that the area could support. Also, the rather complex interweaving of public and private spaces, and of retail shops and office buildings, created problems for getting the enterprise financed.

To overcome these objections the planners, working with architect Romaldo Giurgola who in 1963 made the upper drawing on the left and in 1964 the drawings on the next two pages, developed a second scheme with one dominant air-conditioned, glass-roofed, shop-lined pedestrian esplanade, one level above the street. The esplanade, connected with the subway by escalators, provides dramatic views up and down the cross streets where it bridges them.

The drawing at left shows the effect the building would create from Market Street looking north. On the elevation below, the esplanade (indicated in yellow) extends from City Hall through the department store group. The subway is shown in blue.

This splendid scheme solved the multiple-level problems, but it met with disaster because the department store presidents said that they did not want the people entering their stores at the second story, since this would require a reorganization of their retailing methods. So, once again, the plan had to be rethought and the design restructured.

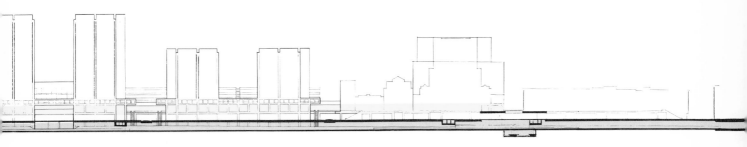

STRUCTURING THE DIALOGUE

The next plan for Market East (above) re-established the level below the street as the dominant plane and obliterated the street plane as a major feature in the central section of the development. In this respect the design turned full circle—back to the original idea for Penn Center (page 272). In the new plan the air-conditioned pedestrian mall rises six stories from the dominant plane. This is bordered on the north side by the bus terminal, parking garages, and commuter railroad station, on the south side by the subway and shops, and above by a diagonal glass wall. The volume of space so defined, running parallel with Market Street, is penetrated by streets passing through glass-enclosed tubes. The streets move onto a bridge structure as they pass north of Market Street between the lower-level courts which serve as pedestrian entrances to the subway and the mall.

On the opposite page, the drawing at top shows a view of a north-south street, looking north from Market Street, which penetrates the sunken mall on a bridge. The drawing below is a view inside the pedestrian mall, looking west. To the left a subway car is visible, to the right above are the bus terminal and parking floors and, in the background, the glass-enclosed street passing through the space of the mall. The drawings on the next two pages show how this plan fits in with the linear development along Market Street.

In accordance with the process pictured on page 259, the planner created a complete, internally consistent hypothesis in the first plan for Market East (page 281) and clothed it in a sufficiently clear image to generate feedback. The negative response to this proposal would have resulted in a standstill had the designer not been able to employ the criticism as a positive force and create a new design with a quite different internal system of order. The negative response to this caused the third restructuring and the creation of yet another design, which turned out, from both an aesthetic and practical point of view, to be vastly superior to the other two. It simplified the financial problems of development and administration, and from the standpoint of planning changed from an expression of regional forces as a system of space organization into one in which those forces are expressed in terms of structure.

Thus, out of the process of dialogue can come a plan of force, provided the planner is capable of communicating, of receiving, of restructuring.

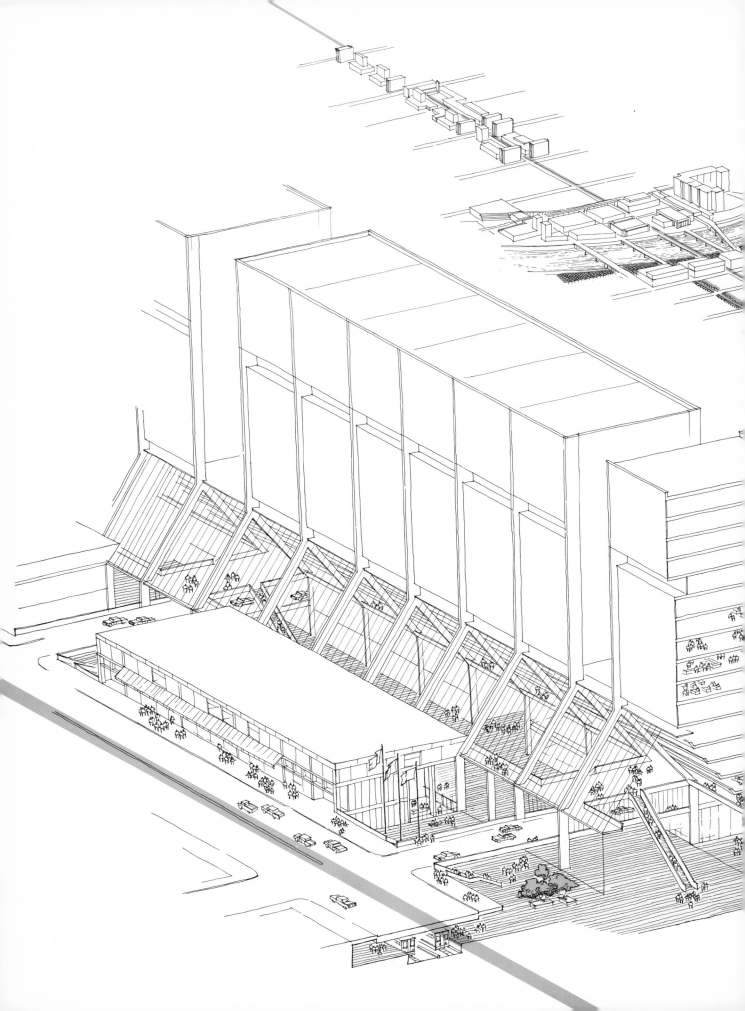

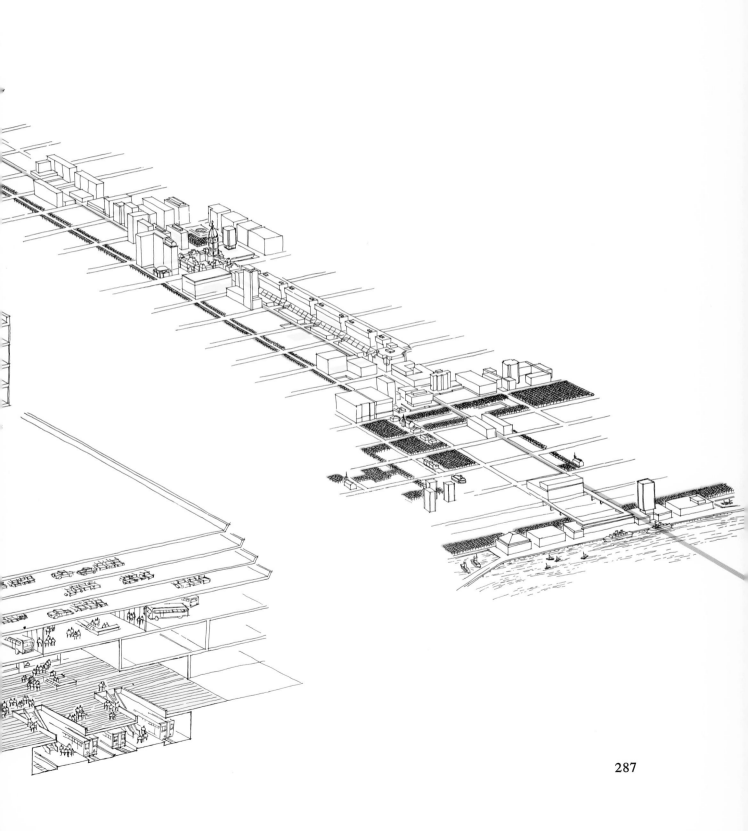

287

THE DIALOGUE CONTINUES

The next step in the evolution of Market East was to subject the Planning Commission proposal to rigorous structural and economic analysis and to carry forward the plan into a more detailed state. For this purpose the Philadelphia Redevelopment Authority engaged the architectural firm of Skidmore, Owings and Merrill.

This firm developed the plan in much greater engineering detail than had previously been possible and through models and drawings such as those on this page and page 276 made the basic idea much clearer than it had been before, and exposed the citizens to a deeper appreciation of the richness of its potential.

Through this process public enthusiasm for Market East was generated, and confidence in it was built up in the minds of the business and political leaders.

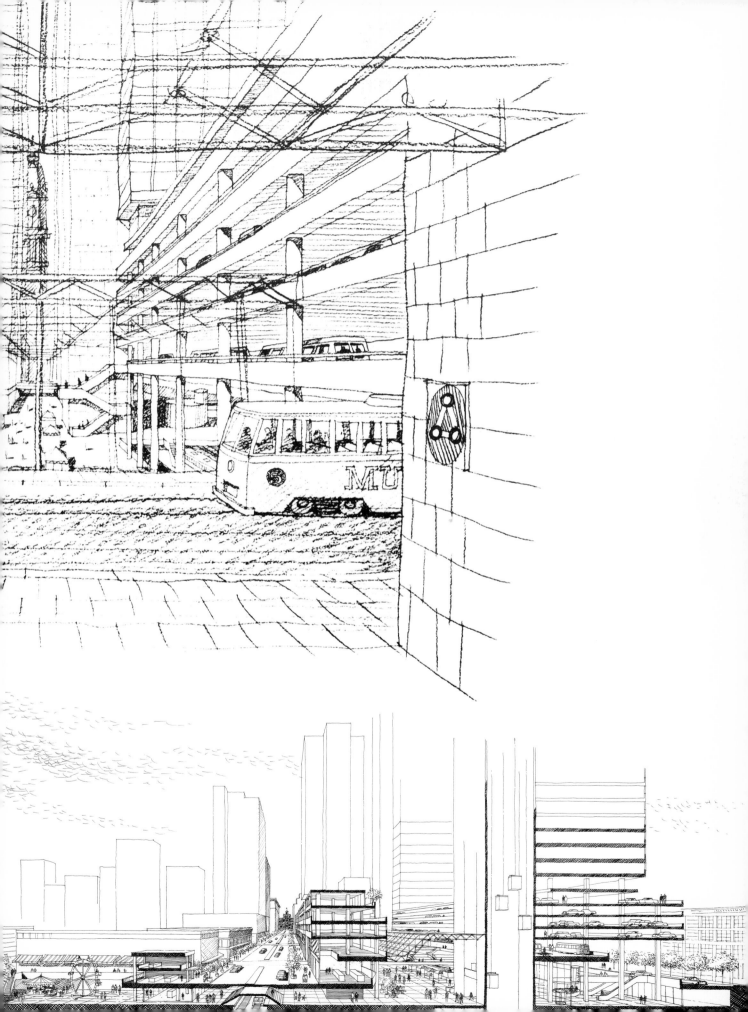

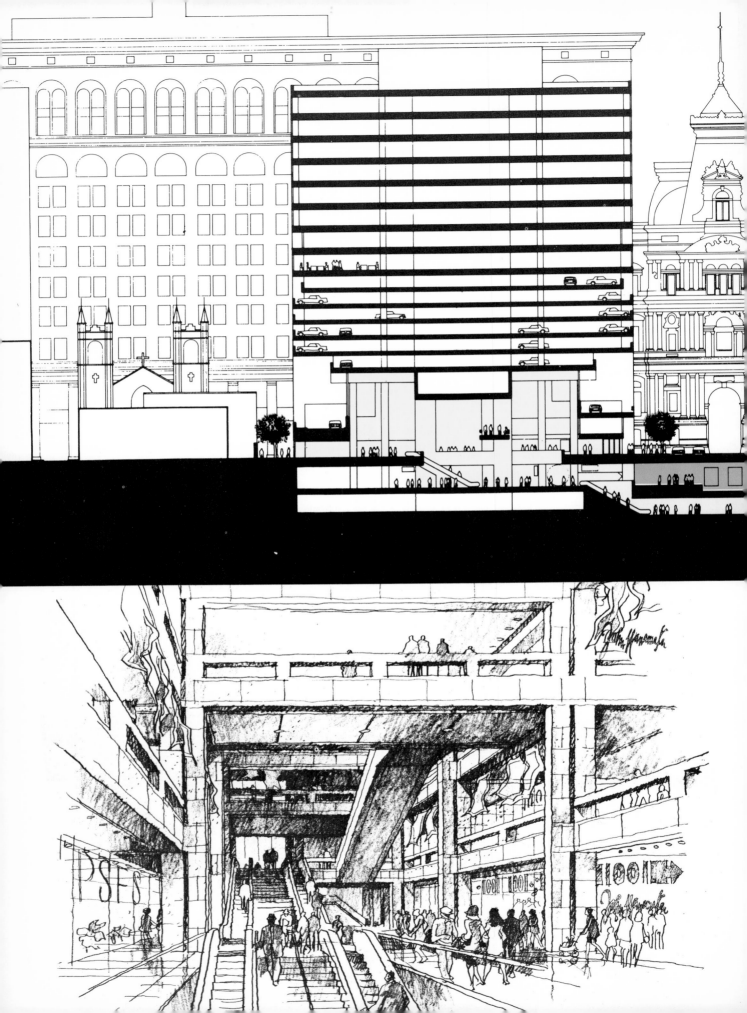

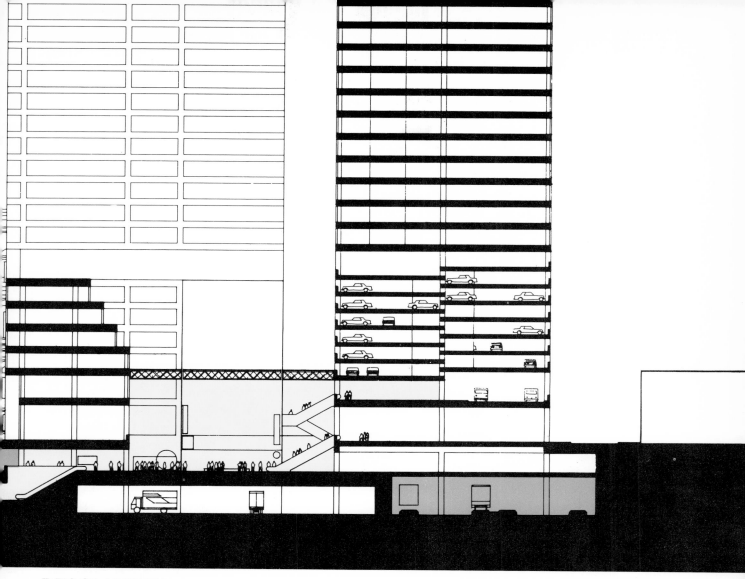

RESOLUTION

Philadelphia by 1969 had become a sort of proving ground to determine whether or not, in actual practice, simultaneous movement systems provide a viable base for urban design. Through the remarkable work of John Bower, a young Philadelphia architect schooled in the offices of the City Planning Commission, and Vincent Kling, now a partner in the firm of Bower & Fradley, which succeeded Skidmore, Owings and Merrill as coordinating architect for Market East, the answer is emerging clearly in the affirmative.

Shown above is the cross section of Bower's plan for a new structure, 1234 Market Street, between the Philadelphia Saving Fund Society, PSFS, and the John Wanamaker Department Store, (left side of the section), connecting them both below and above the street.

The basic concept of Market East on the

right side of the cross section is picked up and carried forward in the Bower design. The enclosed public pedestrian spaces are shown in yellow. The pedestrian walkway with its two escalators passes underneath the Market Street subway (shown in blue), leads into the lower lobby which in turn connects with the two- and three-story spaces which burst upward and outward in both a north and south direction. The pedestrian plane achieves its connection with the sky with an exuberance that establishes a new level of excellence.

The plan has gone through two basic revisions, the final form being illustrated on the left at the subway level looking north. The plan was of such a nature that it developed a kind of confidence in Bower's work, which resulted in his being chosen coordinating architect to continue the work on Market East.

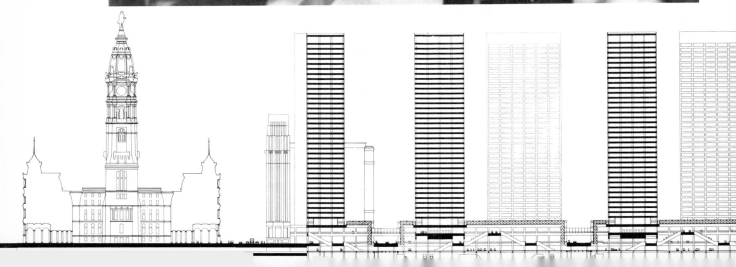

MOVEMENT SYSTEMS
IN PRACTICE

These photographs of portions of the Bower model for Market East show the degree to which movement systems have become the determinants of the Market East design.

The area above is the same as is illustrated in the 1964 design by Romaldo Giurgola at the top of page 284. Twelfth Street here extending north of Market Street passes over the pedestrian plane on its own right of way. The courts on each side, open to the sky, bring fresh air down to the subway level and give abundant light to the glass-enclosed pedestrian mall to the north. The architecture of the buildings which penetrate this space rises clear from the pedestrian level to the level above the street with no expression of the street plane, so oppressively present in Penn Center.

The escalators, so clearly visible, reinforce the direction of movement parallel with Penn's Market Street axis, and give an ever-present central line of orientation effective at all three levels.

The vertebrate structure of the bus terminal and parking garage, an architectural extension of regional movement systems, asserts itself across the composition in the background.

The cross-sectional drawing below shows the richness of interconnection and variety of choice of character and direction of movement that this interweaving of malls, bridges and escalators at many levels can achieve, as well as the clarity of visual orientation and awareness of position at all points which are produced.

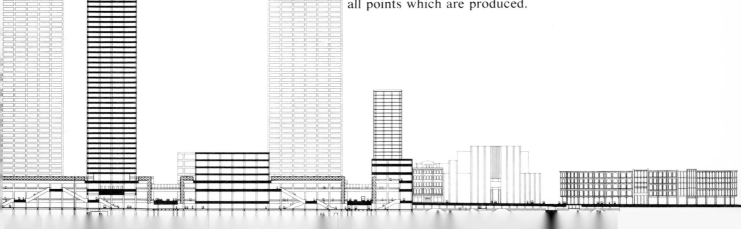

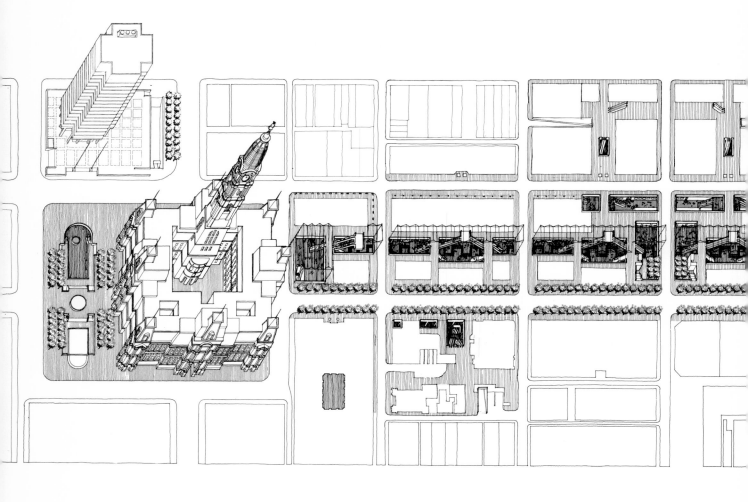

THE PEOPLE STREET

What has been produced by Bower's design for Market East, as this drawing shows, is a new kind of people street, paralleling and reinforcing vehicle-laden Market Street, providing a new kind of experiential continuity in Center City. It accomplishes, in ways undreamed of at the time, all the major objectives of the 1952 Planning Commission's Penn Center plan (conceived in 1947), shown on page 272.

While John Bower is architect for the entire structure, 1234 Market Street, and he has been appointed by the Redevelopment Authority co-ordinating architect for Market East, under his contract he is not permitted to design any of the buildings in Market East, his direct design work being limited to the pedestrian mall, or, as here called, the people street. I believe that, when the project is completed, it will have been deci-

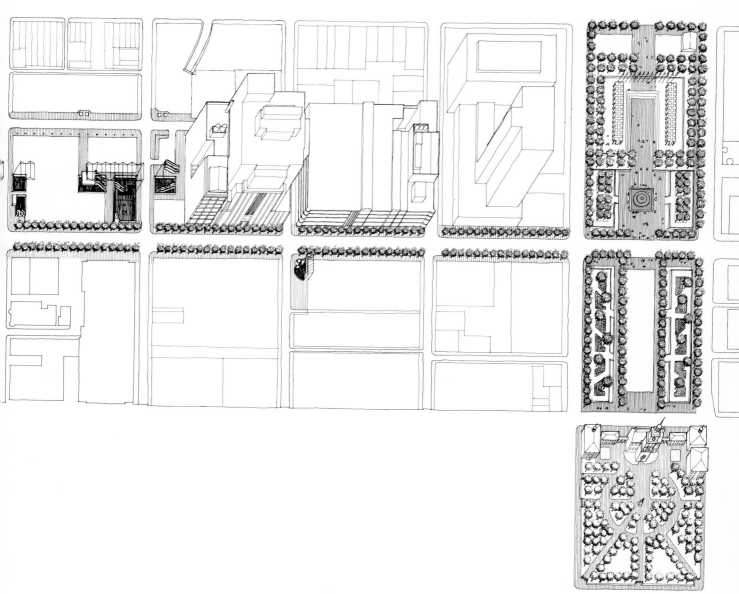

sively demonstrated that the significant architecture actually is contained in the people street and its movement systems, and that the architectural expression of the several buildings along it, each of which may be developed by a different owner with a different architect, hopefully of a high architectural order, nevertheless will be subordinate in importance to the people street.

Here, perhaps as powerfully as it can be demonstrated, exists a central line of movement which became the cohering force for many individual efforts in the sense that it is portrayed in the Klee drawings on pages 252 and 253. And here, as it probably nears its final form, Market East demonstrates, as graphically set forth on pages 258 to 261, the process of hypothesis formation and reformation in the light of community acceptance and rejection of its parts.

THINGS DO GET BUILT

The point of view of many young designers who are considering entering the field of urban design is expressed in this typical remark: "Yes, but I want to see my work built. I cannot face the frustration of the years which will elapse between the completion of my design and its realization on the ground." Because of this attitude there has not been the degree of design talent flowing into the urban-design field that there should have been.

Each man must decide for himself the scope of the problem he will tackle: an isolated building, two or three buildings together, or a total environment. The level of satisfaction will be set by the scale of his objective. What is emerging in Philadelphia is proving that, in the current tempo of things, within a decade there can be achievement on the ground related to the larger order of design.

Although the Society Hill towers of Ieoh Ming Pei represent only a small part of the total construction in the city, they do illustrate some of these ordering principles. The photograph above suggests that the reason for the interrelation of the eighteenth-century Powel house and the twentieth-century Pei towers is the unifying use of glass held within a structural grid. This is true both in the older double-hung muntined windows and in the newer work, where the exterior walls (different in scale but similar in proportion) also form the support for the building and the glass.

In the photograph to the left, the three towers give order to an otherwise confused skyline. When these towers are augmented by the disciplined base line of Penn's Landing they will truly interrelate with the forces of the region, marking the point of juncture of the city design structure with the Delaware River.

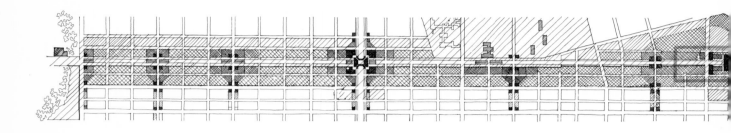

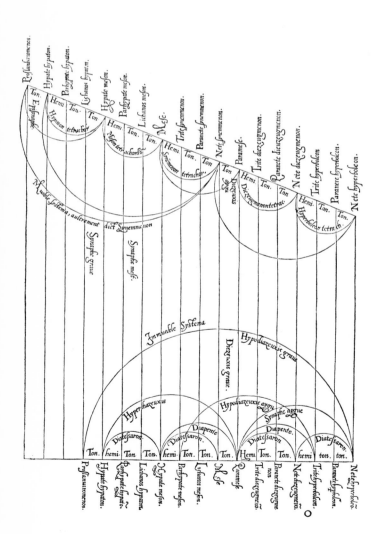

OUTWARD THRUST OF DESIGN

The thrust of design did not stop at the river. It jumped across it and extended right along the channel of the greatest force — the original 1683 Market Street axis of William Penn. Architect Robert Geddes was engaged by the Redevelopment Authority to design a Science Center astride the Market Street axis on the highlands of West Philadelphia, which overlook Center City. Geddes picked up the rhythms of design already existing along the Market Street route between the two rivers and, starting with his design for the Delaware River waterfront, extended the rhythmic pattern on through to the top of a rise at Fortieth Street. His drawing above shows this extension all the way to the city limits. The effect of the design was to thrust the influence of Center City deep into West Philadelphia and give new vitality to that area. Overlaid in green is the perpendicular design force of the proposed park along the Schuylkill River, forming additional branches off the

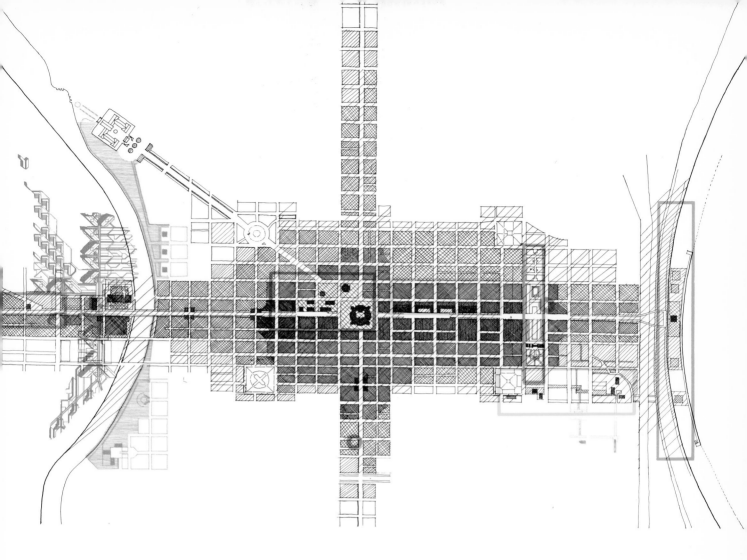

main trunk. Also in green is shown the extension of the design structure to the south within Society Hill.

Superimposed on the plan are a series of "architects' hegemonies," or areas of the city in which one or another designer is dominant. Outlined in dark blue is the area of Vincent Kling's work in Penn Center, and in green is the work of Roy Larson, the Independence Mall. The yellow space is the area of tension between Ieoh Ming Pei's two groups of towers, and the light blue shapes define Geddes' influence. Also in yellow is outlined John Bower's work in Market East. Of themselves, these shapes make a design which encompasses the space in between. The blue plan just west of the Schuylkill River is by Romaldo Giurgola, and the two blue circles mark significant buildings by architect Louis Kahn.

Each of these areas has its own internal requirements of dimensions. These must be large enough to create an environment, but not so large that they create monotony. It may be an accident or it may be the determination of the architect (or indeed of the government) that brings about the initial contact of the architect and the space, the definite commission to construct a single building rooted in the land. If the architect is creative, this should set up an interaction with the environment which can grow to produce a form extending over a larger area. The encouragement of this process is (or should be) a function of the government. And, on the highest level, the design of this kind of activity is, of itself, a work of art.

The drawing to the left (a Renaissance illustration from the fourth book of Vitruvius) reminds us that the rhythmic modulation along a line of movement — in Market Street it is an extent of three miles — can be based on definite proportional relationships, just as it is in the case of a musical composition or a mathematical formula.

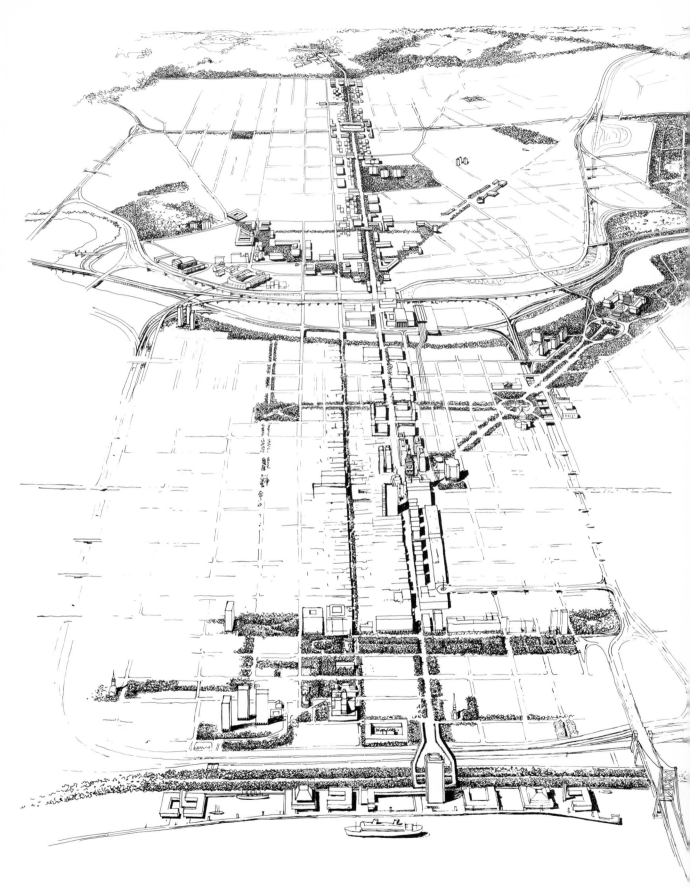

300

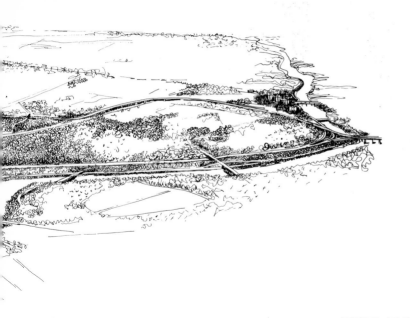

THE TOTAL ORGANISM

On this page is a broad impression of the evolving design structure underlying the growth and development of Philadelphia. This structure did not emerge all at once but was laboriously built up, part by part, over time. It presents unity because each of its parts is related to the other by the principles of an organic growth process. The drawing itself, by its own nature, makes it clear that this is not a final form; the stirring of a new growth and flowering is already present. Many additions and revisions will have to be worked out to meet the new pressures of urban growth. These plans must extend across the land beyond the city limits to provide structure and form to the whole region and channels of energy for the expansion of the city. The objective is to achieve at every moment in time, on the part of every citizen a sense of orientation to a continually enlarging order.

While it makes no claim to finality, the work in Philadelphia has proved that a city can be restructured on a large scale, and that the leaders and the citizens are not only receptive but hungry for the new vision it provides. This is a shared thing, a product of the interaction of the designer's image and democratic feedback. It proves the value of setting up a procedure whereby the process itself involves the citizen in the planning, enriching the plan thereby and building up public acceptance of the plan once it is made.

An important element of the Philadelphia plan is not what is on the ground or what is on paper, but the vision of order that is in the minds of the young people, and the desire for its fulfillment.

301

COMPREHENSIVE PLAN OBJECTIVE

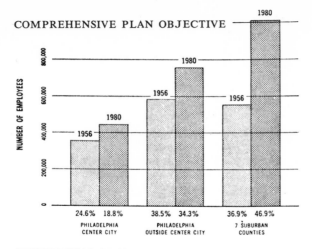

NUMBER OF EMPLOYEES

1956 1980
1980
1956
1980
1956
1980

24.6% 18.8%   38.5% 34.3%   36.9% 46.9%
PHILADELPHIA   PHILADELPHIA   7 SUBURBAN
CENTER CITY   OUTSIDE CENTER CITY   COUNTIES

FUNCTIONAL PLAN

AREA PLAN

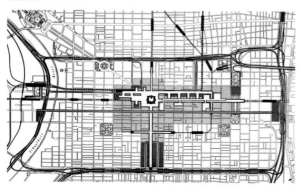

PROJECT PLAN

302

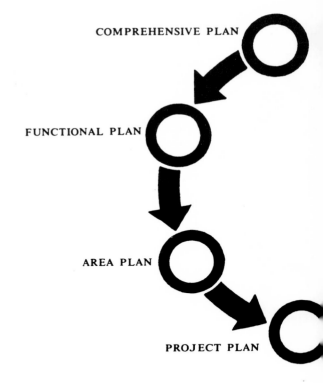

COMPREHENSIVE PLAN

FUNCTIONAL PLAN

AREA PLAN

PROJECT PLAN

DESIGN AS PROCESS

Underlying all the work in Philadelphia is a total process of planning which is a practical application of the principles previously described. Because this planning incorporates many facets of community interests, it involves a large percentage of the community leadership and brings into play a significant percentage of the total energy of the city in a single, integrated process.

I. The Comprehensive Plan, deeply rooted in an understanding of the community, based on both experience and research, sets forth an interrelated, sensitively balanced range of objectives.

II. The Functional Plan sets forth the physical organization, on a regional basis, of a manageable number of factors in their primary interrelation with one another.

III. The Area Plan sets forth, for a limited geographical section of the city, the three-dimensional relationships between the physical factors, correlated with the Functional Plan, which bear on the problems to be solved in order to achieve comprehensive plan objectives.

IV. The Project Plan sets forth, in explicit three-dimensional terms, the essential nature of the project or projects which are necessary to achieve the objectives of the Area Plan.

ARCHITECTURAL IMAGE

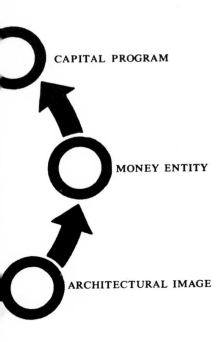

CAPITAL PROGRAM

MONEY ENTITY

ARCHITECTURAL IMAGE

MONEY ENTITY

Line No.	Projects	Estimated Change in Annual Operating Cost	Total Estimated Cost	Cost Thru 1964 Capital Budget	Cost Scheduled Six-Year Period
		$	$	$	$
	DEPARTMENT OF PUBLIC PROPERTY—(Continued)				
	Transit Improvements				
70	Broad-Ridge-Locust Subway system — cars — purchase from Delaware River Port Authority		260,000		26,000x 234,000*
71	Broad-Ridge-Locust Subway system — replacement items		2,000,000	35,000x 315,000	165,000x 1,485,000*
72	Broad St. Subway — South Broad St. and Northeast extensions		98,258,383	(1,220,525f) 7,351,000f 23,238x 209,145	4,983,333f 79,975,000f* 571,667x 5,145,000*
73	Center City Commuter train connection and allied facilities — including land acquisition		43,000,000	30,000x 270,000	18,000,000f 15,700,000f* 900,000x 8,100,000*
74	West Plaza — 15th St. — improvements		4,385,000	*	2,923,334f 146,166x 1,315,500*

CAPITAL PROGRAM

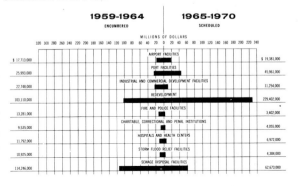

COMPREHENSIVE PLAN RE-EVALUATION

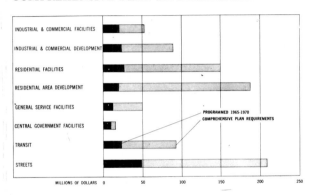

V. The Architectural Image sets forth in human experiential terms what it would be like to see and to move about in the project when it is completed, providing a powerful impetus toward community understanding and popular acceptance of the plan.

VI. The Money Entity, based on cost estimates for the construction of the project, is necessary to give dimension and reality to the project, to provide a definite issue for public debate, and to provide the unit which seeks to find its place in the flow of the capital programming process.

VII. The Capital Program, really an apportionment of time, sets forth the sequence and dimension of public action for project accomplishment, and so becomes a sensitive regulatory device to set the range of comprehensive plan objectives in their proper relationship in space and time.

The Comprehensive Plan is annually reviewed, following the adoption of the capital program by the City Council. This review may cause a revision of the relationships between major divisions of the plan or it may suggest new fields requiring functional plans and so set the entire cycle into motion again with its systematic interactions and feedback.

303

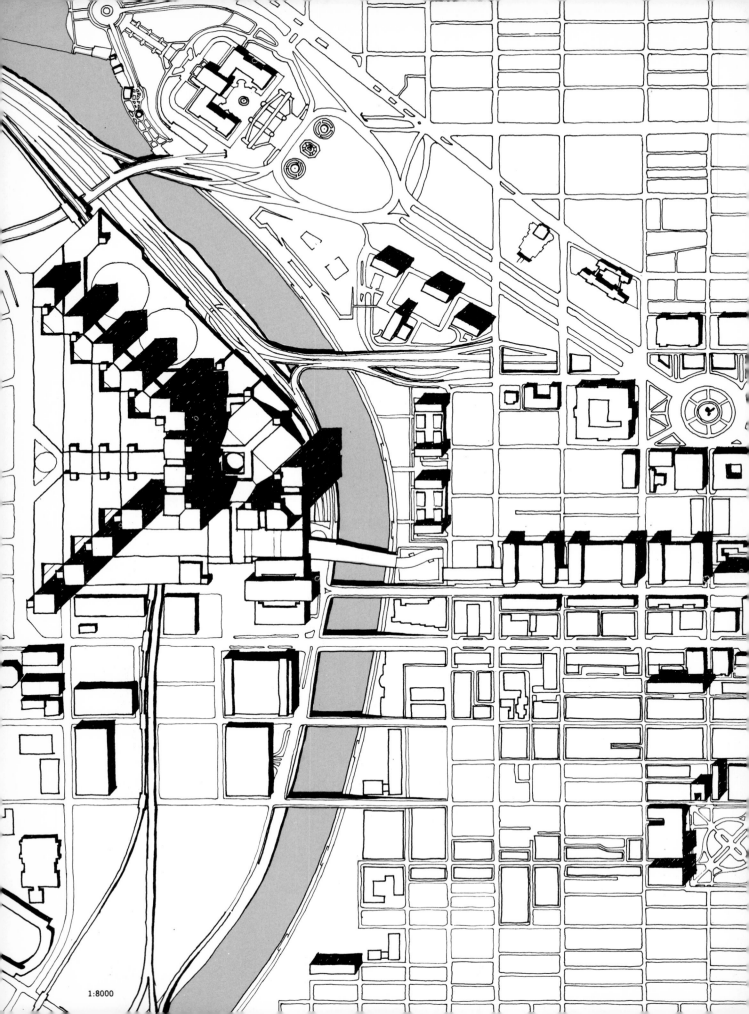

1:8000

MEGALOPOLITAN SCALE

The 1966 design by Vincent Kling which the Pennsylvania Railroad commissioned him to make, in consultation with Robert Dowling, for a projected development over the railroad tracks just north of Market Street and west of the Schuylkill River, has been included on these pages to affirm the continuity of the restructuring and the ever-enlarging scale that underlies it.

City Hall in Philadelphia marks a center created by the intersection of the regional north-south axis of Broad Street with the westerly Market Street axis of William Penn. In this line, moving inland from the seminal point of the riverbank landing from the Old World, is a kind of microcosmic expression of the westerly movement of American development.

Now comes megalopolis and the new lifeline for it — the high-speed transportation line from Boston to Washington, D.C. So it is right that here, at the intersection of the 1683 axis of William Penn and the 1970 or 1980 megalopolitan movement system, a new center should be created in a new dimension of design, pioneered once more by the Pennsylvania Railroad.

But a new scale alone is not enough. There must also be architecture to support it. It is significant that Kling has been able to organize his buildings so that their form reflects the form of the Schuylkill River valley. In his design they act as a kind of design elbow at the river's bend. This solution simultaneously engages the westward movement system of Market Street, the north-south high-speed megalopolitan system, and the slow and ancient movement of the Schuylkill River.

PERMANENCE AND CHANGE

A new design for the area west of the Schuyl-kill River was made by Romaldo Giurgola in 1969, who was engaged by the Philadelphia 1976 Bicentennial Corporation to plan the proposed International Exposition at this site. A visual comparison of this with the Kling plan, which you may obtain by holding pages 305 and 306 vertically, shows an interesting difference in the two approaches. The dominant consideration in the Vincent Kling plan is form, whereas the dominant consideration in the Giurgola plan is movement.

While the program for the Giurgola design has been rendered obsolete by the decision to move the International Exposition elsewhere, the ideas which underlie it are not. A commercial development over the tracks could benefit just as much from the basic organization of the move-ment systems he designed as would the International Exposition.

Here we may learn something about permanence and change. If the architect deals primarily in form, the chance of his work being modified or destroyed in future years is relatively great. If the architect deals with movement systems, if they are well conceived in relation to the larger systems of movement, and if they are rendered articulate, the chances of their survival, and indeed of their strengthening and extension over time, are very good indeed, even if the structures along them are torn down and rebuilt.

Though the leaves go and come each fall and spring, the trunk and branches of the tree remain, and it is they that determine the form of the tree.

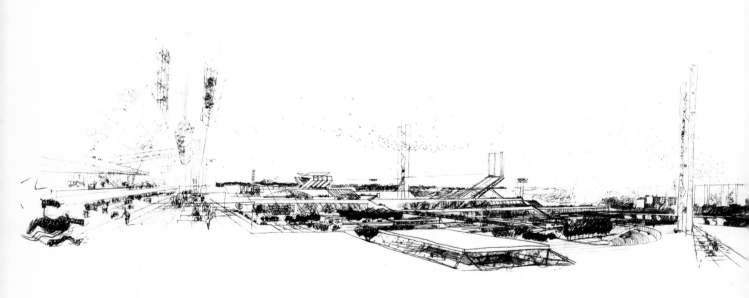

CANBERRA
CAPITAL CITY OF AUSTRALIA
WALTER BURLEY GRIFFIN ARCHITECT

GRIFFIN AND CANBERRA

Many of the examples of civic design in this book were done during periods in history in which autocratic rulers wielded immense personal power. Lest we conclude that this is a prerequisite for great and powerful work, we turn our attention to the conditions which surrounded the development of the capital of the newest of the great nations, Australia's Canberra. Here flourished and continues to flourish one of the greatest urban designs ever produced, conceived, nurtured, and grown in circumstances fiercely democratic. Yet so strong was the original concept of American architect Walter Burley Griffin, long-time associate of Frank Lloyd Wright, that the integrity of the plan survives and reasserts its relevance to the modern day.

The superb drawing on this page, made by Griffin in 1912, shows how he was able to involve simultaneously natural features — Black Mountain, Mount Ainslee, Capitol Hill, the river turned into a lake — and the functional movement system to the various functional focal points — government, commerce, education, recreation, residence — which were basic to his design. The following two pages give a visual comparison of Griffin's plan for Canberra and L'Enfant's for Washington. While there are striking similarities in these two plans, developed more than a hundred years apart, Griffin avoided L'Enfant's problematic acute-angled intersections and lots by modifying the gridiron system to accord with the main arteries. The extraordinary skill with which he did this can be sensed by noting that, of his eight principal nodes four are six-sided, three are eight-sided, and one, the curious focus at Capitol Hill, has nine sides. This is a plan of firm, clear geometry not imposed rigidly on the terrain but sensitively adjusted to its inherent vagaries. Here is a plan that continues to work in spite of enormous changes in the technology of transportation, a system of design which is capable of indefinite extension.

309

GRIFFIN AND
L'ENFANT

The capacity to conceive large systems of urban order simultaneously in their functional and their physical aspects, demonstrated in the work of Griffin and l'Enfant, seems largely to have disappeared, and, indeed, is systematically denigrated by many planners, sometimes ironically in the name of the "Systems Approach," who regard concern for the physical realities as irrelevant and frivolous.

Canberra

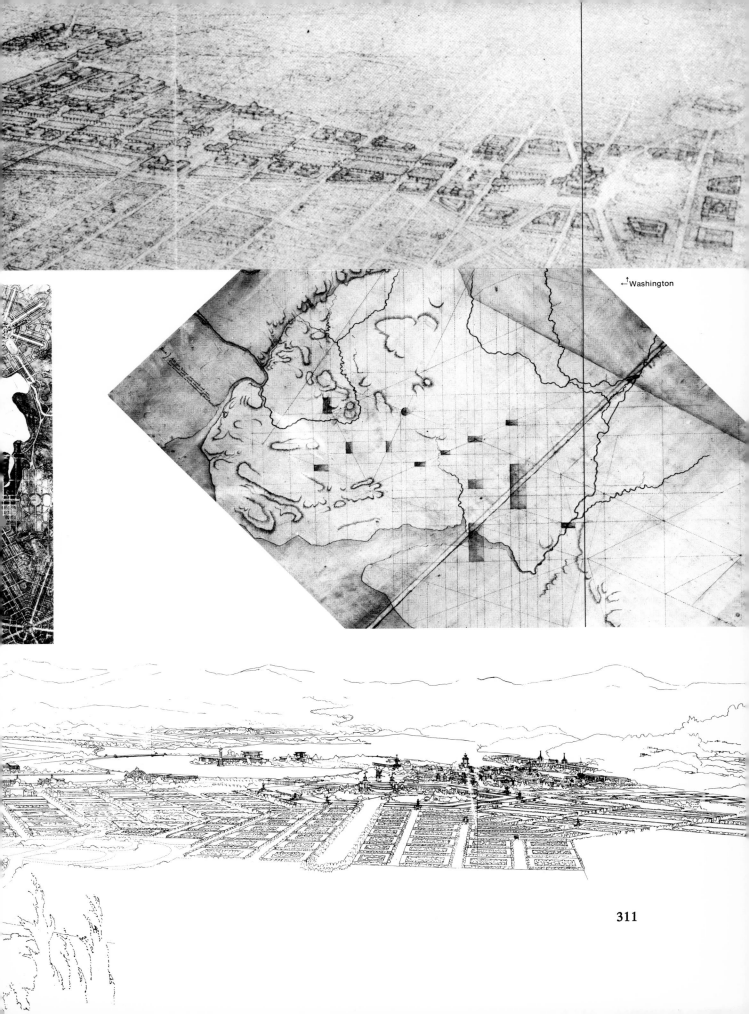

↵Washington

311

CITY FOR HUMANITY – STOCKHOLM

These drawings of Stockholm by David Hell-den present the image of the city as a pleasant place for people to be. They convey something of the spirit of Stockholm and the way in which it is being renewed.

The illustrations are of the lower Norrmalm project (in general form, the work of Hellden), built on top of a subway and growing out of a complexity of movement systems. Below is a drawing of the large pedestrian plaza planned at the south end of Norrmalm to extend from the street down to the subway station and connect with the pedestrian esplanade shown in the drawing opposite. Here is a fine interweaving of buildings of different periods in a city's life. The columned building at the end of the space is architect Ivar Tengbom's Concert Hall with Carl Milles' Orpheus Fountain in front of it. This makes a happy conclusion to the somewhat thinner architecture of the newer shops along the pedestrian way, a fact which Hellden recognized.

As is evident in the drawing, several different levels are used. The rooftops above the shops are filled with trees and flowers, and among these are sitting areas, restaurants, and cafés. Pedestrian bridges span the open space between, and stairways connect the various levels.

All this is the focal center for the movement system which provides the ordering element for the growth of the region. The city of Stockholm owns virtually all the land immediately surrounding the urban area, and across this land it is developing mass rail transit systems. Simultaneously the city is making land available for the planned growth of new communities, which cluster around the new transit stations as they are built. This gives a highly articulate design structure to the extension of the city into the region, reinforced by the restructuring of its point of contact with the older part of the city. Because the Norrmalm project, with its five tall towers, is concentrated, carefully designed, internally logical, and functionally related to the development of the region, the beauty of historic Stockholm is not destroyed. What the new project accomplishes is a powerful counterfoil to the earlier work.

Image labels visible: ...geri ST·ERIK, SAS, SERGELTEATERN, DIOR SCHIAPARELLI Con amore, ...MPER Aftonklänningar VARUHUS, Con amore, Hellden -58

ARCHITECTURAL EXPRESSION AND FORM

The drawing on this page depicts the sense of richness of the multiple movement and various levels of design as they are integrated in Stockholm's Norrmalm project. The drawing opposite gives David Hellden's vision of the area, the five rhythmic towers rising into the upper air, creating an order which would overlie the richness and confusion of the land below.

But the Stockholm government engaged in that great fallacy practiced by many other cities — for example, in the design of the reconstructed area around Saint Paul's Cathedral in London — that form and architectural expression are entirely different and unrelated.

The precise position, form, and size of the five towers were fixed by the government. David Hellden designed the first one himself, according to his own idea of color and rhythm. Then came the second man. The architect of the second building determined what the relationship would be between the two, just as Sangallo decided in Piazza della Santissima Annunziata. He designed a building very similar to Hellden's in materials, color, and design expression, but just slightly different. And with this example before them, the same thing was done by the next and the next, the fifth being strikingly different, as was the original intention. The result is a dissonance, as in a quartet in which each person is performing slightly off key. It is worse than it would have been if the shapes of the towers had been unrelated, and, of course, worse than if any one of the four designs had been repeated four times.

This is simply a restatement of the self-evident fact that an organism is all of a piece, and you cannot deal with one part of it, leaving another part out, except at your peril. There are ways to involve five different designers and still achieve a unity, as has been discovered many times in the studies of the past, but these ways must be organic. Architectural expression emerges as a critical element, just as important as the over-all design structure and form.

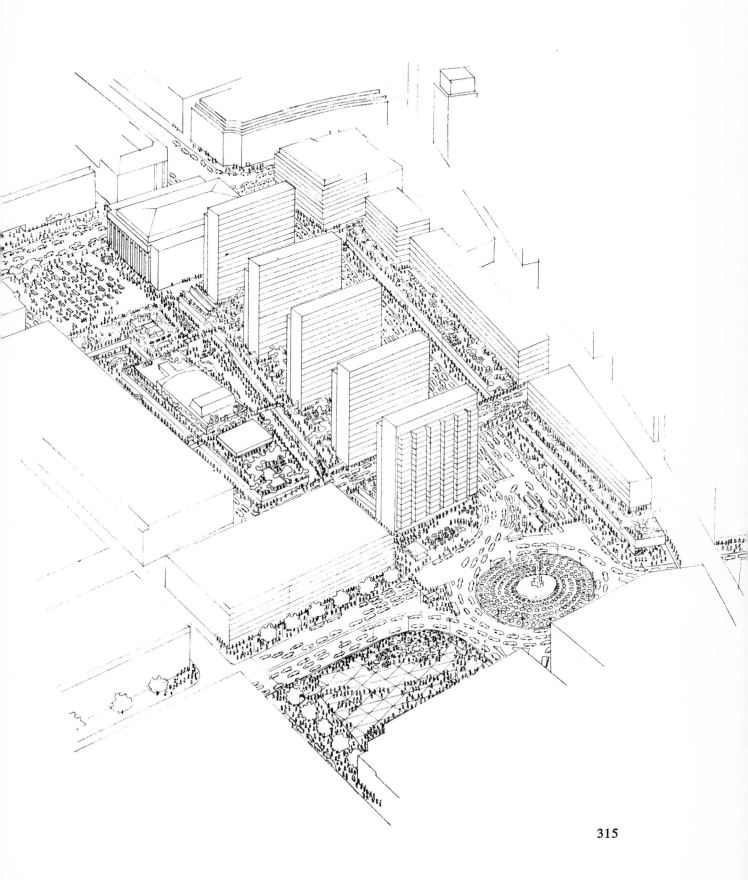

EMERGENT TRENDS

One of the major problems of design today is thinking too early in terms of form. Form should derive from, not dictate, the design structure. The making of arbitrary forms early in the design process tends to stultify thought and to inhibit or stop the flow of basic design creativity. Once articulated, forms are very hard to get rid of and tend to impose themselves where they do not belong.

A brilliant example of the opposite type of thinking is the winning submission by the architectural firm of Geddes, Brecher, Qualls and Cunningham in the 1971 Vienna International Town Planning Competition, models and drawings of which are shown on these pages. The three-phase development of the 2500-acre community pictured on the right shows that the design has a structure capable of growth, that it is sharp and clear, yet flexible and adaptable to change, while holding together as a design.

Paul Klee adds to his list of the formal elements of graphic art: the dot, line, and plane; the spatial element such as a "cloudlike vaporous spot." Usually absent from architects' and planners' thinking, this element has been used with startling success by George Qualls, the principal designer of the submission, in the central open space which extends the length of the project. Sharply intersected by clear, straight transverse roadways, this amorphous space gives a clear orientation for the individual designer of a part of the community, a frame of reference and sense of place without the strait jacket of prescribed form. Virtually all of the other submissions derived from form rather than from the interaction of movement systems.

A way in which to evaluate the relative merits of the various submissions is to place one's self in the position of an architect assigned to design a group of buildings in a part of the community, and consider the degree to which the over-all plan inhibits or inspires creative activity.

The relationship between this model and the subsequent Klee drawings is worth noting.

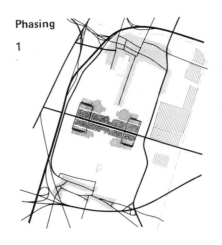

Phasing 1

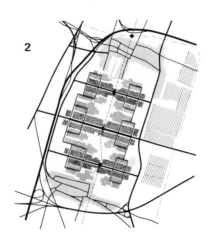

2

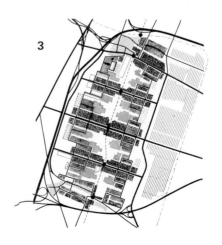

3

Flexible Strip   High Density Residential   Low Density Residential   Greenway   Industrial   Existing Residential   Recreational Facilities

317

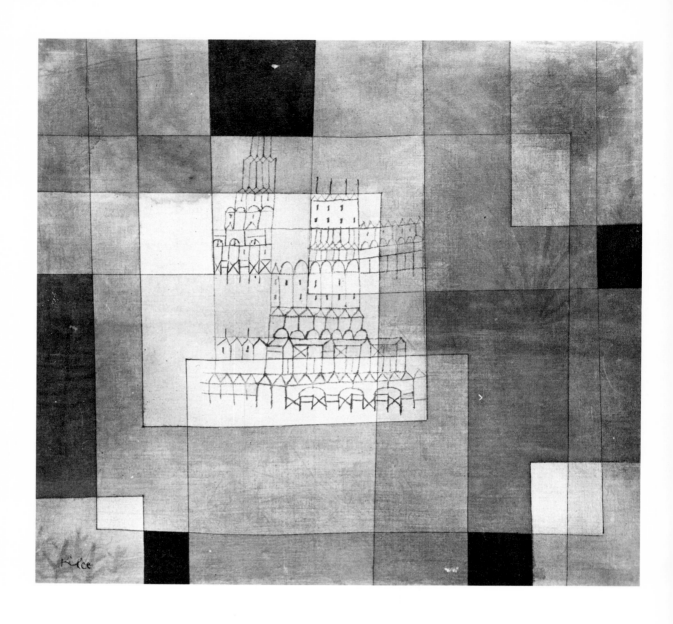

'Any city planning worthy to be called organic
must bring some measure of beauty and order
into the poorest neighborhood.' Lewis Mumford

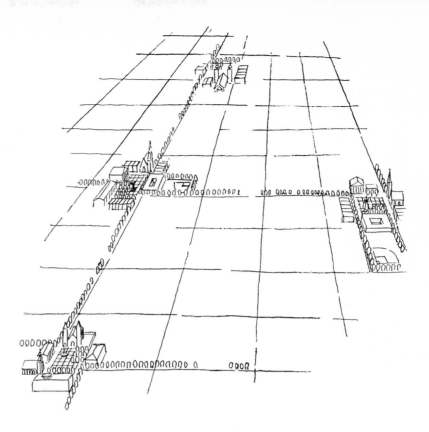

LOOKING INTO THE FUTURE

AMALGAMATION OF PLANNING AND ARCHITECTURE

The water-color by Paul Klee opposite expresses the interrelation of planning and architecture. Here the gray rectangles suggest areas defined in accordance with usual planning procedures, and the architecture gives a glow which illuminates the whole. The architectural rhythms, occupying only a small part of the area, set up a harmony which reverberates through all the spaces, showing that it is not necessary to design in detail every square foot of an area to achieve a great and unified work.

The drawing above represents an attempt by Willo von Moltke and myself to apply these principles to residential areas on a wide scale. The proposal is to create strongly articulated nuclei built around existing beloved landmarks and institutions carefully distributed throughout the residential fabric, to establish powerful architectural imagery and rhythms which extend their influence into the less articulate areas around them. These would generate neighborhood identification, loyalty, and pride, and serve as links for identification with the city and the region.

This approach to urban renewal would make

widespread results possible without destruction of whole neighborhoods, and would give citizens a broad sense of participation in the wider effort. Residential rehabilitation and rebuilding could occur at its own pace and scale in this framework.

The very determination of the point of juncture of the self-conscious architecture and the anonymous city is a sensitive and complicated matter, worthy of the attention of the best designers. It cannot be done by statistics, computer, or Zip-a-Tone on maps. It is a problem the very essence of which is in the nature of design. This is the kind of decision which is usually left to the statistician and the administrator, to be made before the designer starts work. Klee makes it sharply clear that such a procedure of itself lacks life-giving qualities and that, as a procedure, it would defeat its purposes before the essential part of the operation had begun.

Thus we must not only plan but, as suggested in the words of Lewis Mumford, we must design in such a way that the finest of our accumulated experience in city-building is brought to every neighborhood in every part of our cities.

319

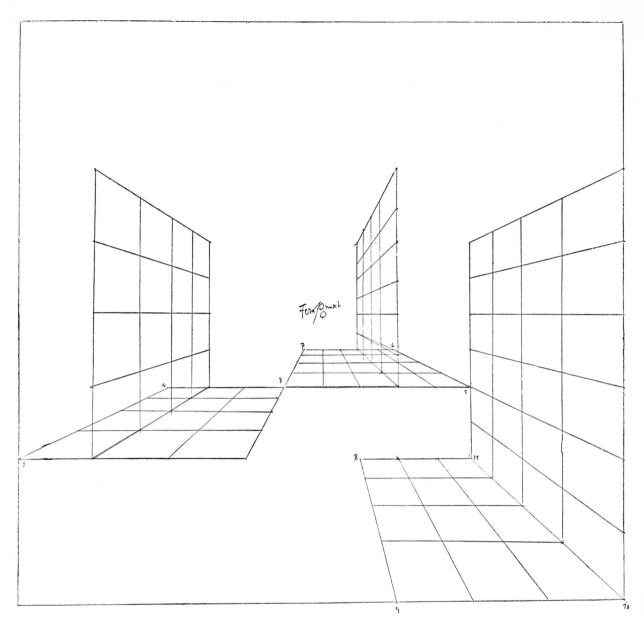

MOVING THROUGH THREE DIMENSIONS

We end as we begin, with the participator. But we see him here through the eyes of Paul Klee, linked to his environment in a way that is very different from the relationships imposed by Euclidean geometry or Newtonian physics. The space he is in and the infinity he seeks are a far cry from those evoked by the stable "Linea del Centro" of the Renaissance diagram on the title page of this book, and are more closely related to those suggested by the elusive "far point" of Paul Klee, shown above. Here are expressed a great new range of awareness, an interaction of emotion and perception, a total involvement that we have only begun to sense. Thus we are able to develop a feeling of what lies ahead, far transcending what we already know.

If I had to represent man "as he is," I should have required so bewildering a tangle of lines that a pure treatment of the element would have been out of the question; there would only have been an unrecognizable blur.

Besides, I have no desire to show this man as he is, but only as he might be. —*PAUL KLEE*

MOVING INTO THE FUTURE

In this book we have discussed movement, the time dynamic, and change. The Klee drawing to the left expresses the concept of movement, of tense lines of progression from one place to another, interwoven into a total fabric. To this have been added points of conjunction, of flowering and enrichment, places of repose. These are important too, and they also call upon the highest expression of architecture, but they can be understood only in relation to the movement to arrive there and anticipation of the movement away.

Together these two elements, the architecture of movement and architecture of repose, make up the city as a work of art, and this is the people's art. The product of city-design can be experienced by anyone, without qualification, on an equal basis. It could become a great democratic statement of the life we share in common.

The test of our achievement is whether we are able to break away from our fragmented approach to this problem and begin to see the city as a whole, dealing with it as a complete organism. Here, again, we may listen to the words of Paul Klee:

Accordingly, a sense of totality has gradually entered into the artist's conception of the natural object, whether this object be a plant, animal, or man; whether it be situated in the space of the house, the landscape, or the world, and the first consequence is that a more spatial conception of the object as such is born.

APPENDIX: THE GREAT EFFORT—BRASILIA

This account of Brasilia was written before I had visited that city. It has been replaced by the account on page 235.

Besides Chandigarh, the one other measure of the maturity of the architectural profession today is provided by the great new capital of its country, Brasilia. Here, also, is a contemporary city built from scratch, entirely freed from the influence of errors made on the ground by past generations, where designers have been entirely liberated to explore the most creative ideas that can be generated. Here, unlike that of Chandigarh, the overall design of the city was the result of a competition, won by Lucio Costa with a sketch made on the back of an envelope.

I feel that no one would say that the basic organization of Brasilia is bad; the colossal difficulties arose in the translation of Costa's sketch into building on the ground, which was to be the task of Oscar Niemeyer. The fact that the city was conceived by two individuals at two entirely different levels of scale meant that the basic problem of the design of open spaces in the sense of scale was dealt with by no one. This problem was still unresolved after the buildings were positioned by Costa and designed by Niemeyer. They are too large to produce an architectural effect, at least in the central core.

During the Baroque period the architect would have conceived the design of the capitol buildings at the end of the mall, and the space before them, as one unified design problem. A comparison of this photograph with the eighteenth-century Wren composition on page 173 shows how this was done. But in Brasilia it was not necessary to compromise in order to tie in with some older building, as in Greenwich. In Brasilia all the elements of space and of the buildings were under simultaneous design control. Since the basic idea of the larger composition is purely a Baroque idea, and adds nothing new, the result can be judged against Baroque standards.

It is evident that, however elegant as a self-contained composition the design of the government buildings may be, it completely fails in its basic assignment to receive the thrust of the shaft of space defined by the ends of the ministry buildings. In fact the space flows right on by, with scarcely a ripple to ruffle it where it should have achieved its climax. Indeed the idea of composing with two towers to contain a narrow space between them, apart from the fact that the offices are placed opposite each other so closely that the occupants can stare into each other's windows, sets up a space movement of such fragility that, where it moves into a juncture with the larger spaces, it expires with scarcely a whimper.

It is amazing that this opportunity to put forward new ideas of large-scale design should have produced no new ideas at all, but rather should have sharply emphasized the skill with which designers applied these same ideas three hundred years ago.

NOTES ON ILLUSTRATIONS

These are in addition to the credits which appear on page 8.

End paper — Detail from small Nolli map of Rome, 1748

Title page — Leon Battista Alberti, *Opuscoli Morali*, Francheschi, Venice, 1568. Courtesy of Lucien Goldschmidt, New York

6-7 — Drawing for the Philadelphia 1976 Bicentennial Corporation by Romaldo Giurgola

10 — G. B. da Vignola, *Le Due Regole della Prospettiva Pratica . . . con i comentarii del Egnatio Danti . . .* Stamperia camerale. Rome, 1611

11 — A Comprehensive Plan for Downtown Buffalo. Prepared for the City of Buffalo by Wallace, McHarg, Roberts and Todd, 1971

19 — Sandro Botticelli, "Noli Me Tangere." Courtesy John G. Johnson Collection, Philadelphia. Photo: Philadelphia Museum of Art

21 — Regional Plan Association. *Urban Design: Manhattan.* The Viking Press, 1969

22-27 — Francesco Guardi, "Architectural Capriccio" (pen and wash drawing). Victoria & Albert Museum, Crown Copyright. Line overprints by author

28 — G. B. da Vignola, *Le Due Regole della Prospettiva Pratica . . .*

29 — Photos: Rolf Hintz; by courtesy of the Stockholm Stads Stadsbyggnadskontor

30 — Andrea Pozzo, *Prospettiva de' Pittori ed Architetti.* Stamperia di Antonio de' Rossi, Rome, 1723

32-33 — Drawings for the Philadelphia 1976 Bicentennial Corporation by Romaldo Giurgola

36 — Kenzo Tange, *Japan Architect,* 102 (November 1964)

37 — Plan of Horyuji, and elevation of central group, Horyuji, Nara, Japan, by Professor Hirotaro Ohta

38–39 — Paul Klee. From *The Thinking Eye.* George Wittenborn, Inc. New York, 1961

40 — Base Maps, U.S. Geological Survey

42 — Detail from *Les Très Riches Heures du Duc de Berry,* The Castle of Saumur by the Limbourg Brothers. Musée Condé, Chantilly

Paul Klee, diagrams. From *The Thinking Eye*

43 — From Walter Holtz. *Kleine Kunstgeschichte der Deutschen Burg.* Wissenschaftliche Buchgesellschaft, Darmstadt, 1965

upper — Burg Karlstein (Böhmen)

middle — Burg Büdingen (Oberhessen)

lower — Bozen-Gries (Südtirol)

44 — Paul Klee, diagrams. From *The Thinking Eye*

upper — From Marie Luise Gothein, *A History of Garden Art.* J. M. Dent & Sons, Ltd. London, 1928. Villa Lante, Bagnaja

upper middle — Giambattista Nolli, *Nuova Pianta di Roma,* 1748

lower middle — Marcel Fouquier, *De l'Art des Jardins,* Emile-Paul, Paris, 1911. Le Château de Petit-Bourg

lower — Environs of Paris, surveyed in 1740. Monsieur Jean l'Abbé de la Grive. Services Techniques et Commerciaux de la Réunion des Musées Nationaux, Paris. Reprinted from original plates

52 — Drawing by author

58 — G. B. da Vignola, *Le Due Regole della Prospettiva Pratica . . .*

59	Paul Klee, spatial study (rational connectors), 1930. From *The Thinking Eye*		*Griechenlandkunde*. Carl Winter Universitätsverlag. Heidelberg. 4th ed., 1962
	Paul Klee, "Sailing City" (water color), 1930. Private collection, Berne. Courtesy of the Klee Foundation, Berne	middle	From A. V. Bunin, *History of the Art of Urban Planning* (in Russian). Moscow, 1953
61	Paul Klee, "Dimensional Operation Combined into a Higher Structure." From *The Thinking Eye*	lower	Based on the plan of Scuola degli Ingegneri of Rome, 1905
62 upper	Paul Klee, "Free-formed Polyphonic Organism" (pencil and crayon). Courtesy of the Klee Foundation, Berne	84	Map by A. Strobl. After *Studi per una Operante Storia Urbana di Roma,* Centro Studi di Storia Urbanistica and Consiglio Nazionale delle Ricerche, 1963, and other sources
lower	"Pergame: l'acropole." From Roland Martin, *L'Urbanisme dans la Grèce Antique*. Editions A. & J. Picard & Cie., Paris, 1956	85	Model of Classical Rome, Museo della Civiltà Romana. Photo: Ernesto Richter, Rome
63	Drawing by Sarantis Zafiropoulos	88 upper and lower	From Heinz Kähler, *Hadrian und seine Villa bei Tivoli*. Gebr. Mann, G.m.b.H., Berlin, 1950
64–65	Photo: Mavroyenis, Athens		
66	After John Travlos, ΠΟΛΕΟΔΟΜΙΚΗ ΕΞΕΛΙΞΙΣ ΤΩΝ ΑΘΗΝΩΝ. Athens, 1960	90–91	Hadrian's Villa. Based on the Plan of the Scuola degli Ingegneri, Rome, 1905
68–69	Paul Klee, drawing from notebook. Courtesy of the Klee Foundation, Berne	92	Engraving by Joannes Blaeu. *Nieuw Vermeerderd en Verbeterd Groot Stodebock van Geheel Italie*. Graaverhaage, 1724
69	Photograph by Agora Excavations, American School of Classical Studies at Athens	93	Ambrogio Lorenzetti, "A Tuscan Town," about 1340. Picture Gallery, Siena. Photo: Anderson (Alinari), Rome
70–71	After Travlos		
73	Photo: Mavroyenis	100–101	Engraving. Origin unknown
74	After Theodor Wegand and Armin von Gerkav, *Milet* (vol. 1, book 6: *Der Nordmarkt und der Hafen an der Löwenbucht*). Stattliche Museen, Berlin. Walter de Gruyter & Co., Berlin and Leipzig, 1922	101	Engraving by Martin Engelbrecht
		104	From A. V. Bunin, *History of the Art of Urban Planning*
		105	From Louis Kahn, *The Notebooks and Drawings*. Eds. Richard Saul Wurman and Eugene Feldman. The Falcon Press, Philadelphia, 1962
75	Model by students at the University of Pennsylvania: Gordon A. Bertrand, Jay N. Cooperson, Lawrence Diamond, Oliver M. Ford, Willard D. Hottle, Paul E. Lusk, Lowell P. Macomber, Richard B. Prudhomme, Josan Russo. Photo: Lawrence S. Williams	106–107 lower	Engraving by F. B. Werner, from which numbers have been removed. Eighteenth century
		108–109	Engraving from Fernando Leopoldo, *Firenze Città Nobilissima*. Florence, 1684
76	Based on publications of l'Ecole Française d'Athènes. *Exploration Archeologique de Delos*. Editions E. de Boccard, Paris	112	Paul Klee, "Irregular Projection." From *The Thinking Eye*
77	Photo: Roger Viollet, Paris	113	Drawn by Giuseppe Zocchi. Engraving by Giuseppe Vasi
78	From l'Ecole Française d'Athènes	115 upper	Paul Klee, diagram. From *The Thinking Eye*
79	Models by students at the University of Pennsylvania: Brigitte L. Knowles, Oscar Martinez, Sherman Morss	lower	Drawn by Maarten van Heemskerck. Fototeca di Architettura e Topografia dell'Italia Antica, Rome
80	Model by students at the University of Pennsylvania: David Cox, Dale Dzubay, Douglas King, Dennis Mann, Dorothy Stelzer, James Wright. Photo: Lawrence S. Williams	116	H. Cock, *Operum Antiquorum Romanorum*. Antwerp, 1562. Trustees of the British Museum. Photo: British Museum
82 upper	From E. Kirsten and W. Kraiker,	117	Anonymous drawing. Ecole italienne, No. 11028. The Louvre, Paris

326

118   Anonymous engraving. Origin unknown

120-121   Neroccio di Bartolommeo, "Storia di San Benedetto." Soprintendenza alla Galleria degli Uffizi, Florence

122   Antonio Pisanello, architectural interior, ca. 1440-45. Louvre, ex Codex Vallardi

123   Piero della Francesca, perspective drawing. From Christopher Tunnard, *The City of Man.* Charles Scribner's Sons, New York, 1953

124 upper   Architectural perspective. Detail of painting attributed to Luciano da Laurana. The Walters Art Gallery, Baltimore, Md.

middle   "Street Scene" (engraving), attributed to Bramante, Italian School, fifteenth century. The Metropolitan Museum of Art, Whittelsey Fund, 1949

lower   Baldassarre Peruzzi, architectural perspective. Soprintendenza alla Galleria degli Uffizi, Florence

125   Francesco Salviati, stage set. Trustees of the British Museum. Photo; John R. Freeman

126   Paul Klee, diagram. From *The Thinking Eye*

     Drawing by Theodore J. Musho

127   Matteo Gregorio de Rossi, "Nuova Pianta di Roma Presente," detail, 1773. Revised and reprinted from plates dated 1668

128   Paul Klee, diagrams. From *The Thinking Eye*

129   Paul Klee, "Illuminated Leaf" (water color), 1929. Courtesy of the Klee Foundation, Berne

130   Photos: The Photographical Archive of the Vatican Museums

131   Paul Klee, diagrams. From *The Thinking Eye*

132   From *Les Eglises des Stations de Roma,* ca. 1650. Engraving by Israel Henriet, Paris

133   Painting by Israel Silvestre. Courtesy of the Fogg Art Museum, Harvard University. Gift of Mr. and Mrs. Philip Hofer

134-135   Giambattista Piranesi, "Vedute di Roma"

136   Antoine Lafréry, "Vedute delle Sette Chiese di Roma," 1575. From *Urbanistica,* June 1959

137   Johannes Gros. Almae Urbis Romae . . . Rome, 1612

138 upper   Taddeo di Bartolo, "Circular View of Rome, 1413-1414." Chapel of the Palazzo Pubblico, Siena

lower   Giovanni Francesco Bordino, "Veduta Schematica del Piano Stradale Ideato da Sisto V," 1588. From *Le Piante di Roma,* Vol. II. Ed. Amato Pietro Frutaz, Istituto di Studi Romani. Rome, 1962

139   Paul Klee, diagrams. From *The Thinking Eye*

140-141   Antonio Dosio, "Rome," 1561. Photo: Biblioteca Apostolica Vaticana

144   Photos: The Photographical Archive of the Vatican Museums

145 upper   Ibid.

146 upper   Ibid.

middle   Paul Klee, diagram. From *The Thinking Eye*

lower   Johannes Gros, *Almae Urbis Romae . . .* Rome, 1612

147 upper   Drawn by Alessandro Specchi, 1702. Nella Stamperia di Domenico de Rossi

lower   Plan of Santa Maria Maggiore from Giambattista Nolli, *Nuova Pianta di Roma*

148 upper   Drawn by Gianlorenzo Bernini. Photo: Biblioteca Hertziana, Rome

lower   From Stanislao Fraschetti, *Il Bernini: La Sua Vita, La Sua Opera, Il Suo Tempo.* Editore Ulrico Hoepli, Milan, 1900

149 upper   Rossi, "Nuova Pianta di Roma Presente"

lower   Plan of Santa Maria Maggiore from Giambattista Nolli, *Nuova Pianta di Roma*

150 upper   Photo: Anderson, Rome

lower   Photo: The Photographical Archive of the Vatican Museums

151 upper   Piranesi, "Vedute di Roma." Metropolitan Museum of Art, Rogers Fund, 1941

152 upper   M. G. Rossi. Engraving, "Veduta della Chiesa e Convento di S. Carlino alle Quattro Fontane"

lower   Giovanni Battista Falda, engravings from *Le Fontane di Roma.* Rome, 1675. Collection of William H. Noble, Jr.

153 upper   Piranesi, "Vedute di Roma." The Metropolitan Museum of Art, Rogers Fund, 1941

154 upper   Antonio Tempesta, map of Rome (detail), 1593. Magnus Gabriel de la Gardie Collection, the Royal Library of Stockholm

lower	Rossi, "Nuova Pianta di Roma Presente"	178–179	P. Patte. *Monumens érigés en France à la gloire de Louis XV.* Details of City Hall added
155	Avelines, "Veue de la Place du Peuple" (engraving). Collection of Plino Nardecchia, Rome	180	From Giovanni Stern, *Piante Elevazioni, Profili e Spaccati degli Edifici della Villa Suburbana di Giulio III.* Antonio Fulgoni, Rome, 1784
156–157	Lithograph, 1880. Origin unknown		
158–159	Giovanni Battista Brocchi, "Carta Fisica del Suolo di Roma," 1820. Biblioteca Nazionale "Vittorio Emanuele." Photo: Fototeca di Architettura e Topografia dell'Italia Antica, Rome	181	Drawings from J. C. Shepherd and G. A. Jellicoe, *Italian Gardens of the Renaissance.* Alec Tiranti Ltd., London, 1953
		183	Photo: Aerofilms & Aero Pictorial Ltd., London
160	Photo: Fototeca di Architettura e Topografia dell'Italia Antica, Rome	184, 185	After Ernest F. Tew, *A Map of Bath,* and Walter Ison, *The Georgian Buildings of Bath from 1700 to 1830.* Faber and Faber Ltd., London, 1948
161	Giambattista Nolli, *Nuova Pianta di Roma,* 1748. (Lettering and dotted lines removed)		
162	Engraving with water color (detail), by Joannes Blaeu	186 upper	Commissaire Delamare, "Lutèce ou Premier Plan de la Ville de Paris, 1705
164–165	Engraving with water color, origin unknown	lower	Commissaire Delamare, "Cinquième Plan de la Ville de Paris," 1705
165 upper	Engraving with water color, by Joannes Blaeu	187	"Les Tuileries, Vue du jardin." Dessin de Perelle
166 upper	Jacob of Deventer, water color, sixteenth century. Martinus Nijhoff, The Hague	188–189	Plan of la Défense. Etablissement Public pour l'Aménagement de la Région de la Défense. Paris, 1971
166–167 lower	J. de Beyer, engraving with water color, 1750	190 left	Paris in 1380. "Plan dressé par H. Legrand." From a reproduction in the *Atlas des Anciens Plans*
167 upper	Jacob van Ruisdael. Rijksmuseum, Amsterdam		
168	Drawing from field survey by Prof. dr. C. S. Kruijt, ir. D. J. de Widt, W. Smeulers, H. J. van Veldhuizen, L. C. Johanns, L. H. Simons, Instituut voor Stedebouwkundig Onderzoek, Delft	right	Paris in 1609. "Plan de Vassalieu (dit Nicolay)." From a reproduction in the *Atlas des Anciens Plans*
		191	Paris, 1734 to 1739. "Plan de Louis Bretez, dit Plan de Turgot." From a reproduction in the *Atlas des Anciens Plans*
169	Water color, 1745. Artist unknown		
170, 171	Steen Eiler Rasmussen, *Towns and Buildings.* Harvard University Press, Cambridge, Mass., 1951	192–193	Plan prepared by I. M. Pei & Partners for la Défense. Paris, 1971
173	Colin Campbell, *Vitruvius Britannicus,* Vol. III. London, 1725	194–195	Environs of Paris, surveyed in 1740. Monsieur Jean l'Abbé de la Grive. Services Techniques et Commerciaux de la Réunion des Musées Nationaux, Paris. Reprinted from original plates
174	Photo: C. Jam, Nancy		
175	P. Patte. Engravings from *Monumens érigés en France à la gloire de Louis XV.* Paris, 1765	196–197	A. V. Bunin, *History of the Art of Urban Planning*
176 upper	Engraving, 1693. Published by le Sr. de Fer dans l'Isle du Palais à la Sphère Royale	200	Based on John Summerson, *John Nash, Architect to King George IV.* George Allen & Unwin Ltd., London, 1935 (second edition 1949)
lower	Modern engraving from old plates. Origin unknown	201	Thomas Fransioli, "Daily Life in London." Private collection. Photo: Milch Galleries
177	From Elbert Peets and Werner Hegemann, *Civic Arts.* Courtesy Architectural Book Publishing Co., New York, 1922	202	From John White, *Some Accounts*

of the Proposed Improvements of the Western Part of London, by the Formation of the Regent's Park.... Engraving. W. P. Reynolds, London, 1814

203, 204   James Elmes, *Metropolitan Improvements.* Jones & Co., London, 1829. Engravings from drawings by Thomas H. Shepherd

205 upper   Ibid.

206   Ibid.

207   London. Balloon view taken over Hampstead, 1851. Bibliothèque Nationale, Paris

208   John White, *Some Accounts of the Proposed Improvements ...* (Color overprint)

209–212   James Elmes, *Metropolitan Improvements*

213 upper   Ibid.

lower   Regent Street Layout Plan. After *Survey of London,* Vol. 29, p. 217. University of London, The Athlone Press. Redrawn by W. Bale

214   James Elmes, *Metropolitan Improvements*

215   La Défense. Paris. Model. Photo-Studio Jean Rabier

216   From Pietro di Giacomo Cataneo, *L'Architettura.* Venice, 1567. Cooper Union Museum

217 upper   Map redrawn by W. Bale

lower   From Map "of 500," 1690, redrawn by W. Bale. From the collections of The Historical Society of Pennsylvania

218   From *Historic American Buildings Survey,* from the work of Richard Carr Peters, and from photographs by the author

219   Engraving by Peter Gordon, 1734. From the collection of Carl Feiss

220, 221   Reprinted from John W. Reps, *The Making of Urban America.* Princeton University Press, Princeton, N.J., 1965

222   Ellicott Map of Washington, D. C.

223   Map drawn by Andrew Ellicott. Reprinted from original copperplate engraving by Thackara and Vallance, 1792. U. S. Dept. of Commerce, Coast and Geodetic Survey

224–225   Williamsburg, Va. "The Frenchman's Map," 1781-1782. From the map in the Earl Gregg Swem Library at the College of William and Mary, by courtesy of Colonial Williamsburg

Engravings of the College of William and Mary, the Governor's Palace, and the Capitol, from the "Bodleian Plate," probably engraved in 1737 (Colonial Williamsburg), are inserted in the map

226, 227   Photos: from the Public Archives of Canada, Ottawa

228–229   Le Corbusier and Pierre Jeanneret, *Oeuvre Complète* 1910-1929, Vol. 1. Les Editions d'Architecture (Artemis), Zürich, Switzerland

230   Drawing by Giroud for Le Concours du Grand Prix de Rome d'Architecture, 1922. Ecole Nationale des Beaux Arts. Armand Guérinet, Editeur, Paris

231   Le Corbusier, *Concerning Town Planning.* The Architectural Press, Ltd., London, 1946

232   Plan by Le Corbusier, redrawn by students, University of Pennsylvania

234 upper   Plan of Brasilia. Shell Brazil Ltd.

237   Drawing by Oscar Niemeyer

244–247   Photos: Colin Penn, London

246–247, 248   Drawings from A. V. Bunin, *History of the Art of Urban Planning*

249   Peking. Model by Students at the University of Pennsylvania: Tim Davis, Andrew Kinsler, Henry Meltzer, Steve Olderman, John Williams

250   Drawing from A. V. Bunin, *History of the Art of Urban Planning*

251   Drawing obtained by R. Osvald-Siren from Professor Ito, Imperial Architect School in Japan, appears in Mr. Siren's *The Imperial Palaces of Peking.* G. Van Oest, Paris and Brussels, 1926

252   Paul Klee, "Free-formed Polyphonic Organism" (pencil and crayon). Courtesy of the Klee Foundation, Berne

253   Paul Klee, diagrams. From *The Thinking Eye*

255   Drawings by author

256   Drawing by office of Vincent Ponte, *Art in America,* Vol. LVII, No. 5 (September-October 1969), p. 64

263   Camac & Susquehanna Neighborhood Development Program, Phila-

delphia City Planning Commission, 1969

264 right   Paul Klee, diagram. From *The Thinking Eye*

left   Society Hill. Webb & Knapp plan for redevelopment of Washington Square East, 1958. Architect, I. M. Pei

265   Society Hill. Better Philadelphia Exhibition, 1947. Model by Panoramic Studios. Photo: Jules Schick

Society Hill. Plan by Vincent G. Kling, Roy F. Larson, and Oskar Stonorov, 1957. City Planning Commission. Photo: L. Williams

Society Hill. Proposal developed by Preston Andrade under contract with the Redevelopment Authority. 1958. Photo: L. Williams

Society Hill. Model of proposal by Webb & Knapp, 1960. Architect, I. M. Pei. Photo: Ibarguen

266   Center City East Design Structure, 1947. City Planning Commission. From *The Architectural Record*, May, 1961

267   Ibid., 1966

268–269   Penn's Landing. Prepared for the Department of Commerce by Geddes, Brecher, Qualls and Cunningham, Architects, 1963

272 upper   Penn Center. City Planning Commission Proposal, 1952. Vincent Kling, Consulting Architect. Photo: Cortlandt V. D. Hubbard

274   Photo: A. Strobl

275   Model of City Hall—West Plaza. Philadelphia Department of Public Property, 1969. Photograph, Lawrence S. Williams

276   Market Street East General Neighborhood Renewal Plan. Prepared for the Redevelopment Authority by Skidmore, Owings and Merrill, 1966

upper   Movement system model

lower   Architectural model

277   A Comprehensive Plan for Downtown Buffalo. Wallace, McHarg, Roberts and Todd

278–279   Drawing by Vincent G. Kling and Associates. Photo: L. Williams

280, 281   Market East Study. Drawn by Willo von Moltke, 1960. City Planning Commission

282–283   Market East Study. Drawn by Romaldo Giurgola (upper) and Donald Jackson (lower), 1963. City Planning Commission

284–285   Market East Study. Drawn by Romaldo Giurgola, 1964. City Planning Commission

286–287   Market East and Market Street Linear Development Proposal. City Planning Commission, 1965

288–289   Market Street East: Skidmore, Owings and Merrill

290–291   1234 Market Street East. Drawings by Bower and Fradley, 1971

292–293 upper   Market Street East. Models by Bower and Fradley. Photo: Harris & Davis

lower   Drawing by Bower and Fradley

294–295   Market Street East. Bower and Fradley

296, 297   Photos: Robert Damora, Bedford Village, N.Y.

298–299 upper   University City, Unit 3, Urban Renewal Area. Prepared for the Redevelopment Authority by Geddes, Brecher, Qualls and Cunningham, Architects, 1964

lower   From Vitruvius Pollio, *Architecture ou Art de Bien Bâtir*. Translated from Latin into French by Ian Martin. Printed by Hierosme de Marnef and Guillaume Cauellat, Paris, 1572

300–301   "United States of America Bicentennial." City Planning Commission, 1963

302–303   Comprehensive Plan, Area Plans, and Capital Program. Philadelphia City Planning Commission

304, 305   New Center designed and drawn for the Pennsylvania Railroad by Vincent Kling, and a model of the plan, 1966

306, 307   Drawings by Romaldo Giurgola. 1976 Bicentennial

308–309   Canberra. Drawing by Walter Burley Griffin. Courtesy Art Institute of Chicago. Photo: Art Institute of Chicago

310–311 upper   *The Improvement of the Park System of the District of Columbia*, edited by Charles Moore. Government Printing Office, 1902

middle right   Drawing by Pierre Charles L'Enfant, 1791. Library of Congress, Map Division

middle left   Plan for Canberra. Walter Burley Griffin

lower	Perspective from Mount Ainslie, drawn by Marion Lucy Griffin. Photo: Art Institute of Chicago
312–315	Lower Norrmalm. Designed and drawn by David Hellden
316, 317	First Prize, Vienna International Town Planning Competition, 1971, by Geddes, Brecher, Qualls and Cunningham
318	Paul Klee, "Polyphonic Architecture" (water color), 1930. City Art Museum of St. Louis
319	Willo von Moltke and Edmund N. Bacon, "In Pursuit of Urbanity." *The Annals of the American Academy of Political and Social Service,* Vol. 314 (November 1957). Drawing by Willo von Moltke
320	Paul Klee, "Uncomposed Objects in Space" (water color), 1929. Private collection
321, 322	Paul Klee, diagrams. From *The Thinking Eye*
323	Paul Klee, "Perspective of a City" (water color), 1928. Ida Bienert, Munich

Photos by author: 53–57, 67, 72, 89, 96–97, 111, 172, 182, 184–185, 233, 234–235, 236, 238–243

Drawings by author: 14–18, 20

Books used for illustrations on pp. 78, 94–95, 134, 173, 175, 180, 187, and 298 were obtained from the University of Pennsylvania Fine Arts Library

BIBLIOGRAPHY

Accademia Nazionale di S. Luca. *Il Campidoglio di Michelangelo.* Milan, 1965.

Ackerman, James S. *The Architecture of Michelangelo.* The Viking Press, Inc. New York, 1961.

Alberti, Leon Battista. *Ten Books on Architecture.* (English translation) Alec Tiranti Ltd. London, 1955.

American School of Classical Studies at Athens. *The Athenian Agora.* Athens, 1962.

Aurigemma, Salvatore. *Villa Adriana.* Libreria dello Stato. Rome, 1961.

Belloc, Hilaire. *Paris.* Methuen & Co. Ltd. London, 1900.

Birrell, James. *Walter Burley Griffin.* University of Queensland Press. Brisbane, 1964.

Boyd, Andrew. *Chinese Architecture and Town Planning.* University of Chicago Press. Chicago, 1962.

Brown, Frank E. *Roman Architecture.* George Braziller, Inc. New York, 1961.

Bunin, A. V. *History of the Art of Urban Planning.* (In Russian) Moscow, 1953.

Burke, Gerald L. *The Making of Dutch Towns.* Cleaver-Hulme Press Ltd. London, 1956.

Cameron, Nigel, and Brake, Brian. *Peking. A Tale of Three Cities.* Harper & Row, Publishers. New York, 1965.

Choay, Françoise. *The Modern City: Planning in the 19th Century.* George Braziller. New York, 1969.

Clifford, Derek. *A History of Garden Design.* Frederick A. Praeger, Inc. New York, 1963.

Conseil Municipal de Paris. *Altas des Anciens Plans de Paris.* Paris, 1880.

Consiglio Nazionale delle Ricerche. *Studi per Una Operante Storia Urbana di Roma.* Rome, 1963.

Doxiadis, Constantinos A. *Ekistics, An Introduction to the Science of Human Settlements.* Hutchinson. London, 1968.

Eaton, Leonard K. *Two Chicago Architects and Their Clients: Frank Lloyd Wright and Howard Van Doren Shaw.* M. I. T. Press. Cambridge, 1969.

Elmes, James. *Metropolitan Improvements: or, London in the Nineteenth Century.* Jones & Co. London, 1829.

Fabos, Julius Gy., Milde, Gordon T., and Weinmayr, V. Michael. *Frederick Law Olmsted, Sr.* University of Massachusetts Press, 1968.

Fontana, Domenico. *Of the Moving of the Vatican Obelisk and of the Edifices of our Lord Pope Sixtus V.* Rome, 1590. (Unpublished English translation by Mrs. Alfred H. Barr, Jr.).

Fouquier, Marcel. *De l'Art des Jardins du XVe au XXe Siècle.* Emile-Paul. Paris, 1911.

Fox, Helen M. *André Le Nôtre, Garden Architect to Kings.* Crown Publishers, Inc. New York, 1962.

Fraschetti, Stanislao. *Il Bernini: La Sua Vita, La Sua Opera, Il Suo Tempo.* Editore Ulrico Hoepli. Milan, 1900.

Giedion, Sigfried. *Architecture, You and Me.* Harvard University Press. Cambridge, Mass., 1958.

———. *Space, Time and Architecture.* Harvard University Press. Cambridge, Mass., 1941.

Giedion-Welcker, Carola. *Paul Klee.* (English translation) Faber and Faber Ltd. London, 1952.

Gosling, Nigel. *Leningrad.* E. P. Dutton & Co., Inc. New York, 1965.

Gothein, Marie Luise. *A History of Garden Art.* J. M. Dent & Sons, Ltd. London, 1928.

Hegemann, Werner, and Peets, Elbert. *Civic Art.* The Architectural Book Publishing Co. New York, 1922.

Hilliaret, Jacques. *Le Palais du Louvre.* Les Editions de Minuit. Paris, 1955.

Hiorns, Frederick R. *Town-building in History.* Criterion Books, Inc. New York, 1958.

Holt, Elizabeth G. *A Documentary History of Art.* (2 vols.) Doubleday & Company, Inc. Garden City, N.Y., 1958.

Hotz, Walter. *Kleine Kunstgeschichte der Deutschen Burg.* Wissenschaftliche Buchgesellschaft. Darmstadt, 1965.

Ison, Walter W. *The Georgian Buildings of Bath from 1700 to 1830.* Faber and Faber Ltd. London, 1948.

Istituto di Studi Romani. *Le Piante di Roma* (3 vols.) Rome, 1962.

Kähler, Heinz. *Hadrian und seine Villa bei Tivoli.* Gebr. Mann, G.m.b.H. Berlin, 1950.

Kahn, Louis. *The Notebooks and Drawings.* Richard Saul Wurman and Eugene Feldman, eds. Falcon Press. Philadelphia, 1962.

Kepes, Gyorgy, ed. *Education of Vision.* George Braziller, Inc. New York, 1965.

————. *Structure in Art and in Science.* George Braziller, Inc. New York, 1965.

————. *The Nature and Art of Motion.* George Braziller, Inc. New York, 1965.

Kirsten, E., and Kraiker, W. *Griechenlandkunde.* Carl Winter Universitätsverlag. Heidelberg, 1957.

Klee, Paul. *On Modern Art.* (English translation) London, 1948.

————. *Klee.* Will Grohmann, ed. Harry N. Abrams, Inc. New York, 1954.

————. *The Thinking Eye, the notebooks of Paul Klee.* Jürg Spiller, ed. (English translation) George Wittenborn. New York, 1961.

Kubler, George. *The Shape of Time.* Yale University Press. New Haven, Conn., 1962.

Lavedan, Pierre. *Les Villes Francaises.* Vincent, Freal & Cie. 8th ed., Paris, 1936.

————. *Histoire de l'Urbanisme.* (3 vols.) Henri Laurens. Paris, 1926–1952.

Le Corbusier. *Concerning Town Planning.* The Architectural Press, Ltd. London, 1946.

Le Corbusier and Jeanneret, Pierre. *Oeuvre Complète.* Les Editions d'Architecture. Zurich, 1937.

Luporini, Eugenio. *Brunelleschi Forma e Ragione.* Edizioni di Comunità. Milan, 1964.

Lynch, Kevin. *Image of the City.* M.I.T. Press. Cambridge, Mass., 1960.

MacDonald, William L. *The Architecture of the Roman Empire.* Yale University Press. New Haven, Conn., 1965.

Marconi, Paolo. *Giuseppe Valadier.* Officina Edizioni. Rome, 1964.

Martienssen, R. D. *The Idea of Space in Greek Architecture.* Witwatersrand University Press. Johannesburg, 1958.

Martin, Robert, and Grosjean, Marc. *Nancy.* Librairie Hachette. Paris, 1959.

Martin, Roland. *L'Urbanisme dans la Grèce Antique.* A. & J. Picard & Cie. Paris, 1956.

McLuhan, Marshall. *Understanding Media: The Extensions of Man.* McGraw-Hill Book Company. New York, 1964.

Meyerson, Martin, ed. *The Conscience of the City.* George Braziller, Inc. New York, 1970.

Moore, Charles, ed. *The Improvement of the Park System of the District of Columbia.* Government Printing Office. Washington, 1902.

Morini, Mario. *Atlante, di Storia dell'Urbanistica.* Editore Ulrico Hoepli. Milan, 1963.

Mumford, Lewis. *The City in History.* Harcourt, Brace & World, Inc. New York, 1961.

————. *Technics and Civilization.* Harcourt, Brace and Company. New York, 1934.

Nash, Ernest. *Pictorial Dictionary of Ancient Rome.* Frederick A. Praeger, Inc. New York, 1962.

Olsen, Donald J. *Town Planning in London.* Yale University Press. New Haven, Conn., 1964.

Pevsner, Nikolaus. *An Outline of European Architecture.* Penguin Books, Inc. Baltimore, Md., 1943.

Portoghesi, Paolo, and Zevi, Bruno. *Michelangiolo architetto.* Giulio Einaudi Editore. Turin, 1964.

Rasmussen, Steen Eiler. *Experiencing Architecture.* (English translation) M.I.T. Press. Cambridge, Mass., 1962.

————. *London, The Unique City.* Jonathan Cape. (English rev. ed.) London, 1937.

————. *Towns and Buildings.* Harvard University Press. Cambridge, Mass., 1951.

Regional Plan Association. *Urban Design: Manhattan.* The Viking Press, Inc. New York, 1969.

Reps, John W. *The Making of Urban America.* Princeton University Press. Princeton, N.J., 1965.

Rosenau, Helen. *Social Purpose in Architecture: Paris and London Compared 1760–1800.* Studio Vista Ltd. London, 1970.

Saarinen, Eliel. *The City.* Reinhold Publishing Corporation. New York, 1943.

Scully, Vincent. *The Earth, the Temple and the Gods.* Yale University Press. New Haven, 1962.

Shepherd, J. C., and Jellicoe, G. A. *Italian Gardens of the Renaissance.* Alec Tiranti Ltd. London, 1953.

Sheppard, F. H. W., ed. *Survey of London;* Vol. XXIX, Parish of St. James, Westminster. Part I: South of Piccadilly. London, 1960.

Sitte, Camillo. *The Art of Building Cities.* (English translation) Reinhold Publishing Corporation. New York, 1945.

Spengler, Oswald. *The Decline of the West.* (2 vols., English translation) Alfred A. Knopf, Inc. New York, 1926.

Spreiregen, Paul D. *Urban Design: The Architecture of Towns and Cities.* McGraw-Hill Book Company. New York, 1965.

Stern, Giovanni. *Piante Elevazioni, Profili e Spaccati degli Edifici della Villa Suburbana di Giulio III.* Rome, 1784.

Summerson, John. *John Nash, Architect to King George IV.* George Allen & Unwin Ltd. London, 1935.

Travlos, John. ΠΟΛΕΟΔΟΜΙΚΗ ΕΞΕΛΙΞΙΣΤΩΝΑΘΗΝΩΝ. Athens, 1960.

Tunnard, Christopher. *The City of Man.* Charles Scribner's Sons. New York, 1953.

Urbanistica, No. 12, No. 27. Rome, 1953, 1959.

Vasari, Giorgio. *Lives of the Most Eminent Painters, Sculptors and Architects.* 1st ed., 1550. (English translation) Philip Lee Warner, Publisher to the Medici Society, Limited. London, 1912.

Vighi, Roberto. *Villa Hadriana.* Rome, 1961.

Vitruvius. *The Ten Books on Architecture.* (French translation, Paris, 1572.) (English translation) Dover Publications, Inc. New York, 1960.

Westermanns Atlas zur Weltgeschichte. Georg Westermann Verlag Braunschweig. Berlin, 1965.

White, John. *Some Accounts of the Proposed Improvements of the Western Part of London. . . .* London, 1814.

Willetts, William. *Chinese Art.* (2 vols.) Penguin Books Ltd. Harmondsworth, England, 1958.

Wittkower, Rudolf. *Architectural Principles in the Age of Humanism.* Alec Tiranti Ltd. London, 1952.

————. *Art and Architecture in Italy. 1600 to 1750.* Penguin Books Ltd. Harmondsworth, England, 1958.

Wölfflin, Heinrich. *Principles of Art History.* (Paperback edition) Dover Publications, Inc. New York.

————. *Renaissance and Baroque.* First published by Benno Schwabe & Co. Verlag. 1961. (Introduction and English translation) Wm. Collins Sons & Co. Ltd. London, 1964.

Wycherley, R. E. *How the Greeks Built Cities.* Macmillan & Co Ltd. London, 1962.

Young, Arthur. *Autugenesis.* (Unpublished manuscript) Philadelphia, 1965.

Yutang. Lin. *Imperial Peking.* Crown Publishers, Inc. New York, 1961.

Zevi, Bruno. *Architecture as Space.* Horizon Press. New York, 1964.

INDEX

Adam, Robert, 185, 201
Aeschylus, 65
Agnolo, Baccio d', 108
Ajax (Sophocles), 11
Alberti, Leone, 124
Aldrich, Robert A., 258
Ammanati, Bartolommeo, 111, 112
Andrade, Preston, 265
Architecture, You and Me (Giedion), 18
Arnheim, Rudolph, 48
Aronson, J. H., 95, 115, 118
Athens, 23, 64, 65, 67, 69–73; Acropolis, 64, 67, 70, 72, 73; Athena (statue), 65, 67; Council House, 70; Dipylon Gate, 64, 67, 72; grottoes of Eleusis, 67; Odeion, 71; Panathenaic Way, 65, 67, 70, 71, 73, 85; Parthenon, 64, 67, 72; Propylaea, 67; Stoa of Attalos, 71, 72; Stoa of Zeus, 70, 71; Temple of Apollo Patroos, 71; Temple of Ares, 71; Temple of Hephaestos, 67, 70, 71, 72

Bagnaja: Villa Lante, 45
Bartolo, Taddeo di, 138
Bartolommeo, Neroccio di, 121
Bath, 29, 182–85, 201; Abbey, 184; Avon River, 185; Gay Street, 184; Lansdowne Crescent, 183, 185; Pulteney Street Bridge, 185; Queen's Square, 184; Royal Crescent, 183, 185; St. James's Square, 185
Bernini, Giovanni Lorenzo, 131, 132, 134, 148, 152, 155, 161
Berry, Charles Ferdinand, duke of, 42
Better Philadelphia Exhibition (1947), 264, 265
Blaeu, Joannes, 163
Boffrand, Germain, 175
Book of Hours, 42
Bordino, Giovanni Francesco, 138
Borromini, Francesco, 152
Boston City Hall, 269
Botticelli, Sandro, 19

Bower, John, 291, 293, 294, 299
Bower & Fradley, 291
Bramante, Lazzari, 109, 118, 124, 132
Brasilia, 237–41; Administration Building, 237, 240, 241; bus terminal, 238; Congress Building, 237, 239; Highway Platform, 239; House of Representatives, 241; Supreme Court Building, 240, 241
Brocchi, Giovanni Battista, 159
Brunelleschi, Filippo, 59, 107, 108, 109, 229
Buffalo, 277

Caccini, 109
Camiros, 81, 82
Canberra, 309–10; Black Mountain, 309; Capitol Hill, 309; Mount Ainslee, 309
Cataneo, Pietro di Giacomo, 217
Chambord, Château de, 269
Chandigarh, 233, 240
Charles V (king of France), 187
Charles VI (king of France), 187
Ciardi, John, 35
Copenhagen, 171–73; Amalienborg Palace, 173; Marble Church, 173
Cortona, Pietro da, 126
Costa, Lucio, 239
"Creative Credo" (Klee), 11
Culemborg, 163, 164, 167

Dawe, Patric, 263
De Architectura (Vitruvius), 217
Delauney, Robert, 18
Delos, 77, 79
Deventer, Jacob of, 167
DNA concept, 258
Dosio, Antonio, 140
Doxiades, C. A., 258
Dowling, Robert, 305

Eaton, Leonard K., 48

École des Beaux Arts, 228, 231
Education of Vision (Kepes), 48
Eigtved, Nicolai, 171
Einstein, Albert, 48
Ellicott, Andrew, 222
Encyclopedists, 45
Erikson, Erik H., 46, 263

Falda, Giovanni Battista, 152
Ferdinand I (statue), 109
Florence, 99, 107–12, 115, 118, 136, 314; Cacus (sculpture), 112; Cosimo I (statue), 111, 112; David (statue), 112; Foundling Hospital, 107, 108; Hercules (statue), 112; Innocenti arcade, 109; Loggia dei Lanzi, 111; Neptune (statue), 111, 112; Palazzo della Tribunale di Mercanzia, 111; Palazzo Vecchio, 99, 111, 112; Piazza della Santissima Annunziata, 107, 109, 118, 314; Piazza della Signoria, 99, 107, 108, 109, 111; River Arno, 99, 107, 108, 112; Santissima Annunziata Church, 107, 108, 109; Uffizi, 99, 107, 111, 112, 136; Via Calimaruzza, 111; Via Vacchereccia, 111
Fontana, Domenico, 137, 150, 155
"Forma Urbis" (map), 160
Francesca, Piero della, 123
Frederik V (king of Denmark), 171

Geddes, Robert, 269, 298, 299
Geddes, Brecher, Qualls and Cunningham, 317
George IV (king of England), 210
Giambologna, 109, 111
Giedion, Sigfried, 18
Giurgola, Romaldo, 32, 283, 293, 299, 306
Greenwich, 172, 204; Naval Hospital, 172; Queen's House, 172; River Thames, 172
Griffin, Walter Burley, 309, 310
Gruen, Victor, 242
Guardi, Francesco, 23, 97, 246

Hadamard, Jacques, 48
Hadrian, Emperor, 82, 89
Haussmann, Baron Georges, 193
Heemskerck, Maarten van, 115, 117
Hellden, David, 312, 314
Henriet, Israel, 132
Henry II (king of France), 188
Henry IV (king of France), 188
Héré, Emanuel, 175, 177, 178
Herulians, 71
Hippodamus, 75
Holme, Thomas, 217
Hottlinger, M. D., 11

"Ideal City, The " (painting), 124
Ischia, 53–57

Jerusalem: Mosque of Omar, 17
Jones, Inigo, 172, 184

Kähler, Heinz, 88
Kahn, Louis, 105, 264, 269, 299
Kennedy, John F., 150
Kepes, Gyorgy, 48

Klee, Paul, 11, 38, 39, 41, 42, 43, 45, 52, 59, 61, 63, 68, 69, 112, 115, 126, 128, 131, 134, 138, 139, 146, 187, 193, 198, 253, 264, 317, 319, 321, 322
Kling, Vincent, 265, 273, 275, 291, 299, 305, 306

Lafréry, Antoine, 136, 137
Lamour, Jean, 175, 179
Langham, Sir James, 206
L'Architettura (Cataneo), 217
Larson, Roy, 264, 265, 299
Le Corbusier, 88, 228–29, 231, 233
Leczinski, Stanislas, 175, 178–79
Leger, Fernand, 18, 54
L'Enfant, Pierre, 222, 309–10
Le Nôtre, André, 187, 188, 191
Leningrad, *see* Saint Petersburg
London, 201–14, 314; All Souls Church, 201, 206; British Broadcasting Corporation Building, 206; British Museum, 201; Buckingham Palace, 201, 209, 212; Carlton House, 201, 208, 209, 210, 212; Carlton House Terrace, 206, 209; Cavendish Square, 206, 208, 209; Charles Street, 212; County Fire Office, 209, 210, 212; Cumberland Terrace, 203, 212; Duke of York Column, 209, 212; Foley House, 201, 206; Golden Square, 206; Great Circus, 203, 204, 208; Great Quadrant, 209, 210–11, 212; Hanover Square, 208, 209; Haymarket, 212; Haymarket Theatre, 212; Inner Circus, 203; Kingsway, 208; Mall, 201, 209, 212; Nash and, 201–212; New Road, 203, 204; North Baker Street, 204; Oxford Street, 206, 209; Park Crescent, 201; Park Square, 201; Piccadilly, 209, 212; Portland Place, 201, 203, 204, 206, 208; Regent Street, 201, 206, 208, 209, 210–11; Regent's Park, 201, 203, 208, 210; St. James's Park, 201, 212; St. James's Square, 212; Saint Marylebone Church, 204, 210; Saint Paul's Cathedral, 314; Soho, 208; Trafalgar Square, 201; Waterloo Place, 212; Westminster, 210; York Terrace, 204
Lorenzetti, Ambrogio, 93, 95
Louis XIII (king of France), 187
Louis XV (king of France), 77, 175, 179
Lowell, John, 253
Lutyens, Sir Edwin, 233

McMillan Commission, 222
Maderna, Carlo, 132
Making of Urban America, The (Reps), 220
Mantua, 93, 101
Mary II (queen of England), 172
McCormick Taylor Associates, 275
Medici, Cosimo de', 99
Médicis, Catherine de, 187, 188
Médicis, Marie de, 187, 188
Michelangelo, 95, 100, 112, 115–18, 132, 136, 140, 141, 144, 150
Michelozzo, 108
Miletus, 75
Milles, Carl, 312
Moguls, 233
Moltke, Willo von, 265, 281, 319

Montreal, 254
Monumens érigés en France à la gloire de Louis XV (Patte), 175
Moscow, 196
Mumford, Lewis, 318, 319
Musho, Theodore J., 126
Mussolini, Benito, 134

Nancy, 175–79; Arch of Triumph, 177, 178; Ducal Palace, 177, 178; Hôtel de Beauvau-Craon, 175, 178; Palace of the Provincial Government, 177, 178–79; Place de la Carrière, 175, 177, 178–79; Place Royale, 175, 177, 178–79; Place Stanislas, 175; "Ville Newe," 175, 177; Ville Vieille, 175, 177
Napoleon I (emperor of the French), 193
Napoleon III (emperor of the French), 193
Nara: Horyuji, 37
Nash, John 201–212
Nehru, Jawaharlal, 233
New Delhi, 233
Newman, Arnold, 273
New York City, 252
Niemeyer, Oscar, 237
Nolli, Giambattista, 161

Oglethorpe, James, 217
Ottawa, 227; Parliament Building, 227; Peace Tower, 227

Padua, 26
Panza, 53–57, 61, 242
Paris, 77, 83, 187–93, 196, 215, 252; Arc de Triomphe, 215; Avenue des Tuileries, 191; Bastille, 188; Champ de Mars, 193; Champs Élysées, 83, 187, 188, 191, 192, 193, 215; Cours la Reine, 188; Eiffel Tower, 193; esplanade of the Invalides, 193; Grande Galerie, 188; Ile de la Cité, 187; La Défense, 188, 192, 215; Louvre, 188, 191, 192, 215; Place de la Concorde, 191; River Seine, 187, 188, 191, 193; Tuileries Gardens, 187, 188, 191; Tuileries Palace, 83, 188, 191
Patte, Pierre, 175
Paul III (pope), 115
Paul V (pope), 146
Pederson, William F., 31
Pei, Ieoh Ming, 264, 265, 269, 297
Peking, 48, 242, 244–51; Altar of Heaven, 246, 247; Bell Tower, 249; Coal Hill, 249, 250; Drum Tower, 249; Forbidden City, 64, 246, 247, 249, 250; Hall of Protecting Harmony, 251; Hall of Supreme Harmony, 249, 251; Imperial City, 249, 250; Imperial Palace, 250; Inner City, 249; Outer City, 249; River of Golden Water, 247, 251; Temple of Agriculture, 249; Temple of Heaven, 249; Throne Halls, 249; tombs, 20; Wu Mên (Meridian Gate), 249, 251
Penn, William, 217
Penn Plan for Philadelphia, 264, 298, 305
Pennsylvania Railroad, 272, 305
Perelle, Gabriel, 187
Pergamon: Acropolis, 63, 253
Perugia, 98

Peruzzi, Baldassare, 124
Peter the Great (tsar of Russia), 196
Pevsner, Nikolaus, 184
Philadelphia, 13, 33, 63, 217, 254, 264–306; Art Museum, 268; Broad Street, 305; Center City, 268, 294; Central Pennsylvania Bank, 273; Christ Church, 264; City Hall, 268, 273, 278–79, 283, 305; City Hall Tower, 273; Delaware Expressway, 264; Delaware River, 264, 297, 298; East Market Street, 277, 279, 281; Eighth and Market Streets, 281; Franklin Square, 264; Friends Meeting House, 264; Greenway System, 264; IBM Company building, 273; Independence Hall, 264; Independence Mall, 264, 299; International Exposition, 306; Market East, 277, 281, 285, 288, 291, 293, 294, 295, 299; Market Street, 277, 279, 281, 283, 285, 291, 293, 294, 298, 299, 305; Municipal Services Building, 273, 279; Parkway, 268; Pei Towers, 265, 268, 269, 297; Penn Center, 272, 273, 275, 277, 281, 285, 293, 294, 299; Penn's Landing, 297; Planning Commission, 263, 265, 272, 288, 291, 294; Powel House, 297; Saint Paul's Church, 268; Saving Fund Society, 291; Schuylkill River, 298–99, 305–306; Science Center, 298; Second Street, 268; Society Hill, 264, 265, 269, 272, 281, 297; Spruce Street, 268; Twelfth Street, 293; Wanamaker's Department Store building, 291; Washington Square, 264, 265; West Plaza, 278
Philadelphia 1976 Bicentennial Corporation, 306
Philadelphia Department of Public Property, 275
Philadelphia Redevelopment Authority, 264, 265, 288, 298
Piranesi, Giambattista, 134, 150, 152
Pisanello, Antonio, 123
Pompidou, Georges, 215
Ponte, Vincent, 254
Pozzo, Andrea, 30
Priene, 80, 81; Assembly Hall, 80; Temple of Athena, 80
Principles of Art History (Wölfflin), 11
Prospettiva de' Pittori ed Architetti (Pozzo), 30

Qualls, George, 317

Rainaldi, Carlo, 146, 148, 155
Rasmussen, Steen Eiler, 171
Reps, John W., 220
Rhodes, 81
Rome, 24, 45, 85–87, 115–18, 121, 126, 131–61, 181; Antonine columns, 138; Bernini Tower, 132; Bernini Triton Fountain, 143; Campidoglio, 109, 115, 116, 118, 138, 142; Canopus, 88; Circus Maximus, 85; Colosseum, 138, 141, 142; Dioscuri (statues), 138, 141, 143, 144, 150; Flaminian Gate, 86, 142; Forum, 142, 160; Fountains of Acqua Felice, 144, 150; Lateran Palace (Vatican), 150; Maderna façade, 132, 137; Marcus Aurelius (statue), 109, 116, 117, 138; Marforio (statue), 117; Palazzo Barberini, 143; Palazzo dei Conservatori, 115, 116; Palazzo on Monte Citorio, 161; Palazzo del Senatore, 115, 116; Pantheon, 138, 161; Pavilion of the Accademia, 88; Pavilion

of the Piazza d'Oro, 88; Piazza Barberini, 143; Piazza d'Espagna, 152; Piazza Navona, 25; Piazza del Popolo, 25, 132, 142, 143, 144, 152, 155, 157; Piazza Quirinale, 143, 159; Piazza San Bernardo, 150; Piazza Sant'Ignazio, 126, 161; Piazza della Trinità, 155; Pincio Gardens, 143, 155; Porta Pia, 141, 142, 144, 150, 159; Porta del Popolo, 137, 140, 142, 155; Porta di Ripetta, 140, 143, 157; Quirinal Hill, 138, 141, 142; Quirinal Palace, 144, 150; Saint Peter's Church, 131, 132, 134, 136; San Carlino alle Quattro Fontane Church, 152; San Giovanni in Laterano, 116, 137, 138, 141, 142, 157, 159; San Girolamo degli Schiavoni, 143, 157; San Trinità dei Monti, 141, 142, 152, 155, 157, 159; Santa Croce, 141, 142, 159; Sant'Agnese, 25; Sant'Ignacio Church, 126; Santa Maria in Aracoeli, 117; Santa Maria Maggiore, 137, 138, 140, 141, 142, 144, 146, 148, 152, 157, 159; Santa Maria dei Miracoli, 155; Santa Maria di Monte Santo, 155; Santa Maria della Pace Square, 126; Santa Maria del Popolo, 137, 155; Santa Maria della Vittorio, 150; Sistine Chapel (Vatican), 150; Sistine Library (Vatican), 131, 144; Spanish Steps, 142, 143, 144, 152, 157; Strada Felice, 141, 142, 143, 144, 146, 148, 150, 152, 157, 159; Strada Pia, 141, 142, 143, 144, 150, 152, 159; Temple of Jupiter, 85; Tiber River, 141, 143, 155; Trajan's column, 138; Trevi Fountain, 138; Triumphal Procession, 85; Vatican Cortile, 109, 118; Via Agostino Depretis, 144; Via del Babuino, 142, 143, 152; Via della Conciliazione, 134; Via del Corso, 86, 142; Via Flaminia, 86, 87, 142, 143; Via Quattro Fontane, 150; Via Quirinale, 150; Via Ripetta, 142; Via Sacra, 86, 87; Via Vento Settembre, 150; Villa Giulia, 181

Ronchamp, 181
Rossi, 152
Rotterdam, 242; Lijnbaan, 242
Ruisdael, Jacob van, 167

Saarinen, Eliel, 128
"Sailing City" (water-color), 61
Saint Petersburg, 196–98; Admiralty, 196, 197, 198; Ministry of War, 197; Neva River, 196, 198; Saint Isaac Cathedral, 197; Winter Palace, 196, 197, 198
Salk, Jonas E., 258
Salviati, Francesco, 125, 126
Sanctis, Francesco de, 152
Sangallo, Antonio da, 108–109, 118, 314
Saturday Review, 35
Saumur, Castle of, 42
Savannah, 217, 219–21; Factor's Walk, 220
Seashore, Carl, 48
Series of Plans for Cottages, Habitations of the Laborer, A (Wood the Younger), 29
Severus, Septimus, 160
Shepherd, Thomas H., 203, 214
Shopping Towns USA (Smith and Gruen), 242
Silvestre, Israel, 132
Sixtus V (pope), 25, 45, 87, 126, 131, 134, 136–44, 146, 148, 150, 152, 155
Skidmore, Owings and Merrill, 277, 288, 291

Smith, Larry, 242
Sophocles, 11
Space, Time and Architecture (Giedion), 48
Specchi, Alessandro, 152
Stockholm, 214, 312, 314; Concert Hall, 312; Lower Norrmalm, 214, 312, 314; Orpheus Fountain, 312
Stonorov, Oskar, 265
Summerson, Sir John, 208

Tange, Kenzo, 36, 241
Tempesta, Antonio, 155
Tengbom, Ivar, 312
Thinking Eye, The (Klee), 11, 45, 59, 138
Tilney, Bradford S., 31
Tivoli, 23, 77, 82; Hadrian's Villa, 77, 82, 88, 89; Villa d'Este, 23
Todd, Thomas, 277
Todi, 83, 95, 96, 98; Garibaldi (statue), 95; Palazzo del Popolo, 95, 96, 97; Palazzo dei Priori, 95
Tokyo: Olympic Sports Building, 36, 241
Towns and Buildings (Rasmussen), 171
Travlos, John, 70
Turgot, Michel Étienne, 191
Tuscany, 93
Two Chicago Architects and Their Clients (Eaton), 48

Utescher, Gerd, 275

Valadier, Giuseppe, 155, 157
Vällingby, 29
Vasari, Giorgio, 59, 99, 136
Vassalieu, 191
Venice, 93, 99, 101, 104–105, 169; Cathedral of Saint Mark, 99, 101; Doge's Palace, 101; Grand Canal, 99, 101, 105; Piazza San Marco, 99, 101, 104–105; Saint Mark's Library, 105
Vienna International Town Planning Competition (1971), 317
Vignola, Giacoma da, 59, 161, 181
Vitruvius, Marcus Pollio, 217

Waddington, C. H., 258
Wallace, McHarg, Roberts, and Todd, 277
Washington, D. C., 31, 48, 222, 309; Capitol, 222; Franklin Delano Roosevelt Memorial, 31; Lincoln Memorial, 222; Potomac River, 222; Thomas Jefferson Memorial, 222; Washington Monument, 48; White House, 222
Watling, E. F., 11
Whitman, Walt, 15, 30
Wijk-bij-Duurstede, 167, 169
Williamsburg, 225
Wölfflin, Heinrich, 11, 30
Wood, John (the Elder), 183, 184–85
Wood, John (the Younger), 29, 183, 184–85
World War II, 203
Wren, Sir Christopher, 172

Zafiropoulos, Sarantis, 63
Zaltbommel, 164, 167; Gasthuys Chapel, 164
Zeckendorf, William, 264
Zocchi, Giuseppe, 112